MW00814604

Winning
CHOICES

A LIFE-CHANGING GAME PLAN

Trust in the Lord.

Get in the Game.

Inspire Right Thinking.

GREG PAPP

FOREWORD BY COACH LES STECKEL,
VETERAN NFL COACH AND RETIRED CEO, FELLOWSHIP OF CHRISTIAN ATHLETES

SMART BUSINESS® BOOKS
An Imprint of Smart Business® Network Inc.

Published by Smart Business Books
An imprint of Smart Business Network Inc.
835 Sharon Drive, Suite 200
Westlake, OH 44145

Printed in the United States of America
Editor: Mark Scott
Cover Design: Lori Scott
Interior Design: RJ Pooch

ISBN: 978-1-945389-81-8
Library of Congress Control Number: 2017958493

CONTENTS

DEDICATION AND ACKNOWLEDGEMENTS

"I dedicate this book to the thousands of devoted volunteers who diligently mentor and coach those who seek to make better life choices."

– Greg Papp

I would like to thank those individuals who contributed their experience, knowledge and skills in helping to make this book a reality—I am forever indebted.

I would especially like to thank the volunteers from the Angel Tree Football Clinic at Stanford University, whose stories and names appear throughout Winning Choices. A special thank you also goes to Joe Avila and Bill Anderson, co-founders of the clinic, and superstar Janna Bowman, clinic event planner, for allowing me access to their world.

Another thank you goes to Rick Isaiah, vice president of field ministry for the Fellowship of Christian Athletes' Great Lakes region, who helped provide valuable connections related to the needs of young people. Rick's connections immensely enhanced the book's content and design as it relates to the needs of young people. I will be forever grateful for his commitment to get this book into the hands of those who can use it as a tool to help others.

In the early stages of development, several people served as sounding boards, including Mike and Heather Green, Scott and Cheryl Smith, and Mark and Karen Wuertz. Thank you for your honesty.

My colleagues and co-authors of the Two Minute Drill, Clint Longenecker and Tim Stansfield, were also instrumental in thinking ideas through and providing feedback.

Sincere appreciation also goes to the publishing team at Smart Business Books, especially April Grasso and Mark Scott, whose editing expertise brought clarity and order to the entire manuscript.

Lastly, I would like to thank my daughters, Laura (and her husband Aaron) and Emily (plus her husband, Patrick, and their children, Emma and Ashley) who politely endured untold hours listening to the ups and downs of this journey. Many hugs to all. Most importantly, I would like to thank my wife Sue, who, in reality, should be considered a co-author of this book. Throughout this effort, she unfailingly served as researcher, editor, encourager and counselor. Her daily prayers provided the power to keep me going and I am eternally grateful for her.

FOREWORD

During my 32-year coaching career, I have faced both great opportunities and daunting challenges. But few of those experiences compare to the challenges faced by today's upcoming generation. In what author Greg Papp terms a "culture of confusion," today's youth wakes up every day to a world seemingly turned upside down. By any measure, this generation is struggling to make sound, successful decisions. In a culture characterized by information overload, a multitude of worldviews, political correctness and a mind-boggling rate of change in technology, they face the reality that they WILL have to make decisions that go a long way toward shaping his or her own future. Unfortunately, many of these individuals also face the hard truth that they lack the skills, experience and guidance to effectively sort through these options and make solid, informed choices.

During my tenure as CEO of the Fellowship of Christian Athletes, (FCA), I saw the dramatic impact of this hard-hitting culture on the lives of countless young people. But, I also saw the upshot of thousands of dedicated coaches who work tirelessly to mentor and encourage them. Winning Choices provides a great set of street level, Biblical-based ideas and tools for making better life-changing choices. Whether you are working with athletes, college or career bound youth, prisoners or simply the individual down the street, you will find a lot of ideas to help you help them.

Values

Foundational to our mission at FCA are four key values: Integrity, Serving, Teamwork and Excellence. Everything we do focuses on developing ourselves and the student athletes we serve in these vital elements of a successful life. Throughout the pages of Winning Choices, these values rise to the surface time and time again. Each is integrated into practical tools customizable to fit a variety of teams. Let me touch on just one of the values - excellence!

Throughout my coaching career, one of the guys I wanted to "be like" was legendary Dallas Cowboys coach Tom Landry. Coach Landry exhibited an inspiring sense of character and class both on and off the field. He once said, "The quality of a man's life is in direct proportion to his commitment to excellence." The apostle Paul also spoke of excellence in his letter to the Colossians, counseling them to "honor and glorify God in all they did" Col 3:23-24. Becoming excellent, however, demands discipline of character plus continually learning and developing new skills. Winning Choices provides insight into skills and tools whether you are new to the game or a veteran with the scars to prove it. You will find excellence portrayed in the model of an H3P3 player and a hero-servant-mentor-leader coach. But most of all, the reader will discover God, himself, to be the author of all things excellent.

God, pizza and football

Every good coach will tell you that to be effective, you must learn to speak the "language of the game" with your players. Good communication is a key part of winning. Confusion on the sidelines or on the field leads to mistakes, turnovers and losses. Same thing holds true for mentoring in life. So, to provide practical tools usable by anyone, Winning Choices employs the metaphors of football (America's favorite game) and pizza (America's favorite food). Together, they provide a no nonsense game plan to move the chains, score and win. Throughout the book, the reader will find advice from more than a dozen former NFL and college players and coaches, plus a wealth of guidance from Scripture.

The Power of Three

There is no doubt in my mind that calling the right plays in life begins with prayer and a search of Scriptures, coupled with good advisers. Greg takes the same approach using what he calls the "Power of Three, namely, a God-coach-player combo as the foundation for winning. He follows that up with several other power plays including seven key elements of a two-minute drill. As a coach, I know the value of having a preplanned, yet flexible, no-huddle game package ready to move fast and score in a tight game. Mastering the elements suggested in this book can help each of us improve our game and be ready to face life's challenges.

Proverbs 3:5-6 sets the overall theme for the book: "Trust in the Lord with all your heart; do not depend on your own understanding. Seek His will in all you do, and he WILL show you the path to take." No coach can offer better advice.

Get in the game ... the game of life

Coaching counts! You can have a huge impact on others whether from the sidelines in an athletic event or, more importantly, in the game of life. I learned the value of a good coach and mentor while still in high school. Growing up in a very challenging environment, I can still recall when my basketball coach, Win Evans, took me aside and spoke such encouraging words to me. To this day, I still remember him convincing me that I had value and should utilize my God-given talents. Isn't it remarkable how a brief conversation can have such a huge impact? That moment with coach Evans inspired me for years to come. It made me feel important and gave me self-worth. Even though I was young, I set out to do exactly what he said I could do.

Later as my coaching career developed, I had the opportunity to be the offensive coordinator for the Tennessee Titans in the year we played in Super Bowl XXXIV. We were set to take home the championship on a last-second pass play. Unfortunately, the receiver was stopped one yard short of the goal. That night, I felt that my play call had gone wrong. But after reviewing my life's game films, I realized that only from a human perspective did it fail. From an eternal perspective, God used it to help redefine what my life was all about. It was no longer about wins and losses; it was about life and death. He asked me, "Do you know how many people out there are one yard short of eternal victory?" Some decisions that we face in life are more important than others. The ultimate choice deals with our eternal destiny. In Winning Choices, you will discover how you can become a hall of famer in the eyes of God and help others join that same roster.

Allow me to play coach once again. We're all in the locker room of life and the scoreboard is not showing the score we want to see. It's up to us to make a play. We need to win back our country - a country built on Christian faith and values. It's time for each of us to share our knowledge, experience and faith with those who need it most. Whether you mentor athletes or couch potatoes, be confident that just like coach Evans told me, you can make a significant difference in this world. My own experiences have taught me that people today are hungry to integrate their spiritual lives with their careers and families. They need guidance and encouragement.

Life is a full-contact sport and we'll need toughness to take action in this world. As I have said, "when all is said and done, more is said than done -- so be bold and very courageous." Let God use you in a mighty way for all to see the difference you can make for him! So, check out the game changers in this book, apply them to your own life and then "get in the game and making winning choices" as a servant for others. Do so, and you will soon discover that God is on the move!

Coach Les Steckel
Veteran NFL coach
Retired CEO, Fellowship of Christian Athletes

AUTHOR'S INTRO

God, pizza and football ...
Can it get any better than that?

"With overwhelming odds, comes overcoming grace."

– Pastor Keith Sholl

Venue:
MOUNT OF OLIVES
AD 30 - 33

In the final minutes of His ministry on Earth, Christ took his disciples, those he had been coaching and mentoring, to the Mount of Olives. There, he gave them some final instructions before they would take the field to win disciples in His name. Known in Christian circles as "The Great Commission," Matthew records Christ's teaching in Chapter 28 of his gospel: "Then the eleven disciples left for Galilee, going to the mountain where Jesus had told them to go. When they saw him, they worshiped him—but some of them still doubted! Jesus came and told his disciples, 'I have been given complete authority in heaven and on earth. Therefore, go and make disciples of all the nations, baptizing them in the name of the Father and the Son and the Holy Spirit. Teach these new disciples to obey all the commands I have given you. And be sure of this: I am with you always, even to the end of the age.'" Matthew 28:16 -20.

With the command to go and make disciples, Christ essentially outlined His game plan for them to follow. Allowing for perhaps a bit of irreverence, permit me to say that had Jesus been speaking to today's sports-saturated generation in those final minutes on earth, He may have simply told them to go and:

GET IN THE GAME AND MAKE WINNING CHOICES!

As the author of this book, I take Christ's commission very seriously as instruction, not only to those original team members, but by extension, to all of us who call on Christ as our God and savior. Throughout the pages of Winning Choices, you will discover that yes, you and I both have an opportunity and a responsibility to coach/mentor/lead others not necessarily in an athletic contest, but in the more serious game of life.

We essentially are to "go and make disciples" just as Christ commanded in the final verses of Matthew. But what does "make disciples" really mean? The command goes far beyond the act of salvation. Making disciples involves teaching, leading, disciplining and various other aspects related to helping an individual follow the principles of Christ in daily activities. Winning Choices focuses the discipleship quest a bit, providing ideas and tools in the art of decision making.

But why has it become important for each of us to make disciples or in our chosen vernacular, to get in the game and make winning choices?

Here's the ticket: A culture of confusion is testing the capabilities of an entire generation!

In a society where absolute truth continues to be viciously and purposely tossed into the dumpster of irrelevance, young individuals struggling to make sound choices face a myriad of obstacles. But with every challenge comes a larger opportunity. Overwhelming odds comes with overcoming grace. Today's challenges must be addressed head on and this book provides street level ideas and tools to take your game, and those you cherish, to a new level. Reading it, you will find real people offering real ideas to tackle the choices of life and win.

If you are already in the game, that's great! Congratulations! At the same time, don't be rebuffed by the book's title. When it comes to helping others, these pages are packed with ideas and tools useful for newcomers and veterans alike. Whether you lead and teach as part of a formal organization or you help individuals in a one-on-one environment, you need to read this book. Whether you are involved with a youth group or a prison release program or you simply offer guidance to an individual facing career, education, marriage or other life-changing choices, the tools from Winning Choices will help you get the job done more effectively.

God, pizza and football ...

Three critical facts: God has been around forever. Pizza was first delivered in 997 A.D. in the town of Gaeta, Italy. And finally, the first NFL broadcast went live in 1939, showcasing the Philadelphia Eagles and the Brooklyn Dodgers. So the question many would ask is: What did couch potatoes do while eating pizza during the 942-year span until football arrived on the scene? I'm not sure and I don't really care. While I talk a lot about God, pizza and football, my focus is on the realities of today and on helping you and those you love.

Although not a sports book, Winning Choices incorporates two powerful metaphors: football and pizza. America's favorite game and America's favorite food will grab the attention of a sports-saturated generation, providing a simple channel to imbed important ideas related to making sound choices. Throughout the book, we will visit 25-plus venues where life really happens. Ranging from Cleveland Municipal Stadium to the Mount of Olives to the shores of Australia, each venue will illustrate a game-changing idea. Additionally, we will hear passionate input from a dozen former NFL and college players and others who are now helping young people get a jump on life.

A lot of learning - a lot of fun

So, get ready for a learning-teaching- life-changing experience. Not only will you discover ways of creating hope, but you will also find tools for achieving that hope. You will have fun as you ...

- ✓ Execute a two-minute drill like a championship NFL team.
- ✓ Find life in a pizza box.
- ✓ Discover the donkey in your locker room.
- ✓ Witness angels wearing football helmets.
- ✓ Become a hero-servant-mentor-leader coach.
- ✓ Incorporate your head, heart and hands in the game of life.
- ✓ Discover how history's initial two questions apply to your life today.
- ✓ Apply 50-plus instructions from Scripture toward making better choices.
- ✓ Learn how the Power of Three (God-coach-player) gets you into the end zone.

Oh, by the way, take a second to reread the final phrase recorded in the Scripture above. What does God promise? Yes, more good news, as He promises to "be with us to the end of the age." We will not have to make this journey alone. When He tells us to get in the game and make winning choices, He assures us that He will be there coaching and leading us every step of the way. That is why I have chosen Proverbs 3:5-6 to be the theme verse of Winning Choices. So, be confident that through His strength, you CAN get the job done.

OK, let's get at it!

—————— Read On! ——————

PART 1
PREGAME

Why Winning Choices is important to you

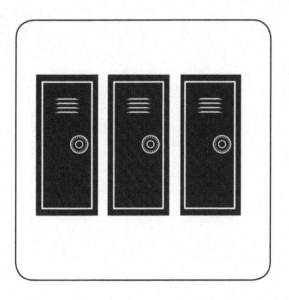

Almost every team spends time in the locker room finalizing its game plan before taking the field. Similarly, we will spend time chatting about the topics outlined below as we prepare to face the challenges of life that will help us make more sound, successful choices. Part 1 delves into the following:

 1. The Donkey in the Locker Room

2. The Gaffe in the Garden

 3. Decisions Happen

4. A Game Plan for Winning

5. Life in the 21st Century Stadium

6. Quick Hit #1 Joe Avila

THE DONKEY IN THE LOCKER ROOM

God has a job for each of us

"You can have an impact anywhere you are."

– Tony Dungy

Venue:
BETHPHAGE, ISRAEL
AD 33

After telling this story, Jesus went on toward Jerusalem, walking ahead of his disciples. As he came to the towns of Bethphage and Bethany on the Mount of Olives, he sent two disciples ahead. Go into that village over there," he told them. "As you enter it, you will see a young donkey tied there that no one has ever ridden. Untie it and bring it here. If anyone asks, 'Why are you untying that colt?' just say, 'The Lord needs it.'"

So they went and found the colt, just as Jesus had said. And sure enough, as they were untying it, the owners asked them, "Why are you untying that colt?" And the disciples simply replied, "The Lord needs it." So they brought the colt to Jesus and threw their garments over it for him to ride on. Luke 19: 28-35 (NLT).

Although it may be a strange way to kick off a football-based book on decision-making and even though the participants in this brief narrative never touched a football, their situation plays out every day in your life and mine. . Let's check it out.

Finding a donkey

In sports, the locker room is typically a refuge where game plans are finalized or, if necessary, modified to take on the opponent and win the game. Among other things, the locker room provides a place to privately discuss player assignments or changes to get the job done right. So, let's take a moment to step out of your personal locker room and wander back in time with your team to the venue described in Bethphage.

Put yourself in their shoes. Imagine their situation on the streets of

Bethany.. For three years, they have been marveling at the words and works of this man they call "master." He has spoken words like no other before Him. He has healed the sick; raised the dead. Now, He summons your team for a task. One may think, "Wow! What could the master want us to do? Would He want us to take a leading role on His team, be His closest advisers or record His every word?" Anticipation grows as you and your team wait for Him to speak.

Finally, He does. His request? "Go get a donkey and bring it to me!" You hear one of your players mutter under his breath, "You've gotta be kidding me." Your immediate reaction to this request is about the same. You think, "Get a donkey? What a lousy assignment. Go find a dusty, stubborn animal that belongs to someone else and drag it through hot, dirty, dung-filled streets. What a great job ... Not!" Also, what about the risk of being arrested as a thief? Would local authorities see this as "grand theft donkey"? The Master's request doesn't sound like the job you really want. In fact, you may be asking yourself: "Why me Lord? Why my team? Why not send someone else? My guys can handle bigger, more important tasks. Send someone else to do the dull and dirty stuff."

So what in reality did the disciples actually do? Did they refuse to obey? Did they complain? Did they try to hand the job off to someone else? No. The passage from Luke 19 says, "So, they went and found the colt, just as Jesus said." They simply obeyed their Lord!

In the face of a downright ugly assignment filled with no apparent glory, the two disciples endured the filthy elements following their master's request. Perhaps thinking their trivial job would be lost in the bigger picture, they followed the will of the man to whom they had given their allegiance. What the disciples may not have known is that they would be participating in the fulfillment of the prophet Zechariah's foresight (Zechariah 9:9) some 500 years earlier. Little did they know their mundane mission would be recorded in history and be read for the next 2,000 years at the kickoff to every Holy Week observance. Little did they know their master and Lord would ride that same donkey in his triumphant entry to Jerusalem a few days later. This mundane task brought huge returns, not to them, but to the waiting world.

Whether serving our creator or, more selfishly, serving ourselves, most of us are willing to accept what we deem to be awesome assignments--doing cool things--requiring minimal efforts that bring acknowledgement (if not fame) to us personally. But what about those donkey assignments? Glory? Fun? Clean? Hardly! These tasks often performed behind the scenes with seemingly minimal importance may appear to be beneath us. These are the jobs that most of us attempt to avoid. No glory, questionable relevance and certainly offering no entertainment value.

But, what if the God of the universe wants you to do a donkey-type chore for Him? What if the task at hand appears mundane, but the one asking is the all-powerful creator? What if he wants you to get in the mud? Would that make a difference? Unfortunately, the answer is too often "not really." We all prefer the big things; the tasks that win the game or save the world. We want to throw the 60-yard last-second winning touchdown pass but not block the smelly 300-pound lineman. Too often, in our self importance leads to self indulgence.. It's a dangerous place to be on the football field or the field of life.

We need to remind ourselves and teach our players to look beyond both themselves and their own needs. We must help them think about the task they are being asked to take on and rather than question why they've been asked to do it.

Creating Hope; Achieving Hope

Check out the reality of history. As Christ rode the donkey into Jerusalem, the crowd cheered Him as their coming savior. He fulfilled a prophecy by creating the hope of salvation for them with every step of that beast of burden. Within the week, however, He moved on from creating hope to fulfilling that hope of salvation by conquering the grave through His death and resurrection. He not only brought a sense of Hope, he brought the actuality or reality of it through what he did on that very first Easter weekend. Had He only completed the Palm Sunday deed, history would have recorded "a nice parade." Instead, He followed the creation of hope with the achievement of it on Good Friday and Easter Sunday.

Consider the dual theme of hope created and hope achieved. As the Holy Week chronicle illustrates, the creation of hope is highly important, but it falls short unless the realization or achievement of that hope follows. Creating anticipation is the first step to realizing victory. Unfortunately, it is only the first step. Imagine yourself once again standing amid the crowd when Jesus rode that lowly donkey into Jerusalem. How would you feel now compared to how you felt days earlier when your team was given the assignment? How would you respond if someone in the crowd wondered aloud as to where Christ got that donkey? Would a little pride seep into your heart as you thought about what your players had done?

Whenever I write, a small ceramic donkey watches over my

keyboard. It stands silently in my peripheral vision as a reminder that no task, if directed by our loving God, lacks relevance. To some, the job may appear boring and the intended outcome obscure. But remember, this is the same God who rode that little brown animal into the pages of history. This is the same God who has, throughout history, fashioned the work of ordinary men and women into extraordinary results.

So, coach, if you fall prey to either the idea that your team is too important to handle the donkey-type jobs or is simply not qualified to lead that donkey to your Lord, shake those thoughts from your head. No task is too small if done for the glory of God. No task is impossible to achieve if done under the power of God. Scripture tells us that with God nothing is impossible.

TIME OUT:

So, I ask you: What is the donkey in your locker room? What task, great or small, stands silently before your players, awaiting them to grasp the reins and take the lead? What assignment will be a game-changer in their lives or in the lives of others? We all need to seriously ask that question and be ready to honestly find an answer.

Each and every one of us has a donkey or two waiting for us to untie. These are tasks that may not be fun or exciting and perhaps no one will notice if they are completed. But they are important and if ignored, over time, they can have a substantial impact on your team's ability to achieve its goals. Going after that donkey may get you a bit dusty and dirty and, yes, perhaps you may need to even step in a pile of dung to achieve the work of the Lord. Perhaps others will recognize you for your efforts. Perhaps not. The point for each of us to carry close to our hearts is that we are here right now to serve the Lord in whatever way He (not us) deems necessary. He has a game plan and within that game plan resides a spot for each of us to play. We are all on the team. We are all in the locker room preparing to take the field to fill our role and execute that game plan.

Throughout Winning Choices, you will find examples (called Quick Hits) of people who have found the donkey in their locker room. From top NFL stars to top 10 criminals to Biblical heroes, you will hear of lives being changed after God sent them to find a donkey. People you will meet are not only helping others to find hope, but also to achieve the results of that hope. We will discuss throughout the book the enablers who help your players untie the donkey that God has waiting for them.

This book will end where it began: the locker room. Between the locker room chapters, you will witness the game that we must all learn to play and the game with an eternal scoreboard in a stadium where the lights never go out!

Game Winning Point: We should revel in any task, large or small, that is the work of the Lord.

Game Changing Verse: Work with enthusiasm, as though you were working for the Lord rather than for people. Ephesians 6:7

PLAYBOOK TIPS

■ Be alert to discover the donkey that God has for you today.

■ Keep yourself in perspective; small jobs often yield huge results.

—————— Read On! ——————

THE GAFFE IN THE GARDEN

History's First Botched Decision

The first two questions in recorded history unquestionably emerge in each of our lives today. They are huge and can drive our decisions and mold our lives. Let's check them out!

Venue:
GARDEN OF EDEN
SOON AFTER CREATION
Genesis 3: 1-10

Now the serpent was the shrewdest of all the creatures the Lord God had made. "Really?" he asked the woman. "Did God really say you must not eat any of the fruit in the garden?" "Of course we may eat it," the woman told him. "It's only the fruit from the tree at the center of the garden that we are not allowed to eat. God says we must not eat it or even touch it, or we will die." "You won't die!" the serpent hissed. "God knows that your eyes will be opened when you eat it. You will become just like God, knowing everything, both good and evil." The woman was convinced. The fruit looked so fresh and delicious, and it would make her so wise! So she ate some of the fruit. She also gave some to her husband, who was with her. Then he ate it, too. At that moment, their eyes were opened, and they suddenly felt shame at their nakedness. So they strung fig leaves together around their hips to cover themselves. Toward evening, they heard the Lord God walking about in the garden, so they hid themselves among the trees. The Lord God called to Adam,* "Where are you?" He replied, "I heard you, so I hid. I was afraid because I was naked."

First-round draft picks blow Game 1

"In the beginning, God created the heavens and the earth," reads the beginning of the Bible. And, looking at it, He declared His creation to be "good." But shortly thereafter, man decided to botch it up. In the first chapter of Genesis alone, scripture quotes God as saying seven times that his creation is "good." But in Chapter 2, things change. The first humans, who may legitimately be called God's first-round draft picks, start exercising their individual free will, and before you know it, everything goes south really fast.

Let's face it. You are not the first person to encounter tough decisions. For thousands of years, men and women, young and old, have molded the landscape of history with choices. Some have produced great results while others have not. Some decisions reflect a lot of thought and some echo none at all. Some choices portray mankind as intelligent beings while others depict us as blundering fools.

So why have some choices been winners and some outright losers? Is there a path that circumvents the blunders and puts our choices in the win column? Absolutely! Is it available to each of us? No doubt about it. You are about to learn how to get in the game and make winning choices, play well (or coach well) and produce winning results. God has created you to be a winner. Your time has arrived.

But first, let's step back in time to check how things went in the Garden of Eden. By the way, we will get to football in a bit. In reality (and they were real people), the first couple to grace the earth didn't do so well with one of their big decisions. Their story, familiar to most of us, illustrates the huge impact of our choices. In Adam and Eve's case, the choice came down to a matter of who to trust. And, wow, did they blow it. That failure resulted in huge consequences for all of us. But God responded with love by providing a solution to their predicament and to ours.

The First Question in Recorded History

How did things come apart in that beautiful garden? It all appears to have started with the first question in recorded history. Was it a question posed by God? Not at all. That first question came not from the God who formed man, but from Satan himself. Take a few seconds to reread the first few verses from Genesis 3. With those four simple words, "Did God really say?"...Satan sowed the seeds of doubt or, in football jargon, threw history's first challenge flag onto the field. He was questioning God's call from the viewpoint of Adam and Eve. He has been throwing similar challenge flags into each of our lives ever since that first confrontation. Be assured he knew the answer. His purpose was not to learn, but to cast doubt. And once doubt was in play, he followed on by creating confusion through deception. And once deception took hold, the game was over. And, as they say, the rest is history.

Is this still happening today? It sure is! Partial truths abound in our culture of confusion. Young decision-makers lacking experience easily fall prey to the folly of deception. That is where you and I and the rest of the "more experienced" people can get in the game and make winning choices. That is where we can bring clarity to the next generation as they make choices. That's where we can lead others to place their trust in the right place.

Question 2 - God's Turn

What about question No. 2? This question was not a question of deception, but one of hope; a father looking over His children. Found in verse 9, it puts forth a simple yet powerful query, "Where are you?" But this time, the serpent's voice was silent. This question came directly from God. But, as with the first, this one offers huge implications for today. In asking, "Where are you?" God was not attempting to locate their GPS coordinates. He is God after all; he knew where they were hiding. More importantly, He was speaking to the reality that the relationship between His creation and Himself had changed. The first man and woman no longer followed His direction by choosing to pursue their own course of action. But God was not finished. In His love, God came looking for them, hoping to rebuild that fractured relationship.

The same situation holds true today. God seeks us. He longs for an eternal relationship through salvation. Plus, he looks to us for a day-to-day relationship, hoping to walk together on this earth. As it relates to making choices, and hence, this book, the question, "Where are you?" projects the idea of being in or out of God's will. Essentially, He is asking each of us if we are following His purpose, or His will, for our lives. Proverbs 3:5-6 gets this point across: "Trust in the Lord with all your heart; do not depend on your own understanding. Seek his will in all you do, and he will direct your paths." Because of its direct yet simple command, Proverbs 3:5-6 serves as the theme verse of this book. We will adopt its foundational wisdom throughout our discussion.

TIME OUT:

Regarding God's offer for an eternal relationship, check out the chapter, titled "On Becoming a Hall of Famer" to find out how. If you have not already addressed this decision, you need to skip to that chapter and do so now. It is the MOST IMPORTANT decision you will ever face.

I am not God and neither are you!

We have been created to enjoy the freedoms provided by God, but we are not free to BE God. Day in and day out, as we travel along our personal journey, we each face the same two pivotal questions posed to Adam and Eve. How we answer, "Did God really say?" and "Where are you?" will determine where we end up and how we get there. Essentially, we must decide if we are in charge or is God in charge? Do we direct our own course or does God? Does our worldview begin with us or does it come from God? Old questions. New questions. Big questions!

Now, if this brief tour of the garden seems to you like simply a "thing of the past," well, I guess one might say that. But do not worry, in the next chapter we will bring the entire sphere of decisions to the doorstep of today. Unfortunately, blundering did not die with Adam and Eve. Instead, it has become the epidemic affecting every one of us. As a coach, you can play the role in helping your players avoid some of the same mistakes you might have made as you grew in your life.

Game Winning Point: You can (and should) learn from the reality of the past.

Game Changing Verse: The Lord God called to Adam, "Where are you?" Genesis 3:9.

PLAYBOOK TIPS

■ Check out God's Word when someone asks you "did God really say?"

■ Never try to hide from God; It can't be done.

Read On!

DECISIONS HAPPEN
Reality tends to surface

"We have learned that we cannot live with the chaos that inevitably results from choices divorced from morality"

– Chuck Colson

Venue:
Highway 99
Fresno County California
September 18, 1992

Today, in large letters, a sign flanking Highway 99 in Fresno County emphatically implores:

PLEASE

DON'T DRINK AND DRIVE

In smaller letters, a second sign mounted directly below it personalizes that plea with the words:

In Memory of

Amy Wall

What's going on here? Why are these signs paired on the same pole? Simply, because decisions happen and decisions have consequences!

On that mid September day in 1992, 17-year old Amy was returning home from a concert when her car was rear-ended into a tree by local resident and business man, Joe Avila. At the time, Joe was driving drunk. And the choice he made led to severe consequences: a teenage girl would die before ever graduating from high school and a husband and father of two daughters would spend the next seven-plus years in prison. Decisions happen; decisions have consequences!

Joe had become a slave to alcohol. Arrested on two previous occasions for DUI, he had managed to talk his way out of those situations, never having served time nor been a part of any rehab program. In his mind, Joe believed that he had beaten the rap and beaten the consequences. Not so. Having avoided the penalties and corrective process, Joe had simply delayed the inevitable. And now, that inevitable had happened with acutely tragic results.

The ongoing saga following this 1992 tragedy reflects intense heartbreak, extreme remorse and emerging forgiveness among Joe, his family and Amy's family.

It demonstrates that God can change hearts, forging a positive outcome from a seemingly dire situation. As Amy's younger brother, Derek, said after several years and emotional struggles following her death, "Amy died... so others may live". It's a statement that we all must respect; a lesson that we all must learn.

Had you attended the Angel Tree Football Clinic, discussed later in Part 2, you may have had the opportunity to meet and chat with Joe Avila. Joe is the same person, but also a very different person than the man behind the wheel on that heartbreaking September day. The person you would have met, as I did, is not Joe the prisoner, but Joe, the Director of Northern California for the Prison Fellowship Ministries (his region has now grown to essentially all of the western United States). So, why is he a different person? Simply put, because Joe followed up on his bad choices with a series of great choices. Those decisions brought physical and spiritual renewal in his own life and allowed him to become a beacon of hope in the lives of countless others.

Joe and I spoke at length about his amazing journey. Check out his comments in the 'Joe Avila Quick Hit' toward the end of this section. His wisdom will bless you as it has me.

But, you may be saying, "I'm not Joe; what does this story have to do with me?" Let's pursue that question a bit.

Decisions Happen!

Paper or plastic? Thin crust or thick? Experts who study human behavior say that we each make hundreds of choices each day. Some actually put the number over 1,000.

Decisions do happen. Some choices are the life-changing biggies;

most address the garden variety day-to-day routines of life. Some choices are great, some so-so, and some downright awful. Making choices is not an option; it is a part of the fabric of life. But, you do have an option and that option is whether you make good choices or not so good ones. It's a recurring theme in the message from a coach to his or her players. We are all faced with decisions each and every day. The decisions we make will shape our lives.

The realization that decision-making has been around for a long time (in fact, since time began) may, to you, seem obvious. But, for those just rolling off the assembly line as teenagers, you can often swap the word "obvious" with "oblivious". As parents everywhere will tell you, "undeveloped brains" truly believe they are the first to ever face the challenges of life. But, for thousands of years, since Adam and Eve decided to pull the first blunder aligning with Satan instead of God, life has been a struggle.

That was then and now is now. So, how are we doing these days in the decision department? Not so good! In fact, as a society, if measured by the outcomes, our choices are downright awful. Allow the following realities to sink in as you get your mind in the groove for the game:

Reality Scoreboard

❑ Divorce rate among young couples approaches 40 percent

❑ Over 60 percent of 20-somethings are spiritually disengaged
❑ Over 2.5 million Americans are in prison, 700% increase since 1970.
❑ Four of ten prisoners are behind bars again within one year of release
❑ More than half of all new businesses fail within five years
❑ The average college student changes their major three times
❑ Still only approximately half will ever graduate

Not a pretty picture. But, there is good news: Something can be done about it! And, you, coach, can play a huge role! Scripture teaches that we are each designed by God, in His image, to lead a powerful, sound life. With a bit of knowledge, a few tools, the right attitude and the help of a coach like you, those in your sphere of influence can put a lot of checkmarks in the Win column.

Time to face reality

What are the realities of life? What forms the skeleton to which we can add ideas and tools to create winning choices? Well, here are five basic facts (or premises) which shape the foundation of all that we will learn and apply. Together these truths allow us to structure and customize a playbook which fits your specific needs.

Reality 1. You WILL have to make decisions

As discussed earlier, decisions happen. Life offers little alternative; we all face choices. Unfortunately, many of us tend to circumvent them through procrastination or outright avoidance. Faced with major uncertainties that we have never encountered before, we all have a tendency to delay making the big choice that seems (and often is) irreversible. That is natural, but it's also a key reason why teams struggle to meet their goals. (It's the people in front of me in the grocery line who take seemingly forever to decide between paper and plastic that tend to put me over the edge.) Part 1 - Figure 1 lists a variety of challenges that make decisions tough, especially for those lacking experience or guidance. Recognize any of them playing out in the lives of those around you (or, perhaps, in your own life)? Think maybe you can make a difference?

Part 1 - Figure 1. Why Are Decisions so Tough?

Lack of street smarts	Emotional roller coasters
Peer pressure	Information overload
Lack of experience	Apathy/boredom
Tendency to procrastinate	Lack of understanding consequences
Lack of knowledge	Lack of understanding risks
Bad worldview	Entitlement mentality
Bad process for choosing	Hazy objectives
Desire for instant gratification	Over confidence

Reality 2. You DO what you VIEW.

This is enormous! For each of us, our worldview determines what we do. In the book of Proverbs, Scripture teaches us that "as a man thinks in his heart, so is he" (Proverbs 23:7). Or, in our terminology, "you do what you view". One may say that "you do what you view" is not a new concept nor one hard to grasp. True. However, in today's pluralistic culture where all views are taught to be equally correct, many in the upcoming generation fail to understand the implications. For those who assert that it doesn't matter what I (or anyone else) believe, most fail to realize that the "do" truly does follow the "view". In a no-right-no-wrong world, misunderstanding that sequence can be fatal.

Our perception and interpretation of the world around us lays the foundation for choices and filters the direction of our course of action. Your players may not realize that they actually have a worldview or, if asked, be able to explain it to someone. But, without a doubt, they do have one, just as you do. We all do. From the moment you wake until you close your eyes at night and, perhaps, even in your dreams, it grinds away setting the course for every move you make.

Reality 3. There is a right way to VIEW and a right way to DO.

As you might expect, all worldviews are not created equal. Nor are all methods for making and implementing choices.

Worldviews typically characterize our ultimate purpose for being here. The standards we live by, our view of both self and those around us, plus ultimately our belief about a supreme being all fall into the box labeled worldview. But, too, often, we all tend to compartmentalize these beliefs, not realizing that they actually work in concert, affecting our daily choices. Fail to understand our worldview and we may fail to understand why we do what we do.

As this book unfolds, we will discover what life has to offer inside a pizza box. Through comparison with other worldviews, you will learn that the Biblical worldview is the deep dish deluxe pie that satisfies our every need. It presents life in the most realistic fashion, offering the best set of principles for making great choices. Truly, the Biblical view may be called the "right way to view".

On the "Do" front, making and implementing a decision can be accomplished in seemingly infinite ways. In a sane world, the approach for choosing "paper or plastic" differs from that of choosing a career, but based on outcomes that we see in the morning headlines, that may not always be the case.

Simplicity is king when it comes to a method for getting the job done. Clarity is much easier to achieve through approaches that are no more complex than necessary to be effective and efficient. Football coaches understand the need for blending simplicity with clarity. We will adopt their wisdom outlining seven proven steps of a football two-minute drill to get the job done right.

Reality 4. Coaching Counts

Going it alone typically produces second-rate results. Research (and common sense) substantiates this reality. Success rates soar when the right people are on the field providing direction and, more importantly, adding accountability for the individual responsible for the decision.

The need to "not go it alone" is precisely why you, the coach, are essential. You do play a crucial role in the game. As a hero, as a servant or as a mentor, you become the lifeblood of the process and the glue that holds it together. We will discuss much more on this later in the book.

Reality 5. God Will Guide

In the third chapter of the book of Proverbs, God offers to provide clear direction in each of our lives. The God of the Bible has provided scripture and the avenue of prayer to support individuals who seek to make sound, consistent, moral decisions. Additionally, He has a way of directing others into our path to meet the countless needs that we face in pursuing solid choices. He designed you to pursue the right path and stands at the ready to help you get there. Believe me, once you realize this reality, you will sleep much better. He has also opened the avenue to developing a personal relationship with Him in the person of Jesus

Christ. Those who have pursued that relationship will attest to the wisdom, strength and peace that accompany that choice.

So, there you have it. Five simple realities that underlie the practical advice that will unfold as you read this short book. As you read, you will learn both principles and practical ways in which you can contribute to the success of others in the short, mid, and long term, helping them to face the realities of the day. You will help them call the next successful play, win the current game and enjoy a successful season.

Game Winning Point: If you avoid making decisions, someone else will make them for you. Not Good!

Game Changing Verse: Show me the path where I should walk, O Lord; point out the right road for me to follow. Psalm 25:4

PLAYBOOK TIPS

■ Periodically, take a few minutes to think through the five realities from this discussion.

■ Understand that you are NOT alone; God and those He sends will help you sort through decisions.

——————— Read On! ———————

A GAME PLAN FOR WINNING

Ideas and tools to get the job done

"Football is an honest game. It's true to life. It's a game about sharing. Football is a team game. So is life."

- Joe Namath

Had you attended Boone County High School in the late 90's, you would have called him Alexander the Great. Later, as an NFL fan, you would recognize him as Touchdown Alexander, superstar for the Seattle Seahawks. In any football venue, Shaun Alexander was a true star, both on and off the field. What you may find both interesting and a bit entertaining, however, is how Shaun decided where to spend his college days. His story will shed some light on how to make successful choices in life. Let's take a look.

Sandwiched between the high school Alexander the Great and NFL Touchdown Alexander was another record-setting phase in his life. Shaun relates an eye-opening account of decision-making that led him to the Alabama Crimson Tide.

In his book, aptly named Touchdown Alexander, he describes how an extremely talented young man decides where to attend college. In his words, "With so many colleges interested in me, I didn't know how to decide which one to attend, so I developed a technique that I know sounds crazy – but it worked for me. Here's what I did: I had stacks of letters in my room, and no matter which college it was that sent that letter, I tossed it over my left shoulder toward the wastebasket right behind my desk. If it landed inside the wastebasket, it stayed there. If it hit the floor, I picked it up and read it. Yes, that was crazy but I didn't know how else to do it. Every offer seemed good – but I had to choose only one, and this strange method worked."

"I didn't know how else to do it"

Good approach? Probably not. You may say it worked for him, but Shaun's football talent alone would make any of the choices appear equally acceptable. His airmail antics may produce a few laughs at after-dinner speeches, but the key phrase to note from his story may arguably be, "I didn't know how else to do it." He knew he had to do something to sort through the maze. But, as he said, Shaun was at loss on how to go about it, opting finally for an off-the-wall approach.

How many young people today can express that same lack of "how" when faced with life's big choices? The number has to be huge. That's where you come in, by adding clarity in a culture of confusion. Fortunately, in Shaun's case, he really did employ additional techniques that helped resolve his dilemma. We will chat about them soon. But, for now, just picture those in your own life who may be (or should be) saying, "I didn't know how else to do it" and may, consequently, get it all wrong. That doesn't have to be the outcome. You can help them get moving toward the end zone. You can help them play a winning game, enjoy a winning season and hopefully become a Hall of Famer.

Franchise You

The question remains: How do you or anyone go about getting the job done? Do you have to be a stellar coach? Or perhaps, a star athlete? Not really. Here's a thought:

Tomorrow morning, wake up thinking of your life as an NFL franchise.

Will you or I ever own an NFL franchise? Probably not. But since we are talking football in this book, we can use the various elements that come together (or fall apart) in the typical franchise to make it a success. We can learn from them to help others manage life in their own stadiums. Simply put, successful NFL franchises breed winning teams.

A Great Franchise

On August 20, 1920, George "Papa Bear" Halas and a group of independent football team owners met in a Hupmobile dealership in Canton, Ohio, to draw up plans and agreements for what would eventually become the NFL. Although only two of the original 11 franchises still field a team today, the league has grown into a powerhouse valued at more than $60 billion. As the league closes in on the century mark, it is important to note that more than 100 franchises have come and gone during the life of the league. As with most organizations, time has created both huge successes and unqualified failures. Superheroes have played the game as have the mediocre and those who endured the weekly boos of short-fused fans. Most franchises have been pillars of the community; a few, not so much. Let's check out one example.

In the world of football, the Pittsburgh Steelers have consistently received accolades as a great franchise. Joining the league in 1933, the team from Pennsylvania has racked up 20 division championships and six Super Bowl wins. Why? Some sportswriters and analysts attribute that success to two factors: stability and consistency (aka loyalty) across all aspects of the organization. For example, in a league where the average head coach's tenure is about four years, the Steelers have employed only three head coaches since 1969. Lack of disruption in style and personality at the top of the coaching ranks leads to much more stability throughout the organization. Speaking of stability, the Rooney family has owned the club since the beginning. Founder, Art Rooney, who died in 1988, left his heirs a simple, three word doctrine: Treat people right! Art's son, the late Dan Rooney, insisted that this philosophy, when put into practice, allowed good people to create great results.

A Game Plan for Winning

So, what should we learn from the practices of franchises to become better mentors or leaders in the lives of those we impact? What elements of those organizations can make or break our own efforts to be relevant?

For the Steelers, or any organization to be consistently successful, a lot of things must work together to make it happen. Achievement requires coordinated efforts in a culture that defines its purpose and values, rewarding activities that support them and penalizing those that don't.

In Winning Choices, we will chat about seven specific elements of a franchise. Undoubtedly, you may conclude that other ingredients exist and I agree. But, these seven are crucial categories that relate to the success of any team. Throughout this book it will become obvious how you can maximize your own contribution if you pay attention to each of the elements. Let's take a quick look at them.

1. VENUE - The venue or stadium represents the culture in which you play your game. Life today differs significantly from life 20 years ago, however, many of the needs and opportunities remain the same. As a coach, characterizing the profile of today's young player will be critical to overall success.

2. MISSION - The mission or purpose in our 21st century franchise describes basic principles that support why the franchise exists. Essentially, these principles form the worldview that serves to energize and limit day-to-day activities. More basically, those principles reflect the "view" in the premise that "you do what you view." Metaphorically, the principles may be viewed as fuel or nourishment, similar to the nourishment provided by a team's pregame meal.

3-5. POWER OF THREE - It may be fair to say that any franchise exists for the benefit of the people related to it. Owners, coaches, players and other staff contribute a variety of skills and resources to make things happen. In our franchise, the discussion will focus on what I refer to as the "Power of 3," namely God (as owner), the coach and the players. You may either be the coach or the player, but you cannot be God. Together, the three roles lead to success. Acting alone, God can handle it by Himself, however, history indicates that He typically employs others to achieve His purpose.

6. TRUST - Trust signifies the organizational glue, either binding people together or, in its absence, sowing seeds of discord. Great organizations learn how to establish and maintain faith in each other and the machinery that drives the engine of success. In our case, with God as the owner, ultimate trust will be placed in Him.

7. PLAYBOOK - Where the mission addresses principles and focuses on the "why," the playbook addresses processes and the "how." In our franchise, we will examine several proven elements of a 2-Minute Drill (or no huddle offense). Every successful football organization devotes significant resources and time to developing a plan for moving the ball quickly when time is short and a score needed to ensure a victory.

We will continue to employ the franchise comparison, not to depersonalize you into an "entity," but simply to help you see how you can impact the lives of others. Once again, the football metaphor will be utilized purely as a tool for communication. Perhaps it will help you create dialogue with those like Shaun Alexander who would otherwise say, "I didn't know how else to do it!"

Game Winning Point: To win big, treat people right!

Game Changing Verse: "Can two people walk together without agreeing on the direction? Amos 3:3

——— Read On! ———

LIFE IN THE 21ST CENTURY STADIUM

A culture of confusion
is testing the capabilities
of an entire generation

Venue:
U OF MICHIGAN STADIUM
ANN ARBOR, MICHIGAN

They call it the Big House for a reason. With an official capacity of 109,901, Michigan Stadium in Ann Arbor, Michigan, tops the list of American football stadiums. In comparison, the largest NFL venue, MetLife Stadium, lists its seating capacity at 82,566. On game day, Michigan Stadium swells with roaring fans to become the third-largest metro area in the state of Michigan. It is home to the team which has chalked up more wins than any school in history, perhaps, in part, due to the impact of the "12th player," the stadium, on the psyche of visiting teams. Vocal-cord ripping screams from the Michigan fans can easily create an environment of confusion for any visiting team unaccustomed to playing in a hostile stadium.

Stadiums date back into antiquity. The oldest known stadium is the one in Olympia, in the western Peloponnese peninsula of Greece, where the Olympic Games of antiquity began in 776 BC. Estimates of seating capacity of approximately 50,000 support the reality that people have always liked to assemble in huge groups to watch events.

On any given fall weekend, stadiums across the country literally erupt into living organisms. Players, coaches, spectators and staff do their best to make it all come together into a huge event. Walls, rules, ticket counters, refreshment stands, restrooms, lights and playing fields are all in place to meet the needs of the throngs of people filling the stadium. For those few hours on that afternoon, the stadium is where life happens. And at the center of the mix, we find the coaches bringing order and purpose to the game by directing events like generals on a battlefield. Although they may be outnumbered by players and refs, they are the ones who call the shots and direct the traffic.

Now, take a mental leap from the football field into the sport you play every day: the game of life. When you look around, what do you find? A stadium? Sure do. We all do. Life happens in our stadium. Personal venues may include an office, a school, a home, a factory or a prison. Each and every person takes the field in their own venue teeming with an assortment of opportunities and challenges. Our stadiums are packed with people, too. Some cheer us on, others hope to see us lose, but most really could care less who comes out on top. We find coaches to guide us and trainers to minister to our needs when we incur the wrath of competition. But, unlike football stadiums, our venues are in full gear 24/7. The lights are never turned out.

A Culture of Confusion - Hard to play today's game in yesterday's stadium

Individuals in today's young generation often find themselves mired in what may be typified as a "culture of confusion." In an environment characterized by information overload, a multitude of worldviews, political correctness and a mind-boggling rate of change in technology, they struggle to face the reality that they will have to make decisions. But for many, they also discover the reality that they lack the skills, experience and guidance to sort through life's options and make solid choices.

As you prepare (or continue) to coach this generation, you may find it helpful to check out a few characteristics of their world. Opportunity abounds but challenges are great. Let's look at a few ways in which today's youth may differ from life back in the day.

Life is different

The stadium may be the same, but the game has changed. Michigan Stadium, was built in 1927. But, is football today the same as football in the early 20th century? Not a chance. The game has radically changed. Equipment, rules, style of play and even the length of the game has transformed the way things happen. Yet, the game has not totally changed. The purpose remains the same: to win; to put more points on the digital (yes that has changed, too) scoreboard than the other team.

How about life in our stadium? Is the game played differently than it was so long ago? No doubt about it. The game is different; the players brandish different uniforms and equipment than previous generations had. Yet, just like football, a lot remains the same. They still hope to win even though their definition of success may differ significantly from their parents and drastically from their grandparents. Their desires may seem unique, but deep down in their hearts, they hold onto the same basic needs that humans have felt since the dawn of time. And that's where you and I come in as coaches. To help a new set of players find their way into the end zone in a culture of confusion.

Generational differences have existed forever. Changes have always happened, but the rate of transformation today appears to be going viral. During the radical changes of the 1960s, Bob Dylan and other singers branded those years with songs that, if you lived through that period, may still resonate in your mind. In his song, "The Times, They are a Changin'," Dylan prophesied:

The line it is drawn, and the curse it is cast
The slow one now will later be fast
As the present now will later be past
The order is rapidly fading
And the first one now will later be last.
For the times they are a' changin'

The times are a changin' and probably more so than Dylan realized when he wrote those prophetic lyrics. As coaches, we must each be aware of the factors that impact our players. In our 21st century culture, we will find the following dynamics reflected in the lives of most players:

He or she probably is experiencing a more secularized education with multiple worldviews. This factor looms large. Flooded with information from school, TV and the internet, this age group is exposed to an overwhelming host of worldviews yet lack the strong principles of discernment necessary to sort through them successfully. Faith-based reasoning, especially Christianity, is under attack throughout all institutions of society. Schools passionately avoid any association with God, prayer or the Christian heritage that originally formed the American culture. A study conducted by the Christian polling firm Barna Group found that "61 percent of today's young adults had been churched at one point during their teen years but are now spiritually disengaged."

He or she is probably experiencing information overload. Today's generation may believe that on the eighth day, God created the blogosphere and said it was "good." The expansion of technology and creation of social media is huge. Even the casual observer will conclude that the digital generation exhibits an addiction to smartphones, tablets and computers. While technology fosters the ability to connect, it also tends to shut out other daily activities, including the formation of meaningful relationships. So whether it is "good" or not so good depends in large part on the user's ability to handle it wisely. Be alert for a player swimming continually in the shallow end of the pool.

He or she may be experiencing a shortfall in life skills. While becoming experts in various surface-level digital skills, the upcoming generation seemingly is falling behind in analytical and reasoning skills. Mark Bauerlein, author of The Dumbest Generation, concludes, "Most young Americans possess little of the knowledge that makes for an informed citizen and too few of them master the skills needed to negotiate an information-heavy, communication-based society." His investigation finds support in a Pew Research study titled, "What Americans Know: 1989-2007." It states that 56 percent of the 18- to 29-year-old age set exhibits a "'low knowledge level" compared to only 22 percent of the older 50- to 64-year-old age group.

He or she is probably more politically correct. The mantra of diversity and tolerance may reside on their lips although the characterization of either term has wandered into a land of the bizarre. Tolerance has morphed from a definition of mutually "agreeing to disagree" in a respectful manner, to forced acceptance that all ideas are equally valid. Diversity has kicked in as a measurement across race, religion, economic status and lifestyles, again demanding that differences disappear in some sort of cultural soup. In essence, while insisting that all views are equally valid, political correctness is making it exceedingly uncomfortable for an individual to sort through information and take a stand when they may disagree with the norm.

He or she has probably taken on the appearance of being more environmentally conscious. Respect for the environment has transposed into an obsession within the education system and media industry. Millions of recycling bins dot the landscape as collection plates at the First Church of Environmentalism. But, if you are a parent of a teenager, the condition of their bedroom probably contradicts their allegiance to cleaning up the environment.

He or she probably is searching for heroes but finding few. We are a people who thirst for heroes in all areas of our lives. In the deep recesses of our mind they provide guidance, hope and in some cases, an escape from the daily hurdles of life. Unfortunately, those champions are becoming more difficult to find and even more difficult to keep. Witness the fall of professional golfer Tiger Woods or world champion bicyclist Lance Armstrong as examples of greatness that went down in flames. One of America's leading organizations, Athletes in Action, works with thousands of young people. Check out what their website says about role models: "Many athletes and coaches once thought to be the ideal role models for today's youth are swept up in a culture that seems to have abandoned limits and a moral compass."

He or she may be dropping out of organized religion. In addition to the loss of heroes, this generation shuns participation or membership in faith-based organizations such as churches and youth groups. David Kinnaman, author of You Lost Me: Why Young Christians Are Leaving Church … And Rethinking Faith and president of the Barna Group, points to the reality that individuals in the 16- to 29-year-old age group are leaving churches in ever increasing numbers. Not a good sign for developing foundational truths.

He or she may be experiencing a high level of anxiety. Dr Robert Leahy, of the American Institute for Cognitive Therapy, points out that today's teen students broadly exhibit similar anxiety levels to psychiatric patients of the 1950s. Challenged by continually increasing pressure from a variety of stressors, the inexperienced decision-maker often flounders through several false starts in education, marriage and other major choices. They don't know the playbook but feel pressure to play in the game.

He or she is probably fascinated with sports and entertainment. Sports blogger Michael Russell insists that "Yes, America is obsessed with sports." Hours spent lying on the couch watching an endless parade of sports shows and other alluring media productions contribute to the deficiency of time dedicated to learning real life skills. A Kaiser Family Foundation study in 2010 found that students spend more than 7.5 hours per day participating in electronic-based activities.

He or she may be the product of a tough family life. Since the day in the Bible when Cain killed Abel, every family has lived with some degree of tension. After all, our entire race consists of fallen creatures blundering through time and space. But, for many young people, their challenges often exceed the breaking point of normalcy. Simply put, life, and in some cases survival, often presents a huge daily challenge. With divorce rates in excess of 40 percent and more than 2.5 million Americans in prison, many individuals in the next generation find themselves alone in a crowded world. Finding reality to be all too real, they struggle to build relationships or find individuals interested in their well-being. The days of the classic 1950s TV show, "Ozzie and Harriet" may never have truly existed but, for sure, they do not exist today.

So where does all of this leave us as coaches? Taken separately, any one of the above factors represents a challenge for today's youth. Taken together, they embody the headwinds of a perfect storm. Essentially, today's fast-paced style of play offers more options for individuals less-equipped to handle them. The situation brings to mind the old adage, "we're making good time, but we're lost."

But, the good news lies in the reality that for these kids, the clock on their adult game of life is just beginning. They truly can become winners and you, the coach, play a key role in that outcome.

Filled with both opportunity and uncertainty, each individual in every generation has sought to find purpose and meaning to their existence. That common ground is a great opportunity for you to coach them through the uncertainties, to uncover the opportunities and do it from your own knowledge and experience. Growing along with them, you will be able to add clarity in the culture of confusion. As former University of Colorado football coach Bill McCartney observed, "All coaching is, is taking a player where he can't take himself."

I once had the opportunity to hear from Derwin Gray, a former NFL standout turned current pastor/speaker standout. We will learn more from Derwin later, but his comments on the challenges young people face in making sound choices in today's culture are pertinent right here and now. He observed, "I think the greatest challenge is the same old challenge that Adam and Eve faced: Do I find my value, significance, purpose and life apart from God or in relationship with God? Cultures change but the enemy and his lies don't."

So coach, our challenge is to help the new generation face the same old problem. Our responsibility is to get in the game and make winning choices when, where and however God calls us. In the end, those you help may drench you in a shower of Gatorade and carry you off the field, celebrating the values and lessons you have brought to their game. Or, they may not. Reality, unfortunately, remains reality.

Game Winning Point: A culture of confusion is testing the capabilities of an entire generation.

Game Changing Verse: With the Lord's authority let me say this: Live no longer as the ungodly* do, for they are hopelessly confused. Ephesians 4:17

Read On!

QUICK HIT 1. JOE AVILA

The journey of a man of God

Personal honesty has become a core competency in Joe's arsenal. At one time that was not always the case. His story, summarized in the Decisions Happen chapter, relates how he fought the reality that alcohol had taken control of his life. He saw no need to change and no need to listen to either the voice within or the pleas from others.

God had a different idea. He had a donkey for Joe to find; a job for him to do! Similar to those disciples who were sent to get a donkey for Christ's triumphal entry to Jerusalem, Joe was sent on a journey to grow God's kingdom.

Today, Joe manages an extensive piece of the Prison Fellowship field operations in the western United States. Every day, thousands of prisoners benefit from the guidance and counseling provided by the team that he serves. Joe's wakeup call involved a human tragedy. His life-changing experience continues to live within him each and every day. But let me emphasize that not everyone who changes the course of their life must go through the depth of sorrow that Joe has had to live through. Joe would tell you that God is not the author of tragedy; we are.

I had the opportunity to ask Joe several questions related to searching for and finding "the donkey in his locker room." Ponder his guidance.

1. Following the tragic event of September 1992, what or who helped you reshape the way you view (life's choices)?

Joe: Before and immediately following the accident, my brain was guided by what I call "stinking thinking." My natural self-kept whispering, or in some cases, shouting in my ear that I could escape responsibility for what I had done. After the accident, I realized that I had committed a terrible act but I assumed that I could selfishly recover from my addictions through a speedy rehab program. Wrong! It took a chaplain and the head of the local Salvation Army to get me moving in the right direction; it took my acceptance of Christ to make it happen. Do not underestimate the need for help from God and those He has placed in your path to make real changes in your beliefs and actions. Alone, I never stood a chance. With these men of God plus an understanding family, my life took on a new perspective. Realizing my guilt, I sought God's forgiveness and direction in my life. The power of Proverbs 3:5-6 energized me as I sought new direction. Since we are talking about "coaches" in this book, allow me to stress two convictions that played out in my life. First for those who coach: Your place in the life of someone in need cannot be overstated. Those in need are often unable to express that need, but, believe me, it exists. As I have already expressed, the presence of others in my life jump-started my change in direction. Second, for those in need of help: FIND A COACH! Lean on someone who can help kill that "stinking thinking." And for both coach and player, seek God's help. In the end, He has to be, in the language of football, your "go-to guy." He truly is the one who offers to occupy your life on a 24/7 basis.

2. How should faith play a role in one's choices in life?

Joe: A sign stands on Highway 99 pleading, in Amy's name, that we don't drink and drive. What wasn't said, is that I drive by that sign nearly every day of my life. Simply put, faith allows me to pass that sign day in and day out; I could not imagine how anyone could drive by it without faith. Knowing God's forgiveness and living with His strength has made that possible. Scripture teaches us that faith in God provides both our way to eternal salvation and the power to live a new life on a daily basis.

3. Following your term in prison, you have relentlessly pursued a life of speaking to others in hopes of deterring them from similar tragic acts. Have you seen material results or feedback from your coaching efforts?

Joe: One of my goals is to allow others to use "my dumb decision to avoid your own." To do so, I have been relating my story at school assemblies, church events, DUI classes and any venue that will allow me to speak. Over the years, I have had numerous personal testimonies from those who have heard my story and made good choices to avoid similar circumstances. For instance, one young man who heard me speak following his arrest on a DUI charge related that one night he began drinking with his buddies again. Fortunately, he realized that he had consumed too much to drive, but, unfortunately he started making his way to his car. As he walked, he remembered my story and rather than getting behind the wheel, he threw his car keys onto the roof of the bar to ensure that he would not let his own "stinking thinking" turn his vehicle into a weapon.

Joe truly understands the impact of both good and bad decisions. He has experienced the consequences of the opposite extremes of those choices. Today, his life has become a huge blessing to those in his ever-growing sphere of influence. Joe will also tell anyone in an earshot of his voice that to make a difference in someone's life you don't need to have a doctorate in counseling or coaching. You simply need to allow

God to direct your path while making yourself available to those in need. You just need to get the donkey when He asks.

—————————— **Read On!** ——————————

Part 2
THE ANGEL TREE EIGHT

THE STANFORD ANGEL TREE FOOTBALL CLINIC

Creating Hope...Achieving Hope....
Meeting Reality at the Street Level

THE ANGEL TREE EIGHT

Introduction

Lift 'em Up!

– Clinic Motto

Venue:
ANGEL TREE FOOTBALL CLINIC
STANFORD UNIVERSITY CAMPUS
PALO ALTO, CALIF.
LATE SUMMER 2013 AND 2014

Talk about getting pumped up! In the eyes of a kid hoping to play football, it couldn't get much better. Take a ride on a luxury bus to one of the best colleges in the country. Have 50 former professional and college players show up to spend the day playing shoulder-to-shoulder with you. Enjoy a great picnic lunch and a ride back home on that same luxury bus. Wow, would that send the "hope meter" skyrocketing or what! When the buses rolled in, it was time to get started as guys who have played the game at the highest level stood ready to teach football and teach life. Until they boarded the buses late in the day, 350-plus kids were the center of attention of a whole lot of people. Read on...

I have chosen to include this inspiring event in Winning Choices because, quite frankly, it's what the book is all about. Every aspect of the day demonstrated how the "good guys" (and girls) can successfully get out of the stands and into the game, sharing their skills, experience and enthusiasm to help younger people make better lifelong choices. The clinic, now in its ninth year, represented a microcosm of the culture in which we live; a lot of eager people helping a lot of other people learn how to get the job done—all under the umbrella of a loving God. Exciting stuff, but not so different than you should be able to expect in whatever game you play.

The Scene

Perhaps dedicated fans across the country would lay claim that their alma mater is the ideal setting for a youth football clinic. An honest person, which excludes most rabid fans, would have to admit that a late summer day on the Stanford University campus in Palo Alto, Calif., would be hard to beat. With ideal weather, a beautiful campus, plus three football fields, complements of the Cardinal athletic department, the venue was nearly perfect. But, the significance of the event was really generated, not by the ideal location, but by the 500-plus people who came together for a daylong event filled with learning, fun and a life-changing message.

Arriving at the Angel Tree Football Clinic as an observer with only minimal knowledge of the "workings" of the day, I was truly impressed by the coordinated effort of an amazing group of volunteers and staff. My first impression was that God was going to do some really serious work here today. Eight hours later, as I left the field, my impression was that God truly HAD done some really serious work here today. During the intervening hours, I was blessed to witness real people making a real difference in the lives of real kids. It left no doubt that God's hand truly was in the mix.

On a summer day that produced memories that would last for a lifetime, HOPE showed up as 200-plus dedicated volunteers walked onto the field and into the lives of more than 350 kids. On this day, an observer could sense that many of them felt that spark of hope. I can only pray that spark takes up permanent residence in their hearts.

The Kids

Though the kids attending the clinic were a bit younger than the target group of this book, their story is quite relevant. The challenges and circumstances faced daily by most of them forced them to grow up long before their time. Many were "child-aged adults," fighting for their relevance in a culture that offers little hope.

Unfortunately, many of them only knew a parent from visits to prison and others would leave the clinic only to return to a homeless shelter. But, for this brief time in their lives, they were stars, playing shoulder-to-shoulder with NFL heroes on a major college campus. At the end of the day, each young participant walked away with three huge things:

Football skills

Life skills and, more importantly,

Hope

So what is my perception of the kids who showed up on buses that day? Face the facts: Through no fault of their own, as a group, they have had a tough start to their game. Call them what you want: the products of our culture; the offspring of the incarcerated; the kids from the wrong side of the track. You make your choice for the label that best fits your own mindset. As for me, I prefer to call them the children of a living God, as valuable in His sight as any human who has walked the earth. And, if my label stands the test (which I believe it will), we owe it to these kids and those suffering similar inequities the opportunity to create a winning life. Our knowledge, our experience and our love must become the tools for helping the next generation have a winning season. We MUST be in the game!

The Volunteers

So, what about the volunteers who got out of bed very early on a Sunday morning? More than 50 individuals offering their time and skills had once played the game of football at the highest levels. They represented a cadre of ex-NFL and ex-college players who had experienced the limelight of thousands of screaming fans and national TV coverage. Today, there were no cameras or reporters trailing them to record their feats of brilliance with promises of headlines in Monday's newspaper. Today, it was just them facing off with kids, teaching them to play better in the game of life; kids whose headlines were yet to be written.

Heroes on this day also came from a broader spectrum of backgrounds, from super-skilled event organizers to first-time show-me-what-to-do volunteers to Prison Fellowship professionals to "hydration assistants," they all came together with a common goal and the enthusiasm to make it happen. Every one of them was there to teach, encourage and guide young kids, from showing them how to hold a ball to explaining how to hold onto hope. Players and speakers provided practical lessons to pump up each kid's game both on and off the field.

Make no mistake, the material recorded in the Game Day Package chapter is not a scripted lesson plan that had been distributed to participants, coaches or volunteers to guide them through the day. What you read is what I heard and saw happening. It records the effect of simply gathering a team of dedicated people and letting them go to get the job done. The only direction from former Stanford standout running back Bill Anderson to the player/coaches was to "teach them football and teach them life." If I may play word games a bit, perhaps

Bill was telling them to mingle football with life, teaching kids the essential skills of "lifeball." In any case, the kids really never knew what hit 'em. They came to learn football and learn football they did. Hanging about the edges throughout the day-long discussion were key skills that would help them be better people on the streets of their neighborhood. I have attempted to capture what I heard and witnessed in eight dynamics, hence, the section title, The Angel Tree Eight. Pump up your game in these eight areas and you will succeed both on and off the field.

The Clinic

Perhaps a few comments on the structure of the clinic would help you visualize the day.

As expected, volunteers were on the scene, briefed and in position long before the busses rolled in around 9 a.m. Once the kids were checked in, assigned teams and given identification badges, the hero in charge of field operations, Bill, assembled everyone for a super-group photo (which each kid was able to take home). Following the photo, Bill introduced the players, sending each them off to their assigned location on one of three fields. Six locations were set up on each field, focused by position (running backs, linemen, receivers, etc.). Each team of kids was assigned a squad leader (typically a high school player) responsible for rotating the team among field locations throughout the day.

After a long morning of training, the entire group descended on a great picnic lunch provided in the shade of a grove of trees near the stadium. Following lunch, several speakers provided hope and challenged each person to be the best they can be in football and in life. They learned that God would always be there for them, even when others let them down. Additionally, Dean Johnson, a noted strong man, entertained everyone by bending steel bars, ripping phone books in half and performing a variety of feats while teaching them to be strong in their faith.

An awards ceremony provided a wrap-up to the day. For each of the 20 or so teams, the assigned squad leader selected one individual on the team who gave it their best during the clinic, exhibiting a great attitude throughout the day. Each winner was recognized with a medal and was lifted up (literally) by several of the former players to honor them in front of the group. Undoubtedly, that hands-on experience motivated them to keep that winning attitude alive.

Kids departed the scene to the waiting luxury buses carrying home a group photo and a head filled with memories. Is that the end? Nope. Churches had been solicited to do some follow up with each participant to help imbed the experience. And, of course, there would be next year when, once again, a bunch of great people would show up to go shoulder-to-shoulder with some great kids.

The Rogue Angel

By the way, if you are not familiar with the Angel Tree ministry, you need to be. As part of Prison Fellowship Ministries, Angel Tree has provided millions of Christmas gifts to children of incarcerated adults around the world. For many, these gifts represent the only expression that someone cares for them. How did it start? One special lady, Mary Kay Beard, a former prisoner and famous for being on the FBI's Top Ten Most Wanted List, decided to follow God's lead and get in the game and make winning choices. Her idea has grown into an inspiring outreach with eternal results. You'll hear more from the woman who calls herself the "Rogue Angel" as you read.

——————— Read On! ———————

COACH BEN PARKS

A Dedication to a Dedicated Man

"Success in life has nothing to do with what you gain in life or accomplish for yourself. It's what you do for others."

– Coach Parks

Volumes could be written about the character and accomplishments of Coach Ben Parks. Being true to character, he would not want us to dwell on him, but rather get on with serving the needs of others. Born in poverty and deserted by his mother, coach Parks learned the blessing of giving one's resources and time from those who took him in. Throughout the years, he has become a hero, mentor, servant and leader crossing racial, economic and cultural boundaries to serve the needs of people in both sports and non-sporting environments. Working formally as a high school coach, he expanded his influence to others, providing training clinics that improve skills at all levels. Professional athletes who have fallen under his influence include household names such as Joe Montana, Ronnie Lott, Jerry Rice and Roger Craig. However, his true legacy is found in his dedication to the youth of America. That commitment has been recognized nationally, earning him the chance to share his ideas with the President's Council, which helps build character in youth via sports.

So, where does coach Parks fit into the Angel Tree Football Clinic?

In 2005, Prison Fellowship Directors Bill Anderson and Joe Avila saw the needs of kids in the Bay Area who lacked parental involvement in their lives. Young kids growing up with one or both parents in prison faced a tough road with little support. Joe and Bill conceived the idea of creating a football clinic which would teach skills while showing the kids that others truly do care about them. As a former football player at Stanford, Bill had access to the right people at the university. But to gain access to the community and to encourage former NFL and college players to participate, both Bill and Joe realized they needed someone who had deep roots into the Bay Area neighborhoods and its players.

Enter coach Parks. He jumped at the opportunity to help make the clinic a reality. Asking and encouraging (or as Bill describes "simply telling") former players to be a part of this worthy effort produced the inaugural talent to kick off the clinic. A host of former players offered their time and skills to get the ball rolling. Coach Parks personally joined them at the daylong event, coaching the kids to "dig deep and play hard" in every part of their lives.

Four-time Super Bowl champion Ronnie Lott (and Angel Tree coach) perhaps said it best: "The motivation that kept me playing well and continues to enthuse me and push me is coach Parks. One thing he says is, 'Life isn't a choice, but living is.' It's inspiring. You have all the choices in the world, why not choose to live life the right way? Why not choose to help people? It makes you stronger within."

In 2011, just prior to the Angel Tree Football Clinic, coach Parks took his story into the book of legends, passing away peacefully in his sleep. Since then, the Angel Tree Football Clinic has established an award presented to Angel Tree coaches who exhibit the spirit of coach Parks.

In his honor, I dedicate this part of the book to him. For without his tireless efforts, the clinic may have only been "a good idea."

———— Read On! ————

BUILDING HOPE
BUILDING TRUST

An Angel Tree Football Clinic leader's example

John Choma will tell you that he is just one of the guys. Maybe so. But, he is also one of the most loyal Angel Tree Football Clinic player/coaches who also played a key role in one of the greatest football moments in Super Bowl history. His story characterizes attributes being taught to the young kids hoping for a chance to play football well, plus play well in the game of life. Let's check it out.

In football lore, it has become known as the greatest goal line stand in Super Bowl history. But, for one of the defenders who played a key role in those four downs, it has become known as the fulfillment of a dream rooted in belief and trust.

On a frigid January day in 1982, the Cincinnati Bengals faced off with the San Francisco 49ers in the comfortable domed confines of the Pontiac Silverdome. At the time, it was billed as the largest stadium in the NFL with a capacity of 82,000 people and it became the first cold weather city Super Bowl venue in NFL history. This was the largest crowd ever in the venue until Pope John Paul II stopped by in 1987 to celebrate Mass, drawing in more than 93,000 people. The 49ers took control of the game early, posting a 20-0 lead at the half on a pair of touchdowns from quarterback Joe Montana and two field goals by Ray Wersching. Quarterback Ken Anderson led a Cincinnati rally in the second half racking up two third quarter touchdowns and moving the chains for a possible third score. But, with first and goal at the 49er three yard line, the Bengals hit a wall, literally a wall of committed San Francisco defenders who planned to fly home winners. In those next few moments, NFL lore would unfold. Fodder for arguments, debates and unending stories of both greatness and failure would come to pass. The greatest goal-line stand in Super Bowl history would go into the record books.

On first-and-goal at the three yard line, the Bengals called a power play. All-Pro fullback Pete Johnson took the handoff from Anderson driving up the middle in an effort to simply use his huge size and powerful legs to cross the goal line. Unfortunately for Johnson, 49er tackle John Choma read the play beautifully and cleanly took Johnson down short of the goal. The YouTube account of the following three downs can best be described as a mass of humanity colliding with little forward movement and, definitively, no points added to the board. Stopped and discouraged, the momentum switched to the 49ers who went on to win their first Super Bowl 26-21.

What does this story of glory (or defeat) have to do with us today as we help young people learn to make better choices? Plenty. The skills and mindset that I observed being passed along at the clinic reflected the same attributes that led John to and through that famous goal-line stand.

His story:

While John still tells the story of this goal-line stand with well-earned exuberance, he also wants us to understand a meaningful lesson that created the opportunity for him to be a part of the record books on that day. It is a story of trust and belief that each of us who mentor others need to learn. As John points out, he should not have been colliding with Pete Johnson on that day.

John had played at both the University of Virginia and in the NFL as an offensive lineman. But, early in the season, San Francisco 49ers coach Bill Walsh ran into a problem which led to an opportunity for John to prove himself on the other side of the ball. The microscopic flu bug accomplished what most offensive lines were unable to do. It knocked several defensive linemen back on their heels and out of the lineup. Short of backups, coach Walsh turned to his offense, namely John, to step up to the challenge. For those of us who have never played at this level, this switch may not seem like a big deal. But, as John relates, the move was a huge deal. A defensive squad is, for lack of a better term, a "closed club" with a great sense of pride. One must earn their way into their ranks and "outsiders" are not typically welcome. John did admit he was a bit unsure of himself as he took on that challenge. But with faith, encouragement and a belief in his abilities, coach Walsh gave him the chance to break into this club and provided the support when he needed it. As the season progressed, the successes of this new short-yardage defense evolved into a strategic advantage for the 49ers. Good decision, coach! It definitely played a key part in its first Super Bowl win.

John was there for that historic set of downs not solely because he had the skills and size. He truly believes that trust and faith played a key role. The type of hope being handed out at the clinic mirrored what John received from his coach; a hope that inspired belief and generated the energy to rise to a new level.

John now spends much of his time mentoring, training and helping youth get their lives together and moving in the right direction. He points out that most young people are not the confident, exuberant, energized decision-makers just waiting to step out on their own and call the shots like an NFL quarterback.

Quite the opposite, John says. "Most young people, especially those who experienced a challenging childhood, are simply afraid to go it alone. They are more confident being part of a team; less confident in being the team leader."

Following the Angel Tree Football Clinic, I had the opportunity to speak further with John to gather his thoughts on the need to help young people as they get into their own game of life. John's response illustrates his commitment to the need for us to get in the game and make winning choices.

1. As a guy with a crowded calendar, why did you add the Angel Tree Football Clinic to your busy schedule?

John: Two reasons: I like football and I like kids. Plus, I have seen enough out there that says these kids need to see that others care for them. These young people are at a stage in life when they will be solidifying their view of the world and acting out that view. The Angel Tree Clinic and other similar venues offer them the chance to see the positive side of life and hear from those of us who care about them. Giving them a few pointers on football was fun; giving them a few pointers on life was essential.

2. As an individual who sees the needs of the young generation, how can the guy on the street help out?

John: I see a lot of young people struggling to make sound decisions. Unfortunately, many of them lack the confidence or personality to step up to the situation on their own. They are uncomfortable taking the lead, often preferring to be part of the team, but not calling the shots. As adults, we all realize that, in many cases, making choices and taking the responsibility for them is an individual thing. But, as these young people learn to move forward, it is important that they are surrounded by people who care enough to encourage, teach and lead them.

I was fortunate in my football career to have coaches and teammates who gave me the opportunity and support to utilize my talents and skills even in positions that were a bit unfamiliar. Kids need that type of attitude from "coaches" in their lives. Each of us who have experienced the ups and downs of life owe this next generation the opportunity to learn from our wins and losses.

Helping kids achieve success depends on a dedicated team. Great teams operate a lot like mechanical watches. The casual observer might be impressed by the largest or fastest gears, but it's the role of the nearly invisible pinions that keep the gears meshed closely and working properly. All members of a world champion team must be closely meshed to ensure that they execute their purpose to produce great outcomes. As a "coach" you have a similar opportunity to help the young generation ensure that the proper people are on the field, working as a team to achieve greatness in their own lives.

3. When it comes to helping young people learn to make better choices, how does faith enter the equation?

John: Faith is huge! It is the basis for a winning season in each of our lives. Even though we have the responsibility to help kids learn, we are human and often unable to offer the right advice. But, the God of heaven is perfect, knowing every need that we have and willing to guide us if we include Him on our team. In fact, each of us must learn to seek God's advice before we make choices. And, if we are able to help others grasp that priority and incorporate it into their daily lives, we will have truly done our job as a "coach."

Every Player Counts

John's observations should strike a note with each of us. As we take on the hero-servant-mentor-leader coaching role, we need to keep in mind that those we help may be reluctant to step up to the challenges of life alone. Through fear, a lack of confidence, or, perhaps, even an attitude reflecting procrastination, many will hang back, not allowing their own uniqueness to shine. That is why we are there. Taking a lead from coach Walsh, we should exude a sense of faith in the capabilities of those we serve by providing support and advice when they suit up for the game. Perhaps the confidence that you impart will be the pivotal act that gets them into the record books of their own Super Bowl.

Though I singled John out for his unique story, everyone volunteering on that August day had their own unique history. What they passed on had been passed on to them in some way earlier in their life. And, I truly believe, that each of them would look you directly in the eyes (and for some that could be rather scary) and tell you that you, too, have unique experiences that need to be passed on to others.

Let's see what I heard them say and do.

———————— **Read On!** ————————

THE ANGEL TREE EIGHT GAME DAY PACKAGE

Eight Game-Changers for Life

Listen Up! Here's the ticket: Game-changing attributes will get you into the end zone

So coach, what do we have here? What did 50 jocks (or ex-jocks) plus a couple hundred other volunteers accomplish? Was it just a good time or did everyone walk away a better person at the end of the day? No doubt about it being a good time. Laughs, smiles, high-fives and even a few belly bumps attested that a good time was had by all. But what about walking away a better person at the end of the day? Good news there, too! The kids (and many of the rest of us) walked off the field with a feeling of hope and some tools to turn that feeling into reality.

Watching and listening to 15 mini-camps happening concurrently on three football fields created a challenge in recording a theme for the day. To keep it simple, I have summarized the overall message into eight points which I have termed "game-changers." Why game-changers? I believe that if you or I or the kids attending the clinic grabbed onto these eight points, incorporating them into their lives, they would truly be game-changers. Relationships would improve. Decisions would improve. Lives would improve.

The eight game-changers listed in Part 2- Figure 1 are discussed on the following pages. You will read the words that I heard and hear the advice of dedicated people working in the hearts of the kids. You will see hope created and hope achieved. You will see God on the move!

Part 2 - Figure 1 - Eight Game-Changers for Life

1. **Show Up and Team Up**
   Every player counts!

2. **Know and Go**
   Have a plan; then act decisively and positively

3. **Focus and Build Momentum**
   Move the chains and manage the clock

4. **Adapt and Simplify**
   Field conditions change; learn to adapt and make adjustments

5. **Suck it Up and Pump it Up**
   You will face failure; deal with it and play with enthusiasm

6. **Finish (Score) and Reflect**
   Don't stop until you achieve your goal; learn from prior plays

7. **Trust and Respect**
   Faith matters; Go deep! Build sound beliefs, place trust & respect in the right place

8. **Get Strong and Go Long**
   Strive to continuously improve your life-long game physically, mentally and spiritually

---

Angel Tree Football Clinic
GAME CHANGER # 1
SHOW UP and TEAM UP
Every Player Counts!

Words I Heard

Come pumped up, ready to play. All players count. Be part of a team.

On the Field

Known as one of the game's iconic coaches, few people have a resume approaching that of coach Willie Shaw. During a career spanning 32 years, he was an integral part of the coaching staff of 14 NFL and college teams. After lunch, coach Shaw, explained to the group that each one of them will be part of many kinds of teams during their lifetime. Whether in sports, jobs, school or family, they will play various roles as part of those teams. Sometimes they will be leaders and sometimes followers, but will always be an important part of the team. He advised them that to be successful, they need to learn to be team players early in life. In addition, he advised that mixing hard work, commitment and trust separates the good from the great. He said that his faith in God was the key in defining his football career and life outside of football.

On the Street

Director Woody Allen once said, "Eighty percent of success is just showing up." I'm not so sure I would agree with the heavy weight assigned by Allen, but the idea you have to show up should not be dismissed. In a world dominated by social media, face-to-face interaction increasingly fades into a distant second place. Sports teams offer an exception to this trend, providing avenues for learning the critical skills of teaming that will serve each of us through life. As coach Shaw suggested, however, teaming goes far beyond sports. He advised that paying attention to your parents, your teachers, your coaches, and most importantly, your God will reap huge dividends. So stop and ask yourself, "Where is my next opportunity to team up either as a player or a coach? Who do I need to listen to and who needs to listen to me?"

In God's Playbook

"Just as our bodies have many parts and each part has a special function, so it is with Christ's body. We are all parts of his one body, and each of us has different work to do." Romans 12:4-5

From the Legends

"Treat a person as he is, and he will remain as he is. Treat him as what he could be, and he will become what he should be."

- Jimmy Johnson, former NFL player, coach and Pro Football Hall of Famer

Angel Tree Football Clinic
GAME CHANGER # 2
KNOW and GO
Think, then act decisively and positively

Words I Heard

Face reality...move fast...hit hard...take a hit...concentrate...collide.

On the Field

Super Bowl champion John Choma explained to the kids that football is an explosive sport, but you need to think before you explode. Moving fast gives you an advantage, but doing it right comes with experience. So keep practicing. You must know the plays before you try to execute them. Otherwise, you will fail at doing your part to making the team successful.

Former Indianapolis Colts running back Brian Allen headed up the session for offensive backs. He explained (and showed them) the importance of knowing how to hold the ball before you collided with the defense. Here again, know before you go was the advice of the day. "Holding the ball wrong will lead to a fumble and a fumble hurts the entire team," Brian told them, "You can't score if you can't hang onto the ball."

On the Street

"Know and go" represents good advice for more than just football. Life on the street is more demanding than on the field. Knowing what to do and why to do it before acting is a huge lesson that needs to be conveyed to players. Snapping the ball without knowing the play (aka shooting from the hip) leads to disaster. Life on the street reflects a "you do what you view" mentality. It is important to get the "view" right before you "do." More on "right viewing" as the book unfolds. Additionally, as Brian said, you must be able to hang onto the critical elements (like the ball) of whatever you are doing in life to create a positive outcome. Getting into the end zone without the ball is easy; crossing the goal with it is a different story. It's a message you need to deliver again and again because it's so critical to achieving success in life, no matter the path you take.

In God's Playbook

"The godly person thinks before he speaks (acts)." Proverbs 15:28

From the Legends

"The dictionary is the only place where success comes before work."

- Vince Lombardi

"We didn't tackle well today, but we made up for it by not blocking."

- John McKay of USC

Angel Tree Football Clinic
GAME CHANGER # 3
FOCUS and BUILD MOMENTUM
Move the chains and manage the clock

Words I Heard

Keep trying...manage the clock...hustle up and never give up.

On the Field

As a former linebacker at Cal, David Shaw knows the importance of focus and time management during a drive. Actually, as a linebacker, one of his key goals was not so much to create focus but to disrupt the offense's efforts to generate it. David explained to the kids that focus begins long before the game. You need to learn to visualize your goals during practice and in the days leading up to the game. On game day, you must concentrate on playing just as you visualized earlier and if you do make a mistake, put it behind you and focus on the game. David's advice: Listen to the coach; pay attention to what is happening on each play; keep your mind on the game and don't daydream.

On the Street

David explained to me that every game or major event in life has a defining point; a point where focus and concentration vaults you to victory or where a lack of it allows your game to come apart. David said he believes life IS time management," that is, how we choose to use the 24 hours of each day and how it defines us as a person. For a young person, a lot of time remains on the scoreboard. If you have spent it unwisely, there is still time to get your game (and life) back on track, play well and finish strong. Momentum equates to sustainability. Every team knows that losing momentum breaks focus, making it difficult to play well as an individual or as a team. In life, almost anyone can start a task; the real skill comes in keeping it going and in finishing it.

In God's Playbook

"Look straight ahead, and fix your eyes on what lies before you. Mark out a straight path for your feet; then stick to the path and stay safe. Don't get sidetracked; keep your feet from following evil." Proverbs 4:25-27 (NLT)

From the Legends

"Once you learn to quit, it becomes a habit."

– Vince Lombardi, legendary player, coach and executive in the NFL

Angel Tree Football Clinic
GAME CHANGER # 4
ADAPT and SIMPLIFY
Field conditions change; learn to adapt and make adjustments

Words I Heard

Observe...Flex...Improve...Respond...Form counts...Keep it simple... Don't get fancy.

On the Field

As the thermometer began to rise, I'm not sure if the veterans or the kids showed the most sign of fatigue as water breaks became more frequent. John Cato, former Cal linebacker, told the participants, "There's no shade trees on the football field." If you want to play well, you must be willing to sweat. John explained that successful players practice in all types of conditions so that when game day arrives, they will be able to adapt to everything that nature throws at them. Practice when it rains, suck it up in the heat, run drills in the mud and learn to play in the snow. "Fair weather" players are in for a surprise: Life in the stadium changes with every set of downs.

On the Street

Life on the street (aka your stadium) also changes daily. How you handle or adapt to that change may spell the difference between a winning and losing season. Bill Anderson, former running back at Stanford, drew a parallel between football and life, explaining that the stadium you play in today will not be the stadium you play in next week. Successful football teams learn to play away games well, adapting to noisy crowds, unfamiliar turf and living in hotels. Even on home turf, Bill explained, weather changes present challenges as the game wears on. Similarly, the venues and playing conditions that we face as life progresses will undoubtedly change. We cannot play tomorrow's game with yesterday's game plan. We must learn to adapt to a myriad of challenges including different people, new living conditions, more or less money and growing responsibilities. We must each be alert to changing circumstances, adapting how we play the game while not sacrificing our principles. Establish sound principles and stick with them. As Bill said, "Only change your principles if they are out of sync with God's principles."

In God's Playbook

""Don't copy the behavior and customs of this world, but let God change you into a new person by changing the way you think." Romans 12:2

From the Legends

"If you align expectations with reality, you will never be disappointed."

-Terrell Owens, former NFL wide receiver

Angel Tree Football Clinic
GAME CHANGER # 5
SUCK IT UP and PUMP IT UP
Deal with failure; play with enthusiasm

Words I Heard

Keep trying ... hustle up and never give up ... put mistakes behind you.

On the Field

Ron Johnson, a former standout wide receiver for the Philadelphia Eagles, taught the kids to "play the ball" concentrating on the front point of the ball as a pass came their way. Chatting with him after the clinic, he confessed that he, like all receivers, occasionally dropped a pass he should have caught. I asked him how he would get back in the game mentally after such a blunder. He said that when he dropped a catchable ball, he knew he let the team down. All he wanted to do is suck it up and get another opportunity to make a play. In Ron's words, "I can't get down on myself because I would not be ready for the next opportunity if I stayed in a funk. My college coach used to say that if you dropped the ball, forget about it because we are coming right back at you."

On the Street

All of the players working the clinic, like all of us, had experienced failure as individuals and as members of a team. Several of them advised the kids: You, too, will make mistakes in athletics or in life. The real sign of a player, however, is how they handle a tough blunder. Do you dwell on it? Or, do you learn from it and move forward? Good players learn from errors then look for another opportunity. Poor players dwell on their mistakes, or play the blame game, by losing focus and subsequently, the game. Champions play with a game-winning, contagious enthusiasm.

In God's Playbook

"Work hard and cheerfully at whatever you do, as though you were working for the Lord ..."Colossians 3:23.

From the Legends

"All of us get knocked down, but it's resiliency that matters. All of us do well when things are going well, but the thing that distinguishes athletes is the ability to do well in times of great stress, urgency, and pressure."

-Roger Staubach, NFL Hall of Fame quarterback

Angel Tree Football Clinic
GAME CHANGER # 6
FINISH and REFLECT
Don't look back until you cross the goal line; learn from your game films

Words I Heard

Keep moving. Think. Learn with every play. Keep your eyes down field.

On the Field

Volunteers Brian Allen, former NFL running back with the Indianapolis Colts and Todd Spencer, former tailback at the University of Southern California, coached the kids on basic running back skills. After taking them through some high-stepping drills, they then turned to developing "accelerate and find the running lanes" exercises. Many of the kids initially responded well, blowing past the line, but then slowed or stopped completely. "Keep running, keep running!" the coaches would shout. "Don't stop until the play is over!" Their point: You need to crank up the speed and finish the play. Don't slow down; keep grinding out the yards. Never look back before you cross the goal line! There will be plenty of time to celebrate after you score!

Brian also told them to learn from their mistakes. In football and life, he explained, we all make mistakes. Great running backs learn from their blunders and deliberately decide not to repeat them. Be honest with yourself when you check out your game films.

On the Street

Later in the day, the kids heard the same message. Following a great picnic lunch, Pastor Ebara, a Bay Area minister with a great personal and spiritual message, spoke with the group. Having grown up in a tough environment himself, Pastor Ebara bonded well with the kids offering them a future filled with hope. His message: NEVER GIVE UP! Knowing that it is easy to say but hard to do, he coupled his message with practical advice. He asked each of them to promise that if they feel like giving up or quitting, they'll talk with five people before doing so. Never quit without seeking the advice of others. The power of accountability with and to others will help to keep your players from quitting when they are at an emotional low point. Share your own experiences with failure and disappointment and those moments when you wanted to quit. Be a leader, but demonstrate that you don't have all the answers. You struggle, too, but you found a way to overcome those low points.

Pastor Ebara also counseled the young men on the need to find time to be alone with God. In a world filled with challenges, spending a brief time in silent reflection can help slow an angry response plus will energize you to face whatever comes your way.

In God's Playbook

"It is better to say nothing than to promise something that you don't follow through." Ecclesiastes 5:5

From the Legends

"I learned that if you want to make it bad enough, no matter how bad it is, you can make it."

- Gale Sayers, former NFL Hall of Fame running back for the Chicago Bears

Angel Tree Football Clinic
GAME CHANGER # 7
TRUST and RESPECT
Faith matters; Go Deep! Build sound beliefs, trust and respect the right people

Words I Heard

Good attitude...Strong faith...team unity...love.

On the Field

Back to John Choma's story. When he stood still for more than 10 seconds, the kids would flock to him looking for autographs, photo ops or a chance to try on his Super Bowl ring. I was chatting with John during the picnic lunch when a bunch of eager kids descended on him in a swarm. Some brought jerseys, some footballs, all seeking a big-time autograph they could show off to friends.

And then there was Marcus. A little guy, a big jersey and an even bigger heart. Marcus (not his real name), wore a jersey obviously too large for his physical stature. But he brought a big lesson for all to hear. Chuckling politely at the size of the jersey, John asked the 10-year-old if he planned to grow into it and wear it on the football field. Without hesitation, the small guy with a big heart smiled saying, "No, it's not for me. It's my present for my dad. He couldn't be here. He's in prison." Wow. That comment, coming from the heart of a young man, put a perspective on why we were all there. John bent his 6 foot 5 inch tall frame a bit deeper, looking Marcus directly in the eyes and told him that giving his dad a present was a really great thing to do and that his dad would remember it for a long time. John then personalized the jersey with Marcus' dad's name, adding in huge font, "May God Bless You!" above his own signature.

That brief encounter summarized the meaning of the day at many levels: A big man encouraging a little guy to encourage, love and respect his imprisoned father. It was definitely a coaching moment where the child coached the coach!

On the Street

Throughout the day, a subtle (and, at times, not so subtle) theme of trust and respect wound its way into discussions on and off the field. The points being made: Trust God and respect and love your parents. Knowing full and well that those kids often found it tough to trust anyone in their life, the speakers emphasized that God will never betray you. Friends or even parents may let you down, but God truly has your best interest in mind. When you feel alone in the world, remember the voice of God is with you. But, God also tells each of us to love and respect our parents even though they may not always treat us right. Why? Because God loves us even when we let Him down and we should follow His lead and do the same.

In God's Playbook

"Two people can accomplish more than twice as much as one; they get a better return for their labor. If one person falls, the other can reach out and help. But people who are alone when they fall are in real trouble." Eccl. 4:9-10

From the Legends

"Every team requires unity. A team has to move as one unit, one force. If the team doesn't do this, it goes down in defeat. You win or lose as a team, as a family."

– Jack Kemp, football player/statesman

Angel Tree Football Clinic
GAME CHANGER # 8
GET STRONG and GO LONG
Skills count; Learn to block and tackle, then, pump up all aspects of your game

Words I Heard

Stay strong...pump up your spirit...endure for the long haul.

On the Field

Countless times at the clinic, big-time players insisted that the kids learn the basics before moving on to more advanced skills. But once mastered, it is critical to move beyond the basics. Craig Awbrey, former nose guard at Stanford, counseled them to learn skills in practice before you need them in a game because your opponent will not cut you any slack.

Following lunch, the kids were entertained by strongman, Dean Johnson. Dean ripped phone books in half, bent steel bars and broke a baseball bat over his leg all to the amazement of some wide-eyed kids. But, more importantly, Dean wove a critical message into his presentation. His message: Continue to develop ALL aspects of your life. "Work the body; work the brain; work the heart". He told them that God will utilize His strength in their life if they will simply ask Him. Knowing God and spending time with Him is the first step to a life of strength.

On the Street

Just as the kids were advised, each of us must be ready to play BEFORE the game begins. No smart coach tries new plays on game day without first running them successfully in practice. Similarly in life, developing convictions and life skills BEFORE the crisis comes is huge! In football, attendees were soundly advised to stick with the basics and not try the "fancy stuff" until they had the blocking and tackling mastered. The same holds true for life. But, as in football, each and every person needs to move beyond the basics, especially spiritually. God has a purpose for us to fulfill; He expects us to hone our God-given capabilities to enable us to achieve that purpose.

In God's Playbook

"Having gifts that differ according to the grace given to us, let us use them." Romans 12:6

From the Legends

"We have a lot of players in their first year. Some of them are also in their last year."

- Coach Bill Walsh

Read On!

MOTIVATE AND SERVE

Coaching Counts!

Coaching counts; share your experience by serving others; they need a hero

Note: The eight Game-Changers in the prior chapter actually apply to both players and coaches. But, in listening to the chatter, I picked up some thoughts that apply primarily to those assuming the role of coaches. Let's check them out.

Renowned NFL coach Tony Dungy once remarked, "I've always tried to coach people the way I would like to be coached; positively and encouragingly rather than with criticism and fear. I've tried to be as fair as possible." The former players coaching the kids at Angel Tree, undoubtedly, have seen it all when it comes to coaches. Throughout their careers they have been challenged by the screamers, the lecturers, the task masters, the philosophers, plus a host of other coaching styles. Most coaches think their own personal style is God's gift to the team. Many players would tend to disagree. But in observing the guys on the field and speaking with them afterward, they tended to agree that an approach similar to that described by Tony works best in today's world.

I had the opportunity to spend some time with Craig Awbrey, former nose guard at Stanford, who currently helps young men develop both football and life skills. While at Stanford, Craig had the opportunity to play for legendary coach Bill Walsh. "Coach Walsh provided a great example of a successful coach who did not scream at his players," Craig said. "In fact, coach Walsh intentionally practiced humor as a communication style to teach and motivate the team." Craig was adamant that in today's culture, screaming at players only creates problems, not victories.

In our discussion, coach Awbrey threw several practical ideas of wisdom my way. Most of them were on display during the clinic. Consider the following thoughts as you work with others in sports or in any activity of life:

• The primary task of a coach is to prepare the player for the game.
• Be creative; every player learns in a different fashion. Be a teacher,

120

not a teller.

- Never teach advanced concepts and techniques to a beginner. There is an epidemic of coaches teaching inexperienced kids far too advanced concepts which they attempt to try and subsequently fail.
- If it can't be done consistently in practice, it can't be done successfully in a game.
- Players should be responsible for making and achieving their own goals. Coaches should monitor their progress as the season progresses.
- Be an encourager and most of all, "love 'em up!"

In God's Playbook

"Iron sharpens iron, and one man sharpens another." Proverbs 27:17

From the Legends

"The Lord has a plan. We always think the plans are A, B, C and D, and everything is going to be perfect for us and it may not be that way, but it's still his plan."

-Tony Dungy, NFL coach

———— Read On! ————

GET YOUR DUCKS IN A ROW

"The wise look ahead to see what is coming." Proverbs 14:8

Big-sized events (aka Angel Tree Football Clinics) don't just happen. They require a significant amount of planning, coordination, solicitation, execution, communication and funding, plus a host of other activities to successfully pull them together. And, unless you are God, these critical activities involve a myriad of people bringing a variety of skills, plus the ever-needed element of dedication to the party. They are not accomplished alone. But, at the center of this vortex, you will always find the individual responsible for planning and managing any successful event. On that sunny day in Palo Alto, that individual was Janna Bowman.

Although she will humbly admit she is not God, event planner/manager Janna Bowman brought many of the skills and experiences that, in the eyes of those present, may have earned her that title. Well, almost. As the head duck (yes, that's her title) of J Duck Productions, Janna makes the complex appear simple. But, believe me, pulling off an event involving hundreds of volunteers, most of whom have never met each other, and making it happen with the efficiency that I witnessed at Stanford, does not come easy. But, for individuals hoping to make better decisions, watching Janna in action does offer an example of how to, if I may use her words, "get your ducks in a row." On game day, Janna moved effortlessly and calmly throughout the three football fields being utilized for the clinic. Composed, with clipboard in hand, one could easily mistake her for a casual observer rather than the individual responsible for much of what was going on. Take note as a lesson to all of us: No need to run about with your hair on fire. Prepare thoroughly and properly, and you will be ready for action on game day.

Her planning encompassed both ends of the spectrum, outlining the big picture and filling in the details. In chatting with her, Janna emphasized a coach truly needs to be flexible. More often than not, the original game plan must be adjusted to meet the game day realities. Sometimes it's tweaked or occasionally ripped up and totally replaced.

For instance, shortly before the clinic started, Stanford informed the planners of a new policy requiring any organization working with kids on the campus to have background checks for each volunteer. That meant having 200 volunteers agree to complete all of the paperwork necessary to certify their background, which seemed not possible at that late date. So, to ensure the clinic moved forward, the planning team met with Stanford and worked out a compromise. In lieu of background checks, the organizers would instead hire several police personnel who would have freedom to roam throughout the event, observing and creating a visible presence. Additionally, other controls were established to ensure that no young person was alone with an adult for restroom breaks and the like. The plan worked.

Later in this book, we will discuss the elements of a 2-minute drill utilized by NFL teams to rapidly move the chains when time is short and they need a score to win. In planning and conducting the clinic, Janna and her cohorts essentially mirrored those seven steps:

1. Know your field position and set your goal.
2. Get the right players on the field matched up with the right skills.
3. Create and maintain a sense of urgency and focus.
4. Create a game winning game plan.

5. Snap the ball and execute the play.

6. Build momentum and move the chains.

7. Get into the red zone, score and win.

You, or those you coach, may never be responsible for an event the size and complexity of Angel Tree, but at some point in your life, you will have to coordinate the activities of others to get the job done. Finding a college, planning a marriage, starting a career or just getting from point A to point B often involves many of the skills Janna exhibited at the football clinic.

So, I took the opportunity to chat with Janna following the clinic to glean ideas from her that may help each of us get our act together. Specifically, I asked her:

1. How do you determine you have planned enough?

Janna: I tend to err on the side of being a perfectionist. I diligently plan, establishing processes, lists and putting the details together. I firmly believe that people thrive on structure, so as a professional, I try to build a high level of organization into an activity. Part of the planning is to over plan, allowing you flexibility and resources to make changes at the last minute as circumstances demand it. But, from a standpoint of personal faith, I have learned that I often need to step back and see if I am forcing my plans (things aren't working) or if I need to stop and ask God to direct my plans, allowing Him to change or alter the original plan. Self-imposed deadlines should defer to a dependence on God.

2. Do you suggest having plan B in place in case circumstances call for it?

Janna: Definitely. In fact, plan A may be my plan while plan B is actually God's plan (which, in retrospect, was there all along). Not only do you need a plan B, but you must be open to the idea of being willing to change. An unwillingness to change can easily lead to failure.

The God of the universe is a God of order, but he also has designed us to be capable of changing when He wants us to pursue something differently. Proverbs 16:9 teaches that "we can make our plans, but the Lord determines our steps."

3. What should each of us do if we feel overwhelmed by the size and scope of a task?

Janna: First, stop, take a deep breath and don't panic. On occasion, feeling overwhelmed is a normal response to a new challenge. However, each of us needs to realize when we are in over our head from an experience or capability standpoint. Scripture teaches us that we should depend on others in the body of Christ to help us as we follow God's path in our lives. The theme verse of this book should also provide peace when we face seemingly huge undertakings. Proverbs 3: 5-6 teaches us that God will direct our path if we simply trust Him and acknowledge His presence in our lives.

The Bear

Another plan B kind of person was legendary University of Alabama head coach Bear Bryant. With a bit of a different twist, coach Bryant advised, "… have a plan for everything. A plan for practice and a plan for the game. A plan for being ahead and a plan for being behind 20 to 0 at the half, with your quarterback hurt and the phones dead, with it raining cats and dogs and no rain gear because the equipment man left it at home."

The point: Be ready to flex your plan. In any endeavor, winners flex, losers don't!

———————— Read On! ————————

QUICK HIT #2
BILL ANDERSON

The Stadiums of Your Life

Co-founder of the Stanford Angel Tree Football Clinic Bill Anderson provides a real example of a finding the donkey in his locker room. Following a record-setting college career as a running back at Stanford, Bill moved very successfully into the business world where he was responsible for global sales in the high-tech semiconductor industry.

Bill said his successful revenue-building business career took him on a worldwide adventure. Filled with trappings of success and the rewards of completing deals, that lifestyle was also physically, mentally and spiritually demanding. Returning from the completion of a particular multi-million dollar deal in Asia, Bill found himself sitting alone in his plush Tempe, Ariz., office questioning the course of his life. Totally exhausted, Bill said he felt tired of the game. He sensed something (or someone) pulling him in a different direction.

Here comes the donkey!

Nearing the "Big 4-0," Bill told his boss he was done and needed to move on. The boss asked him to take some time off and reconsider his decision. He wanted Bill back. But God had a different idea. He had a donkey for Bill to find and a job for him to do. In his football days at Stanford, Bill had earned the "Unsung Hero" award for his game-changing play. Now, he was about to follow God's lead becoming a hero in the lives of those who need a hero most of all.

Following an extended period of contemplation (plus volunteering for Prison Fellowship), Bill was approached by Chuck Colson to become a full-time director within the Prison Fellowship organization. After resisting Colson's (or perhaps God's) pursuit for a year, he finally relented, offering to join Prison Fellowship for two years. Fourteen years later, he was still working on his two-year stint when God sent him off to get yet another donkey. Bill now utilizes his experience and God-given talents to help manage the Children of Grace organization, which helps marginalized youth overcome barriers and challenges.

The stadiums

Winning Choices portrays our lives as being lived in our own particular stadium, the environment in which we "play" on a day-to-day basis. As we have discussed, throughout his life, Bill has played and worked in extremely challenging stadiums or settings. I thought his comments would help each of us as we both live and coach in our own stadium. Take a minute to check them out.

Over the course of my football career, I have had the opportunity to play in a myriad of enormous stadiums packed with the "enemy." In several cases, perhaps, the word opportunity is stretching it. Many of those venues were downright scary, especially for a 19-year-old kid. Most of us are familiar with the phrase "though I walk through the valley of death" described in the 23rd Psalm. To draw a parallel, many of those huge stadiums throughout the nation seemed at the time like a valley of death. But, we had great coaches. And, part of their job was to pump us up, ensuring the team that we possessed the skills and attitude to win in any arena. At the time, football WAS life and life WAS football.

After graduation, as my football playing days transitioned into other less physically demanding but more mentally demanding activities, I realized that life continues to play out in a stadium. Having spent much of my career working with prisoners, the families of those incarcerated and kids from disadvantaged situations, I began to appreciate that the daunting stadiums from my football days were not so scary after all. Simply put, a lot of people face some really tough challenges on a 24/7 basis. Those of you who work in various ways to make their stadiums friendlier and perhaps give them the home-field advantage often face major challenges. But, as I can personally attest, you also receive major blessings.

A few practical tips:

1. Be Alert! In your own stadium or in the arenas of those you coach, you must continually be alert to activity around you. Stadiums do not present static environments; neither does life. People change, playing conditions change, goals and aspirations change. Those who become complacent find themselves in a fourth-and-long situation far more than necessary.

2. Find Good People! Too often, we fail to team up with the many good people who are out there. We tend to focus on the "bad guys." not realizing that a whole host of "good guys" are willing to help us get the job done. As coaches, team members, advisers or whatever, they possess the skills, experience and, most importantly, the willingness to make things happen. Find them. Get them on your team.

3. Seek Spiritual Guidance! Not only are there good people out there. There is a great God out there who offers to guide us in every decision in life. If we are going to take the snap and run successful plays, it is critical that we all trust the one who knows all and promises to deliver.

Check out Proverbs 3:5-6.

Quick Hit Point: As Bill has pointed out, every day brings a new "stadium" in which we must each suit up to play. Be alert, find good people and seek spiritual guidance and you will be on your way to a winning season. And, by the way, be ready to act when God sends you to get yet another donkey!

—————————— Read On! ——————————

THE LADY IN THE BIG FLOWERY HAT

A testimony to the powerful grace of God

A story of a life redeemed

Venue:
CHUCK COLSON MEMORIAL
LANSDOWNE, VA.
MAY 16, 2012

For now, let's just call her the "Lady in the Big Flowery Hat!" So, how does a gentleman conduct social small talk with a pleasant lady, perfectly garbed and wearing a large-brimmed, flowery hat? Not too sure about that. But, here's my account on how not to do it!

A bit of relevant background: As a member of the centurion's class of 2009, I enjoyed the opportunity to study under the sponsorship of Prison Fellowship founder Chuck Colson and other great teachers in the program. When the Lord decided that this dynamic man-of-God's work on earth was done, I also shared with thousands of others in the opportunity to honor Chuck and his work at a memorial service at the National Cathedral in Washington, D.C. To accommodate the large crowd, hundreds of us were bused from Prison Fellowship headquarters to the cathedral. On my particular bus, I noticed a nice lady wearing a large flowery hat.

As a self-proclaimed (and soon to find obviously flawed) observer of people, I simply assumed she was Chuck's friend from the office. Following the service, the group returned to Prison Fellowship's offices for a reception. Once again, I saw the lady in the big flowery hat. Approaching her to engage in typical reception small talk, I asked how she came to know Chuck. Her surprising answer: "I met him after prison." Okay, I thought. Now trying to act intelligent, I continued with: "Oh, were you a volunteer?" "Nope," she said, "I was a prisoner." "Oh!" I falteringly muttered, trying to rationalize the conflicting mental picture of the flowery hat with the vision of this nice lady in stark, orange prison garb.

Thinking she must have been doing time for backing over the neighbor's cat or offending the local sheriff, I continued my downward spiral, inquiring as to why she had spent time behind bars. She offered in a frank, but lady-like tone, "bank robbery."

Not knowing exactly how to proceed, I simply stammered, "Oh, of course, which bank did you rob?" To which she explained, "Most of them were in the Southeast parts of the United States." "Right," I said, once again searching for a way to address the polite eyes peering from under the flowery hat, "there are a lot of banks in the South."

Tripping over my own words, I gave up any attempt to mimic television host Larry King. So, I simply stuck out my right hand and said, "Hi, I'm Greg, one of Chuck's Centurions." "Hello," she said, "it's nice to meet you. I'm Mary Kay Beard, founder of Angel Tree." "Of course you are," I replied, hoping someone would save me from continuing embarrassment, "Of course you are."

Fortunately, others did join in, sparing me from a further descent into fooldom.

The point here is not my ineptness, but the reality of the saving grace of God. For those unfamiliar with Mary Kay or the Angel Tree initiative, she is proof positive of the changing grace of Christ. Yes, she did spend time in prison for armed robbery and yes, she is the founder of Angel Tree, an organization dedicated to helping the families of those serving time.

Mary Kay's story can be read in brief online or in a fuller sense in Rogue Angel, her outstanding biography. From an early life as an abused child, to a runaway teen, to a hardened criminal, Mary Kay sought to prove her independence. Partnering with a man who himself was determined to satisfy his vanity through crime, she developed a hunger for risk by seeking to find relevance and pleasure that had escaped her as a child. Bank robberies became their core competency, earning her a spot on the FBI's Top 10 Most Wanted list. As with most criminals, her pursuits eventually led to her capture.

Tried and convicted of multiple crimes, Mary Kay was sentenced to 21 years in an Alabama prison for women. But, God had different plans for her. Following her conversion to Christ, she began to study and lead a changed life. Through the Gideon's organization, she learned scripture, eventually becoming a leader and speaker for the group. Through God's power, she received a full pardon after serving only 6 years of her original 21-year sentence.

While in prison, Mary Kay was impressed by other female inmates who were desperately trying to acquire Christmas gifts for their children. Lacking money and access to shopping, they were saving soap, shampoo, plus other incidentals, and wrapping them to send home as gifts. Appreciating their efforts, Mary Kay wondered if these trivial gifts really meant much to the kids on Christmas morning.

Mary Kay's heart was moved, but while on the inside, she could do little to help. But, once on the outside, things changed. Determined to make a difference, she single-handedly decided to collect money to buy presents for the children on behalf of their incarcerated parent. Dubbed Angel Tree, she collected over $10,000 to buy gifts on behalf of mothers at the prison where she had spent the last 5 years. The idea worked. God was on the move! The loving effort gained the attention of Chuck Colson and the Prison Fellowship organization, going national in 1982. As of this writing, more than 10 million presents have found smiling faces on Christmas morning.

Mary Kay exemplifies the redeeming grace of God. He utilizes each and every person who seeks to follow Him. As coach Shaw told the kids at the football clinic, everyone can be on the team! Mary Kay was not only on the FBI's Most Wanted list; she was also on God's most wanted list. And peering out from under the big flowery hat, she would be the first to tell you that you, too, are on that list. Mary Kay died in April 2016.

But the story of her life as portrayed in Rogue Angel speaks of a lady filled with great advice for each and every one of us. Here are a couple of thoughts that would help all of us, but may be critical to a young person climbing out of a tough situation:

1. The Book - Following her conversion, she began to intently study Scripture (which she refers to as The Book), seeking guidance for her new beginning. Her habit has become her counsel to those wanting to know how to handle any particular situation: Check the Book! She has learned the Bible provides insight in all circumstances and has learned to search for direction on a decision before taking action.

2. Bitterness - Having been immersed in a childhood teeming with bitterness, no one is more qualified than Mary Kay to appreciate the consequences. But, with her conversion came a change in attitude and advice: Do not let bitterness take root. But how? Again, she has an answer. At the first sign of bitterness, pray for the person for whom you sense the emotion. God works through prayer. He will help. Mary Kay stands as a testament to that!

From Flowery Hats to Football Helmets

Sometimes, God appears to enjoy weird ways of getting to the hearts of individuals like the kids (and adults) who attended the Angel Tree Football Clinic. Think about it this way: If the nice lady in the big flowery hat had not taken God's lead in starting the Angel Tree program, these big, rugged guys who previously wore helmets for a living may not have been here on that August Sunday. Angel Tree may not have even been a thought, let alone a reality. God is always on the move, but sometimes connecting the dots is beyond us. Sometimes He converts flowery hats into football helmets to achieve His purpose. The lesson: If God tells you to do something, do it! If He asks you to go get a donkey, be confident that He has a plan for that donkey.

When you see one of the thousands of Angel Trees that dot the country as Christmas approaches, take time to recall how Christ can work in the heart of an individual to carry out His work. Thank Him for Mary Kay and others like her who get the job done. And then, dig into your wallet and buy an angel to help those who in need.

Read On!

THE END ZONE BANNER
Truth in your face

"To succeed, you need to find something to hold on to, something to motivate you, something to inspire you."

- Tony Dorsett, NFL Hall-of-Famer

What better way could there be to end this section than to discuss an end zone banner.

When Coach David Shaw, Coach Willie Shaw's son, took over the head coaching reigns of the Stanford Cardinal football program, he installed a 100-foot-long banner on the fence in the end zone of the team's practice field. It reads:

> ## YOU ARE GETTING BETTER OR YOU ARE GETTING WORSE. YOU NEVER STAY THE SAME!

An outstanding program for many years, the Cardinal football team does not dwell on mediocrity. On the contrary, coaches and players set lofty preseason goals such as winning the Pac-12 Conference Championship or perhaps the national championship. Neither is an easy task. A lot of other great teams annually pursue the same goals. So, the end zone banner serves as a constant reminder to the team as to why they spend hours on that practice field, namely, to get better! Practice sessions can be long and tough. Sweat happens! But, any coach will tell you that time spent on the practice field drives performance on game day. Legendary Alabama coach Bear Bryant put it this way: "It's not the will to win that matters – everyone has that. It's the will to prepare to win that matters." From a player's perspective, former NFL All-Pro receiver Jerry Rice spoke of time spent preparing when he said, "Today I will do what others won't, so tomorrow I can accomplish what others can't."

As we wrap up the lessons learned from the Angel Tree Football Clinic, perhaps it would be a good idea to ask ourselves what banner would we want to see displayed in the end zone of our field? Do we believe what coach Shaw believes? Or, is there another mantra that drives our way of thinking; our view of reality? Take five minutes and think through what slogan would appear on your banner. You may want to jot it down in the space below:

Now, let's consider another banner that you may wish to hang in the end zone as a constant reminder of how God wants you to play or coach the game:

TRUST IN THE LORD WITH ALL YOUR HEART; DO NOT DEPEND ON YOUR OWN UNDERSTANDING. SEEK HIS WILL IN ALL YOU DO AND HE WILL DIRECT YOUR PATHS

In God's Stadium

God's banner can be found in Proverbs 3:5-6. In a few words, it provides straightforward direction for making decisions on any field. It's a game plan for success. Before you call the play, snap the ball and move the chains, you should take a moment to remind yourself of what the owner is telling you to do. Then, with trust and confidence, take that snap and move forward. Because of its clear-cut guidance, you will find Proverbs 3:5-6 as a theme throughout the book. For me, it provides clarity but also challenges. So often, my own understanding, or my foolish ideas, get in the way. For most of us, total dependency on God is a lifelong challenge. God knows our limitations yet His offer remains open.

Stanford's banner, aimed at inspiring a football team, may also apply to our own personal spiritual reality. With each passing day, every one of us is either improving in our spiritual walk or getting worse. We are either getting closer to God or further from Him. As we read earlier in the Gaffe in the Garden, like Adam and Eve, we are either seeking Him or hiding from Him. Perhaps the banner that God would choose to hang across the end zone in our stadium would repeat that second question in recorded history: Where are you? Are you hiding from Him or seeking Him? Think about it.

Hang onto God's wisdom as we move forward in the book. Ahead, you will find ideas and examples from the football field, from life and, yes, from Scripture on how to pump up your game.

One final point. As I reflect on the interaction among nearly 600 people that day at the clinic, I recall seeing a lot smiles, no frowns, a lot of laughing, no crying, a multitude of high-fives and only a few stare downs. I even witnessed a few excruciating belly bumps by guys who were old enough to know better. Wrapping an understanding of football, life and God into a day of learning can be a refreshing experience. Offering hope can be rewarding as well as stimulating as you reach into the hearts of others to Lift 'em Up!

——————— Read On! ———————

PART 3
THE POWER OF PIZZA

THE PREGAME MEAL
OF CHAMPIONS

Finding Your Worldview in a Pizza Box

Only if we get the "view" part right do we stand a chance of success when the "do" part kicks in. In the lingo of academia, we must understand our worldview and its impact on our actions. Unfortunately, the scholarly jargon can hastily send us plunging down the rabbit hole into a world of unending complexity. That is fine if you hope to become an authority in the field, but not for our purposes. It becomes even more difficult for those struggling to find their way along life's path; individuals who are in dire need of guidance to find direction in their lives. We're going to hang out at the street level where real decisions are made and real life happens. Our intent is not to pursue an exhaustive study of the wide-ranging aspects of the topic. Rather, our intent is to focus on those points critical to making sound, effective, real world choices and put ourselves in a stronger position to not only clarify our own sense of purpose, but that of others clamoring for leadership.

To get at the matter, we need a simple, universal language that adequately covers the topic.

We're going to talk about pizza. That's right, pizza. Pizza is simple! Pizza is universal! Pizza, in reality, is life! Fortunately, everyone understands pizza and can talk the language of it. We were born eating it; we will die eating it (possibly, the more you eat, the faster you get there). Every birthday party, every football bash and every cheap date taught us to speak the language.

Fortunately, pizza and worldviews share a lot in common. As we open the box, we find that every pizza has a crust loaded with tasty toppings, all sliced and ready to consume. Guess what? So does every worldview. As with pizza, we build our worldviews by adding various personal beliefs (toppings) and then slice the total pie to fit the situation at hand. The metaphor is close to perfect. And, it is simple. So get ready to become a worldview guru and get ready to discover the Power of Pizza.

Earlier, we discussed that "you do what you view." We also said there is a "right way to view and a right way to do." In this part of the book, we will take a look at the "right way to view" portion of that fundamental statement. By setting the Biblical worldview as our baseline, we will check out three contemporary alternatives which replace God as the ultimate authority for making choices. Throughout today's culture, young people are being hammered with human secularism, environmentalism and political correctness. A healthy respect for humanity, nature and government is being molded into an unhealthy threesome of idols perched on the altar of confusion.

We will open the pizza box in five sections:
- The View is Great - The definition of worldviews
- In the Eye of the Pie - Why the metaphor works
- The Pizza Palooza of Worldviews - How four contemporary views will affect your game
- The Four Dudes - Worldviews matter; Coaching matters!
- Quick Hit #3: Derwin Gray - A change of heart
  Let's chow down.

--------------- Read On! ---------------

THE VIEW IS GREAT

Worldview Blocking and Tackling

"As a man thinks in his heart, so is he."

– Proverbs 23:7

On Feb. 20, 1962, American astronaut John Glenn became first the American to orbit the Earth. As part of the team of seven original astronauts selected to take America into space, he was enamored by his view of Earth. Glenn's assessment: "To look out at this kind of creation out here and not believe in God is to me impossible. It just strengthens my faith. I wish there were words to describe what it's like." Six years later, the first Apollo team to orbit the moon quoted similar Scripture to express their own awe. Circling the moon on Christmas Eve, the trio of Jim Lovell, Bill Anders and Frank Borman publicly read the first 10 verses of the first chapter of Genesis, describing the wondrous creative work of God to a watching worldwide audience..

Before we sit down for our pregame pizza, let's spend a few minutes chatting about worldviews. Why? Simple. For each of us, our worldview presents itself as a blueprint for action. How we view the culture surrounding us drives what we do. That which lives in our brain eventually surfaces in our deeds. And as we will see, there is a "right way to view," which leads to "right decisions." Unfortunately, the opposite also holds true. Understanding our own view, ensuring that it is right, then making it a habit has to be a priority for each of us.

From outer space to inner space

No group of humans has enjoyed a more breathtaking view of Earth than the small fraternity of astronauts who have admired creation from space. Undoubtedly, the awesome spectacle has emotionally moved each to ponder why we are here. As America's first person to orbit the earth, the specter and awe of our planet inspired Glenn to articulate his worldview on both the creator and His creation.

View of the world or worldview or both?

John Glenn's account may be one of the best examples of expressing both a view of the world and worldview in the same sentence. A casual reader may miss the duality. Is the term worldview another way of saying, "view of the world?" Not quite. In fact, not at all. One is an outer space experience, while the other comes from the inner space. One term represents what the eye sees, the other, what the mind sees. One is a simple assessment of the beauty of creation; the other a belief in the author of that creation. Had Glenn simply described the awesome wonder he saw, he would have been describing a view of the world. When he adds, "To look out at this kind of creation out here and not believe in God is to me impossible. It just strengthens my faith," he is making a true statement of his worldview that God created our world.

While this outer space view may seem to be an awe-inspiring out-of-body experience, let's turn our attention, not to the physical image of the world, but to the worldview that lies within the mind of our souls. Here we will uncover this internal vision that drives the engine of your life and mine. We will find the power-generating view that can take your game to a new level.

What in the world is a worldview?

Can you describe your favorite pizza? Is it the simple pepperoni version of early childhood or a more flavor-packed, calorie-packed variety of adulthood? Given our predictable human tendency to stay in a rut, most of us can name our preferred pie without giving it much thought. Now, switch gears and consider the same question about your worldview. Can you describe it? Can you identify the key beliefs that drive your life? Probably not. At least, not without a couple hours alone putting thought to paper.

Perhaps the clearest definition of the term worldview can be found in a video series titled, "The Truth Project," where educator Del Tackett refers to a worldview as "truth claims" that guide your life. Those claims address your beliefs in God, your fellow man, the physical world, moral law and essentially any fundamental aspect of your life. Those claims serve as your foundation and your filter for making choices. For example, if you believe mankind is essentially good, you may choose to trust everything that everyone says, only to be disappointed if your best friend lies to you. On the other hand, if you believe everyone is evil, you may trust no one choosing to live a life of isolation. What you believe really does matter.

Alternatively, another way to depict or define the term, would be to think of your worldview as your lens on life. It's the reason you get out of bed in the morning (or at the crack of noon). It's the basis of your actions throughout your day. And finally, it's the attitude that allows you to sleep (or not sleep) when your day is through. Your worldview can motivate you or drive you deeper into apathy. It can be a framework for achieving success or a reason for achieving nothing. It can build lasting relationships or drive you into loneliness.

Employing everyday slang, you might say your worldview is what "floats your boat" or "turns your crank." Whether you are helping someone whose car has broken down, deciding on a career or robbing a store, your worldview lurks in the background of your mind. It pushes you forward or holds you back. It feeds your conscience and strengthens your resolve. Consequently, understanding this cornerstone of choices is not a theological or academic exercise. Knowing why we do what we do lives at the street level of our brains. It leads each of us to success or drives us to failure at every turn. It will protect us or expose us as we face reality each and every day.

Where does your worldview come from?

A person's view flows from their heart. Call it principles, morals, ethics or whatever. As the decision wheels start churning and the juices begin to flow, there is a resident set of beliefs manifest in our heart that defines what will eventually be manifested in our actions. Does Scripture support this idea? Yes. Check out Proverbs 27:19 which says, "As water reflects a face, so the heart reflects the person." Or, in Proverbs 23:7, we find, "As a man thinks, so is he." God recognizes the significance of our heart. Sticking with the principles found in Proverbs 4:23, we find God advising, "Above all else, guard your heart, for it affects everything you do."

How often have we heard a sports announcer say, "His heart is just not in the game today," to describe a faltering player? Most of us would interpret his comment as a lack of emotion or commitment on the part of the athlete. Most of the time that would be fair and probably true. But from a worldview standpoint, the heart idea goes much deeper, essentially defining those foundational beliefs that drive your life.

Are all worldviews created equal?

Hint: Not even close! Because "you do what you view," your beliefs lead to your actions. Not all beliefs are created equal. They do not all get you to the same place. If you doubt that, be sure to check out The Four Dudes at the end of this chapter. There, you will discover how four perceptions of reality led intelligent, skilled young people to divergent careers. More importantly, it led them to extremely different and in some cases, fatal decisions. Based on their view of reality, the four chose to either become a successful business person, a legendary rock star, a superb athlete or a deadly terrorist. As their lives illustrate, worldviews matter! What you believe drives what you do. It's true for me and true for you. In terms of football, your worldview may help you choose your team, define your rules of play and, ultimately, express the objective of the game itself, all of which will influence how you call the plays.

Game Winning Point: Your view is up to you. Make it a good one.

Game Changing Verse: "As a man thinks in his heart, so is he." Proverbs 23:7

PLAYBOOK TIPS

■ Remember, your worldview comes from within.

■ Continue to stress right-thinking with young minds.

Read On!

IN THE EYE OF THE PIE

Seeing the World Through the Lens of a Pizza

America's favorite food has been around for a long time. The first trace of pizza dates back to 997 A.D. in the southern Italian town of Gaeta. However, flat breads with toppings date back far before Gaeta, crossing a variety of cultures. Popularity of what we term pizza took off in the Italian city of Naples in the 18th century. People living in the poor sections of the city began adding tomato paste to the previously dry pizza. Amazingly, tourists began to flock to the city in anticipation of this new style of food to feed their new-found appetite. Thus, modern pizza was born.

But nowhere in the world has the famous pie flourished as it has in the good ole' USA. More than 62,000 pizza joints serving more than 3 billion pies annually confirm our love for the palate-pleasing delight. More than 90 percent of Americans admit to eating pizza on a regular basis with each consuming an average of 23 pounds per year. A Gallup poll indicates that kids between the ages of 3 and 11 prefer pizza over all other food groups. How do we like it? Pepperoni convincingly leads the way as the topping of choice for nearly one-third of all pizzas sold. When do we like it? Always! However, Super Bowl Sunday clearly tops the list of popularity (which, by the way, validates our discussion of both football and pizza in this book). The overwhelming presence of pizza in our lives has even led to culinary theories such as the Pizza Cognition Theory (more on that later).

Reality: In America, we are born eating pizza; we die eating pizza.

The Big View Six-Slice Pizza

Starting from a humble beginning as a basic food of southern Italy, the shape, size, style of crust and number of toppings on pizza has grown exponentially to meet the needs of today's consumer-driven world.

Competing for every potential mouth, pizza companies have marketed their products to attract consumers who can only be satisfied by "different and more". Let's face it, purveyors of pizza do not market their product as health food. TV ads portray happy, skinny people wolfing down multiple slices of a calorie-laden, deep-dish concoction while cheering on their favorite football team.

From the worldview perspective, at the point of creation, God imbedded one worldview into man's mind and soul. Like early forms of pizza, it was not a complicated theological dogma, but simply a relationship between creator and created. But in His wisdom, God also designed us with a free will allowing us to accept His perfect way of thinking or create our own. Guess which way we went?

As with pizza, the assortment of worldviews has skyrocketed throughout time. That growth, just like with pizza, essentially reflects our attempt to satisfy a never-ending hunger to fulfill our own desires. But unfortunately, that new and expanding menu has come with a price: a culture of confusion. We find ourselves in a culture in which billions of people hold thousands of views, most of which bear little resemblance to God's original menu.

Sifting through the resulting culture of confusion requires discernment; discernment requires experience; experience calls for coaching; and coaching calls for you.

But, coaches need skills and tools to get the job done. Let's see what we can do about that

Getting to the basics: pizza and your worldview

Check out the illustration below. Pretty simple, huh? You have a crust, piled with a few toppings, cut into six slices. If we are looking for a tool to explain worldviews to those we coach, it doesn't get much simpler than a pizza. Imagine the opportunities that unfold when you mentor someone while sharing a pizza. Face it, food creates dialogue.

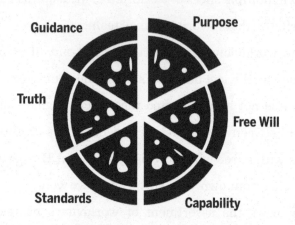

The Crust.

A pizza without a crust is a salad. A worldview without a foundation is chaos.

Both pizza and worldviews begin with a crust. Essentially, the crust defines the pizza. Check out any menu at the 60,000-plus stores throughout the country. Most begin by describing the crust: thick crust, thin crust, stuffed crust, square crust, just to name a few of the options. Now, imagine ordering a pizza sans the crust. Opening the box, you will just find an unappealing concoction of peppers, olives, onions and pepperoni swimming in tomato paste and cheese. Quite obviously, the crust makes the pizza, serving as the foundation for everything else.

The same deal holds true for worldviews. Each and every individual's worldview is grounded in a crust or foundational set of beliefs. These beliefs support the toppings that we all tend to pile on to gratify our personal tastes. But, unlike the typically cluttered carry-out pizza menu, in our world, our crust selection is a bit more limited. Limited, yes, but extremely important.

We will, essentially, limit our discussion to four contemporary viewpoints that offer radically different approaches to making choices. We will not look at major religions such as Islam or Buddhism which offer alternative perspectives on life. Those topics are important but lie beyond the scope of our discussion. The viewpoints behind each of the four crusts on our menu can be found in each of our daily lives. We cannot escape their influence, hence, we need to understand them if we hope to make great choices. The crust we choose will, undoubtedly, influence our choice of toppings. The four menu options define ultimate authority as:

1. The God of the Bible (The Big He pizza)
2. Me (The Big Me pizza)
3. Nature (The Big Tree pizza)
4. Government (The Big PC pizza)

In "non pizza" vernacular, we will check out Christianity, human secularism, nature worship and political correctness. Said another way, life is all about He, Me, Tree or PC.

The Slices &Toppings

While the crust forms the foundation, the toppings produce the flavor or taste. They differentiate your desires from mine. Some toppings will make you salivate; others will make you gag. Serve my wife a slice of deluxe pizza and within seconds, you will have a slice of less-than-deluxe pizza, plus a pile of mushrooms. She hates mushrooms and will search until the cheese turns hard to make sure they never make it into her mouth.

Our worldview pizza falls prey to a similar fate. We add, remove or change the toppings based on personal preferences. For some, the world is black and white. For others, 50 shades of gray. For many, a single topping satisfies; for others, a five-cheese, six-meat order is the only way to go. In the end, the topping combo that satisfies our individual tastes may, like our fingerprints, be totally unique. And being so truly identifies and differentiates each of us as we make choices in our daily lives.

Our Big View pizza is cut into six slices. As labeled in our illustration, each slice represents a key element that defines how we will make decisions. Each can be piled with a variety of toppings. For example, let's look at the slice labeled 'truth'. Depending on the crust you select, your view of truth will differ if you are honest and consistent. If you choose the God crust, then you will tend to define truth as absolutes coming from God. On the other hand, if you order the "me" pizza, your view on truth may be quite personal. Perhaps the contemporary adage, "what's true for you, may not be true for me" will ring true. If your pizza box contains the "tree" or "PC" pies, you may consider that truth emanates from nature or government. Or for any crust, you may tend to waver, depending on the topic under consideration, believing that truth is a situational trait. In any case, your topping represents your preference, your viewpoint and your worldview. Make sense?

In the following chapter, we will check out the typical toppings that can be found on the four contemporary crusts on our menu. Doing so will help you appreciate your personal beliefs and those of whom you coach. That discussion will help you recognize what you eat and what eats you.

Before we go there, however, here are a couple other things to remember as you coach others to life's victories

1. Our tastes for both pizza and worldviews may change over time

In his landmark book, Pizza: A Slice of Heaven: The Ultimate Pizza Guide and Companion author Ed Levine deals with every aspect of America's favorite food, including the Pizza Cognition Theory put forward initially by Sam Sifton of The New York Times. On the one hand, the theory claims that whatever topping you enjoyed on your first slice of pizza will be the one you order for the rest of your life. Food for thought? Possibly. But on the other hand, if that theory holds true, I'm not sure how any of us get from birthday party pepperoni to the Hawaiian pineapple, artichoke deluxe pies later in life. Then again, does it really matter?

In reality, our taste for pizza changes as our taste buds mature. Same may hold true for our view on life. As children, we are strongly influenced by parents, teachers and others as to what we believe or don't believe about the world. That input builds strong roots into the soil of our consciousness. But as our exposure to the myriad of influences outside of our basic family group enters the picture, we tend to question those roots, often ripping them out of the ground and altering our foundational beliefs. Bearing witness to the magnitude of this transformation, recent polls by both Gallup and Pew researchers found a huge and growing church dropout rate among millennials. Once again, proof that coaching matters in helping to make a difference.

2. Both pizza and your worldview can keep you awake at the night

Consume three slices of a five-meat pizza with jalapenos at 10 p.m. and see how well you sleep. The gut-rumbling noise alone will keep you awake. Adopt the wrong set of beliefs and, in similar fashion, you may toss and turn until dawn. Pizza, loaded with wicked spices, will leave a bad taste in your mouth and the "breath of a dragon" for days. Friends may seek shelter elsewhere. Same holds true for wrong thinking. Mental belching plus a noxious tongue may drive your friends away. But, a solid worldview, based on Biblical principles, will ease your sleep and guard your heart. Psalm 3:5 enlightens us with these words: "I lay down and slept. I woke up in safety, for the Lord was watching over me."

Game Winning Point: The churning in our mind surfaces in our actions.

Game Changing Verse: "Show me the path where I should walk, O Lord; point out the right road for me to follow." Psalm 25:4

PLAYBOOK TIPS

- Understand that your beliefs drive your actions.
- Do not ignore any slice; eat the entire pizza.
- Be honest as you choose a crust.

——————— Read On! ———————

THE PIZZA PALOOZA OF WORLDVIEWS

Your Slice of Life Pizza Parlor

"Sell more pizza; Have more fun."

- Dominos mission statement

Venue:
DOMINOS WORLD HEADQUARTERS
PRESENT DAY

Check out their website. In a mere six words, "Sell more pizza; Have more fun," the world's largest pizza delivery company outlines its mission. Thousands of employees from delivery people to the CEO can easily understand what criteria and beliefs drive the organization. Ideally, everything that happens throughout the company can be traced back to that simple statement. Those six words form the foundation upon which all else is built. In other words, they represent the viewpoint of the world of the company as it relates to how it will sell pizza.

In the last chapter, we introduced the six-slice pizza, proposing that each and every time we approach a fork in the road, those slices provide questions to help sort out the right path to follow. Successful organizations like Dominos dedicate huge levels of resources, monetary and otherwise, to establish a culture that supports its overall mission. Why? Simply because the company also realizes that people of all levels 'do what they view'. The company leaders understand that the ideas and principles existing within the minds and hearts of associates eventually (or quickly) manifest into actions, both good and bad.

In their own way, they fully understand that each of our six slices comes into play day in and day out. Offering five crusts, four sizes, 27 toppings and a myriad of sauces, Dominos must be on top of its game to deliver an exceptional product to each and every customer. Regions, departments and every other conceivable organizational structure are comprised of employees who understand their purpose, utilize skills and resources, function within established guidelines and know where to turn for help in achieving their goals.

The Six Slices "Elevated"

Now, step back for a moment from making day-to-day choices. Let's take those same slices to a to a life-level status. At that point, they rise from simply being a checklist for choosing alternatives to being foundational characteristics that define your philosophy of life and your view of the world. They become the lens through which you observe and interpret life. In our "do what you view" world, they formulate the playbook for your game.

So, what questions might we find topping each slice of our Big View Pizza? Here are a few:

Purpose - Who defines your overall purpose in life? Does God have a purpose for you being on Earth? Do you define your own purpose of being here? Is there really no purpose, thus, you are simply a collection of atoms produced by nature?

Free Will AND Responsibility - Are you free to do whatever you wish? Who made that determination? Again, is it God? You? The government? How much freedom do you have? Total? Limited? Plus, who is responsible for your actions? You? Your parents? Society?

Capability - Do you have personal or other resources to fulfill your purpose in life? If so, who is responsible for providing them? Nature? God? Yourself? Who is responsible for developing them?

Standards - Are there limitations or guidelines related to how you achieve your purpose? Are they self-determining? Set by the government? Set by God? Natural laws?

Truth - Does truth exist in your stadium? Are those truths true for everyone? Who or what makes them real?

Guidance - Is there an ultimate source for guiding your life's journey? God? Nature? You? Your friends? If so, how do you relate to that source? Is it infallible?

How you and I (plus those we coach) answer each of these questions forms a belief system which will cascade downward into our daily lives. Get it right at the top and produce excellent results at the bottom. Establish inconsistency at the top and create chaos at the bottom. Consuming the right pizza will take our game to a new level. Select the wrong pizza and life will be one gooey, greasy, runny mess.

The big question we must face: How do we know which pizza promotes a winning life? Is there a taste test that helps us to select the right items off the menu? The answer is "yes." The answer is reality!

Reality ... Separating the good, bad and ugly

Throughout the summer, in a multitude of cities across America, residents are treated to an event known as a Pizza Palooza. At these tasty happenings, young and old alike sample a variety of concoctions. Voting for their favorites, they ultimately crown one pizza maker and one pie the best of the year.

At a Pizza Palooza, the winner is decided by the vote of the masses. The reality, however, is that there is no one right pizza. Right is determined simply by a vote, not by a concrete set of measurable standards. The concoction that is right for you may not be right for me. And if we are going to share a pie, then we may have to load different toppings on each half to make us both happy.

Personal preference works great for pizza. It's a disaster for worldviews. Unfortunately, in today's culture, many of us tend to treat basic principles (standards, truths and responsibilities) as a Pizza Palooza, voting on which ones the crowd likes best and changing at the whim of the masses. But, that approach typically fails without fail. The evidence is overwhelming.

So, how can we separate the good, the bad and the ugly? Is there a label or skull and crossbones warning against toxic beliefs? Not quite, but, there is a measure that works; a measure called reality. Reality screams loudly that there is a right way to view. Simply put, the surest measure of the validity of a specific view is basically an honest consideration of how well it describes the certainty of the world around us. For example, how well does a "we're all good people" assumption stack up with the morning news? That's an easy one. Or, better yet, how does an "I can do whatever I want" attitude work when it comes to paying taxes? Do I see a certified letter from the IRS in your mailbox? The reality we must face is that reality is real!

The reality of reality has been around for a long time. Step back to those days in the garden to ask Adam and Eve if their decisions had real implications. They quickly found out the reality of God's creation. Want more confirmation from Scripture? Check out Romans 1:20 which explains the invisible reality and attributes of God can be clearly seen in His creation. And, as such, we are without excuse.

Reality replicates

Do past successes help us choose the route of the future? The first day you drive to work in a new city, you may wonder if that route will get you there. But, after a thousand trips down that same route, that question no longer exists. Why? Repeated success ensures that today's drive will get you to the right spot. The same holds true for your worldview adventure. Reality tends to repeat itself; hence, seeing the world through the lens of realism helps select a path that leads to success. On the other hand, a worldview steeped in emotion or uncertainty projects a route shrouded in fog.

Today's upcoming generation faces both a myriad of opportunities and challenges. Leveraged by social media and the multitude of information floating about the internet, these young minds are poised to absorb new opportunities amid a culture of confusion. They truly consume a cultural pizza unlike any previous generation. Assaulted by an educational system that infuses extreme environmentalism, political correctness, plus a distorted view of tolerance, these individuals are consuming a pregame meal of questionable nutritional value.

What can you and I do as coaches to help bring clarity to the confusion? As we prepare to coach millennials and other generations, it is first important for us to understand the menu, and secondly, help them choose wisely from it. In the balance of this chapter, we will look at four types of pizza, checking out the ingredients for the crust and toppings. Will they nourish the consumers or lead to more confusion and poor choices? Does any single pizza stand out as a superior representation of a worldview that leads to success?

FCA Leader.....

Thanks for taking a moment to read this brief memo. Accompanying this note is your complimentary copy of *Winning Choices, A Life Changing Game Plan.*

I created *Winning Choices* to provide ideas, illustrations and tools for individuals such as yourself who work with others to help them make better life-changing choices. The book utilizes 'street-level' metaphors of pizza and football to increase the appeal to a sports-saturated generation. Pizza illustrates how one's worldview affects their decisions and football (a two-minute drill) provides a disciplined method for getting winning results. Additionally, I have gathered life-changing advice from a dozen former NFL/college football players and a myriad of stories from sports, scripture and life to provide illustrations for you to utilize in working with those you mentor.

Former FCA CEO, Les Steckel, wrote the Foreword and FCA Executive Director, Rick Isaiah, contributed significant content including a discussion of FCA values. Rick and I agree that the content of *Winning Choices* supports this year's 'STRONG' camp theme.

Please enjoy reading the book. By the way, it is constructed in a format that you can pick and choose topics that are relevant to a particular discussion, thus, you do not have to read it from cover-to-cover to benefit from it.

If you wish to obtain additional copies to distribute to your team, Amazon carries both hard cover and e-book versions.

Prayers for all of the work that you personally do to help others make *winning choices!*

Greg Papp

Winningchoices.net

Your Slice of Life pizza parlor offers four items on the menu. As we have discussed, worldviews, or in our case, pizzas, can be infinitely customized. Thus, our four specialty pizzas may not always be totally distinct. It is possible to share toppings among them. But, I believe you will get the point.

**Your Slice of Life
Pizza Parlor
MENU**

PIZZA	INGREDIENTS
It's All about HE	A Biblical Outlook
It's All about ME	Human Secularism
It's All about TREE	Extreme Environmentalism
It's ALL about PC	Political Correctness

For each of the four menu selections, we will check out the good and bad news from a nutritional perspective, plus assign a reality rating, representing my personal view on their effectiveness as a foundation for making sound choices.

———— Let's Go! ————

THE BIG HE PIZZA
It's All about HE!

"The image of the Great Hero is tattooed on your soul."

\- Derwin Gray, former NFL player and founding and lead pastor
of Transformation Church in South Carolina

Worldview Starting Point: He. God reigns supreme

In the first 10 words of Scripture, "In the beginning, God created the heavens and the earth," we find the essence of the Biblical worldview. This straight-to-the-point opening captures several foundational realities:

- There is a God.
- God is distinct from the universe that He created.
- God is universally powerful
- There is a beginning to time for the universe.

Scripture goes on to richly provide a historical, moral and redemptive roadmap indicating the God of creation stands ready to personally interface with each of us in our daily walk. His creation itself speaks of His power and sense of order reflected in the many natural laws (like gravity) that repeat methodically, day in and day out, from that first day of creation. The God of the Bible does not shout out that He is a god among other gods. He shouts that He is a God above all others.

As Scripture relates, His crowning achievement was the creation of mankind in His own image, which again was done with great purpose, that being for an eternal relationship with Him.

Volumes have been written about the power and truth of the Biblical worldview. If you were to peruse the literature, you would find hard evidence of the impact of this worldview on science, government, the arts and, essentially, all aspects of Western culture. A belief in a creative God and an orderly universe brought us the scientific method and the resulting explosion of our understanding of nature. Developments in technology can be traced back to strong Christian beliefs among scientists. Western government and legal systems offer the same genealogy. Even the founding of the United States--the legal system that we enjoy; the three-part system of government and the major early universities--all reflect a strong adherence to the Biblical worldview.

The HE Pizza

Looking at the Biblical worldview, from the perspective of our six-slice pizza, how well does it support the needs for making wise choices and implementing them successfully throughout our lives? Let's take a brief look inside our pizza box to check out the contents: Does the Biblical worldview offer a hot six-slice deep-dish deluxe pie?

Slice 1: Purpose

As with anyone who designs and creates something, God accomplished His act of creation with purpose. In doing so, He has created each of us with a specific purpose. Reflecting on God's achievement and His purpose, Jeremiah 29:11 states, "I know the plans I have for you." Logically, if an all-powerful God has plans for you, He will help you figure them out. Scripture (check out 2 Corinthians 3:18) teaches us that God has created us for His glory, thus, whatever purpose He has for our lives will bring glory to Him.

Slice 2: Free Will and Responsibility

This couplet of parameters outlines two critical aspects of the relationship between maker and man. God has designed us with purpose, giving us the freedom to pursue that purpose or reject it and chase after our own ideas. Secondly, He has created us with responsibility to make good choices and ultimately find and pursue the purpose that He has for each of us. In essence, we have the choice to eat this slice or trash it.

Slice 3: Intellect and Capability

A God who would create us with purpose and insist we have the responsibility to go after it while not embedding the capabilities to get there would not be a loving God. He would be more of a buffoon, challenging each of us to do something He knew we could not do while laughing all the while. In that case, failure would not be an option, it would be a reality. But, fortunately, God has provided us with the capability to achieve our purpose whether you may be a homemaker, a brain surgeon or an NBA star. Unfortunately, some of us tend to drop this slice on the floor by attempting to pursue our own ideas. Check out what Romans 12:2 has to say about renewing of our mind to achieve good things.

Slice 4. Standards

Again, whether you are an engineer designing a car or the God of the universe creating man, you develop operating criteria for your creation. If a car must achieve 30 mpg in the city, then that standard guides designers in such things as weight, gear ratios and engine size. If you are the commissioner of the NFL, then you or your predecessors have created standards for the game. Those standards help the teams know how to play, setting limitations and expectations. Similarly, God in His benevolent wisdom has provided us with standards in both Scripture and nature, creating an envelope in which to play the game of life. Those ground rules are not our ideas, they are His. They are not suggestions, they are realities. They do not change and they are timeless.

Slice 5. Truth

Today's culture increasingly refuses to believe in absolute truth. Survey after survey describes a shift of young minds toward a worldview in which relativism has replaced reality. Imagine if that belief was actually true. Think about a world in which truth does not exist. If natural laws changed randomly, we would all fear pulling out of the driveway. Similarly, if moral laws were not consistent, today's answers may be totally wide of the mark tomorrow. Fortunately, the God of the Bible has provided unwavering truths we can both know and follow (or not). The ultimate truth entered the world in the person of Christ who stated, "I am the way, the truth and the life." John 14:6.

Slice 6. Guidance

This may be the most appetizing slice in the box. We all seek mentors who can help steer us along the path. And that is a good thing. None of us has experienced or knows every aspect of life's serious choices. Guidance is good. In the Biblical worldview, God, Himself, the one who does know all, has explicitly stated that He WILL guide us. Proverbs 3: 5-6 is one of many verses which confirm His commitment. As the theme verse of the book, this portion of Scripture tells us to trust in the Lord with all of our heart; refrain from depending on our own understanding; acknowledge Him in all we do; and he will direct our path.! That's hard to beat regardless of how you spend your waking hours.

So there we have it. Six slices, each loaded with the nutrition and power to get the job done. An honest person would conclude the Biblical worldview delivers a deep-dish deluxe pizza, loaded with all that we need. It may be ordered anytime and arrives hot, ready for consumption. No doubt about it, the Biblical worldview is a full box. Menu 1 summarizes this amazing dish.

Don't simply take my word for it. Let's check out a renowned apologist. Born in the Hindu-dominated culture of India, Ravi Zacharias has become one of the most respected apologists for the Christian faith. An expert on world religions, philosophies and worldview, Ravi has unequivocally stated, "Only the Judeo-Christian worldview would create a constitution based on life, liberty and the pursuit of happiness. Naturalism, Islam and others would fail to provide the freedom to write those words or the freedom to believe or not believe."

Thus, it may actually be fair and reasonable to insist the Biblical worldview represents the baseline of reality against which other viewpoints should be measured. Do the other three philosophies meet the mark or do they fall short in content or delivery? While the Biblical worldview is built on a crust formed by God, the remaining outlooks start with some form of crust built by man.

Another way to judge each of these pizzas would be in terms of "surrender of control." In other words, to whom or what does an individual ultimately surrender control in making choices in life? The Biblical worldview ultimately surrenders control to the God of the Bible. The individuals adhering to that view realize the power of their maker and the danger of assuming they are in control. But what about the other pizzas? Where do they associate power? To whom do they surrender control? Let's see how they stack up. Remember as we do, you can choose your response to reality; however, you cannot choose your reality.

Recommendation: Great, deep-dish deluxe. Get it now!

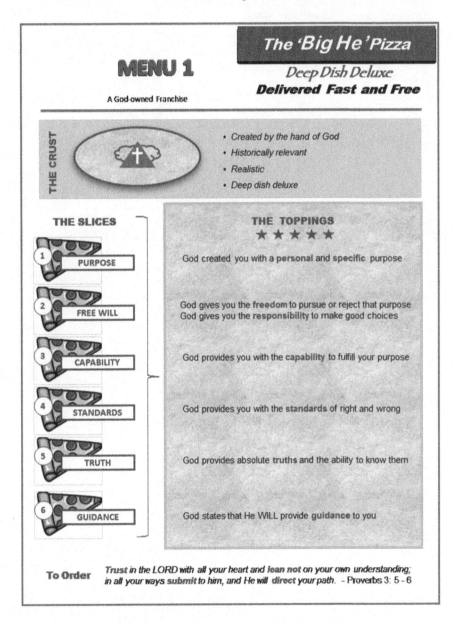

The 'Big He' Pizza

MENU 1

Deep Dish Deluxe

Delivered Fast and Free

A God-owned Franchise

THE CRUST

- Created by the hand of God
- Historically relevant
- Realistic
- Deep dish deluxe

THE SLICES

THE TOPPINGS
★ ★ ★ ★ ★

1 PURPOSE — God created you with a personal and specific purpose

2 FREE WILL — God gives you the freedom to pursue or reject that purpose
God gives you the responsibility to make good choices

3 CAPABILITY — God provides you with the capability to fulfill your purpose

4 STANDARDS — God provides you with the standards of right and wrong

5 TRUTH — God provides absolute truths and the ability to know them

6 GUIDANCE — God states that He WILL provide guidance to you

To Order — *Trust in the LORD with all your heart and lean not on your own understanding; in all your ways submit to him, and He will direct your path.* - Proverbs 3: 5 - 6

Next on the menu: The Big Me Pizza.

THE BIG ME PIZZA

It's All about ME

"And you will know the truth, and the truth will make you free."

- John 8:32

Starting Point: Me. Humanity reigns supreme.

Confidence-based competence is a good thing. Make no mistake about it, as the Biblical worldview pointed out, each of us have been created in the image of God, bursting with intelligence and skills. But the Big Me pizza promotes each of us to a new level of importance. In this view, the All About Me perspective goes way beyond measured competence. Essentially, it puts you, or me, at the top of the food chain.

In Exodus 3:14, God, when responding to Moses, unequivocally affirms, ""Ehyeh-Asher-Ehyeh," or in a language more understood by most of us, "I am that I am." In the ancient blockbuster, The Ten Commandments, Hollywood employs a deep off-screen booming voice to emphasize the magnitude of this proclamation. So who is the "I am?" In Exodus, the answer is easy. The "I am" is God. In each of our lives; however, the answer may play out a bit differently. Based perhaps not on our statement of faith, but on our statement of action, many of us see ourselves as No. 1. But really, does the world spin because of God or does it spin because of us?

This is a big one! Known more formally as secular humanism, this worldview effectively replaces God with humanity. Although we all, including believers in the supreme maker, occasionally fall into the "It's about me trap," most of us see this as selfishness and not our true vision of life. But human secularism goes far beyond selfishness. Again, replacing God with humanity, true adherents express no belief in or a need for the supernatural or for divine providence. All authority and morality is simply defined by each of us individually or by society collectively.

Human secularism is sweeping the country. In a land that has throttled prayer or even the discussion of God in the public arena (including schools and sporting events), young people are taught that the secular world is the true natural state. In the absence of God, students learn that only mankind can solve mankind's problems. How's that approach working out? Check the morning headlines and the answer is obvious--not so well.

So, how would the worldview of human secularism stand up to the six-slice pizza assessment?

To a human secularist, life's purpose comes from within the person. While this may sound noble, just think about how you may have defined purpose when you were 10 years old versus now. For adherents to this belief, purpose arises primarily from the emotions of the day, not by an overarching belief in a supernatural meaning to life.

Standards and truth emanate from within the individual, leading to a what-works-for-you is not necessarily what-works-for-me definition of reality. The "I'm OK, You're OK" perception leads to situational ethics and cultural chaos. It's tough to discern valid choices in that environment.

Where do individuals proposing this view find guidance and hope? For those true to their beliefs, there is no one to light their path other than themselves or others of similar convictions. Without a belief in the supernatural creator, they make choices with the understanding that death brings finality. In other words, there is no need to live your life in a way that extends beyond the horizon of the grave. Despair replaces hope and choices reflect the belief that life is a short journey. Easy to become selfish? You got it! That's how it becomes, "All about me!"

Check out the toppings listed on Menu 2. Without going slice-by-slice through the entire pizza, generally, what do we find in the box when the "BIG ME" pizza is delivered to our door? Or, how does it compare to the deep-dish deluxe variety in the box labeled "Biblical worldview?"

Pizza Palooza Rating:
Crust: Inadequate
Topping: Messy

Not much in the box when it arrives. Maybe two or three slices piled with toppings that aren't recognizable. Definitely, the slices representing standards, truth, and supernatural guidance have fallen out of the box somewhere along the way. We may find our purpose, but that purpose may be vague and changing with time and circumstances. We do have intelligence and capabilities because, regardless of our own belief, we were created in the image of God. But have we matched up those capabilities with our purpose? Maybe, maybe not.

Biblical worldview assessment

The human secular view of life is totally at odds with the Biblical worldview. Man sits on the throne, not God, hence all morality and truth hinges on the combined beliefs of the millions of people occupying the planet. The tenets of this system fall short of reality on physical, moral and spiritual levels. Although it is not taught as an overt brand of faith, human secularism tends to lead the pack if one eliminates God from the scene. It sort of becomes the default choice in a secular environment, creeping menacingly across broken borders of reason and reality.

Be extremely wary of falling into this belief system. It's not the playbook for a winning game. It may lead to a few first downs, but lacks the credibility to generate a win. Check out the verse John 8:32 quoted at the beginning of this chapter. It provides the winning game plan ... know the truth (God) and you will be set free for a winning game of eternal life.

The Bible according to me

The theme verse of this book is Proverbs 3:5-6. How would an adherent to the "All about Me" view of life rewrite this pivotal verse? As a refresher, Proverbs 3:5-6 provides comfort to each of us with these words: "Trust in the Lord with all your heart; do not depend on your own understanding. Seek his will in all you do, and he will direct your paths." From the all about me perspective, this verse would read, "Trust in yourself with all your heart; depend on your own understanding. Seek your own will in all you do, and you will direct your own paths." Wow! Big assignment huh? Surrender control to no one. Do you think you can handle it? Many have tried. All have failed.

Recommendation: There is a God and it's not you or me. Enjoy your God-given skills and resources.

MENU 2

An All-About-Me Franchise

The 'Big Me' Pizza

Thin Egocentric Crust
Delivered to Me by Me

THE CRUST

- Created by me
- Changeable by me at any time
- Based on my perception of reality
- Thin crust with inconsistent ingredients

THE SLICES

THE TOPPINGS
★ ★ ★ ★ ★

1. **PURPOSE** — You decide the purpose for your life based on your own needs

2. **FREE WILL** — You personally select your own degrees of freedom and responsibility

3. **CAPABILITY** — You are innately entitled to fulfill your desires

4. **STANDARDS** — You create your own personal standards of right and wrong

5. **TRUTH** — Truth is a personal belief; absolutes rarely exist

6. **GUIDANCE** — You are the ultimate source of personal guidance in your life

To Order — *Trust in yourself, with all your emotions. Acknowledge no one else in anything you do. And you will run (or ruin) your own life. Proverbs 3: 5 – 6 RESTATED*

Next on the menu: The BIG TREE Pizza

194

THE BIG TREE PIZZA
It's All about TREE

*"The Lord God placed the man in the Garden of Eden
to tend and care for it."*

- Genesis 2:5

Starting Point: TREE. Mother Nature reigns supreme

In this scenario, nature IS God. On this pizza, we find the natural world is all that exists and has come into existence through some unknown natural process. Mother Nature represents more than an offhand comment on the nightly weather report. Nature finds itself elevated to an object of true worship.

Depending on the agenda of supporters, this worldview may be labeled Darwinism, naturalism or a selection of other titles. Believers, exhibiting some level of universal intelligence, range from passé to fanatical in their devotion to the idea that nature trumps all. In most cases, it begins with the idea that God does not exist, backing into its beliefs through science or human reasoning. Its roots stream backward into ancient history, but have been leveraged by the writings of Darwin and the adoption of his theories in our education system.

You will not find churches built to the God of nature, but you will find a growing system of beliefs promoted through the educational system, the media and governmental legislation. The green movement, Gaia and other save-the-environment organizations have become the churches of this system, dedicated to advancing the cause. One may ask, with a bit of humor, if the millions of recycling receptacles are their collection plates.

Too often, adherents have created or distorted scientific facts (e.g. global warming data), twisting them to move their agenda forward. Unfortunately for their cause, as science unfolds exposing the reality of nature, it continually points to an orderly, created universe, not one that sprang from chaos, chance and time. Unfortunately, the tenets of this faith have a stranglehold on much of the education and entertainment system, driving an agenda more so than hoping to face reality.

The pizza reality test

But in the world of decision-making, how does the "All About TREE" stand up to the pizza test? Under honest scrutiny, the report card is not good. Let's take a brief look.

In this worldview, slice 1 (purpose), is rather messy. Essentially, we are the result of random interactions of some undefined goo, and, in the view of many philosophers who support this belief, life is essentially meaningless. In their view, we are simply one of the many combinations of molecules in the universe. If anything, we belong to some mystical force that is the combination of all elements of nature.

From a freewill standpoint, each of us can do whatever we wish, but lacking real meaning, those choices themselves become meaningless.

Standards reflect whatever we each want them to be in our own world or, at best, some amalgamation of natural laws. Consequently, everyone can live by their own standards which essentially says there really are no standards of right and wrong.

And finally, from a guidance standpoint, in the absence of God, everyone is pretty much on their own. We may seek the advice of others; however, in this faith where truth and standards are lacking foundation, who knows where this counsel may lead us. You might even try talking with a tree, but good luck getting an answer.

Biblical worldview assessment

Long before the green movement drove college students giddy, and eons before the stuffed shirts of pseudo-scientists developed their godless body of beliefs, God himself had some things to say about nature. In Genesis, we find God's wisdom. Right out of the box, (in fact, it is the first command recorded in the Bible) mankind was given charge for tending the garden (Gen 2:15) and having dominion over the earth and everything that lived in it (Gen 1: 26-30). Both of these commands give man the responsibility for caring for God's creation. In that respect, each of us must care for the resources of the world and not abuse them. But, Scripture also warns against worshipping the creation instead of the creator (Romans 1:25). Unfortunately, much of the environmental movement has forced the pendulum to swing toward worshipping the creation. It follows that if you don't believe in a creator, you truly must fill the vacuum with something.

The Bible according to TREE

Once again, let's take a shot at how this worldview would recast Proverbs 3:5-6. Perhaps it would read, "Trust in the Earth and universe with all your heart; do not depend on your own understanding. Seek nature's will in all you do, and it will direct your paths." Sounds like those who adhere to this belief system surrender control of their choices to some form of nature! Good luck with that one.

Recommendation: Take care of God's creation but don't worship it!

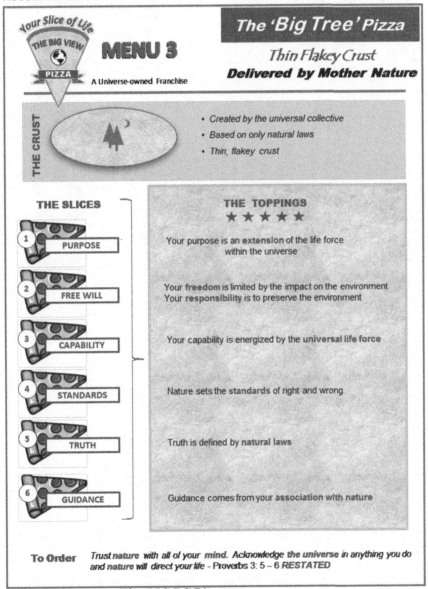

Next on the menu: The BIG PC Pizza

THE BIG PC PIZZA
It's All about PC

"Keeping an open mind is a virtue, but not so open that your brains fall out."

- James Oberg

Starting Point: PC. The government reigns supreme

It's all about who you trust. In this case, an adherent to the PC, or politically correct worldview, places their trust and faith in the government.

PC defines the faith of this worldview. Congregants of this conviction believe that governmental bodies retain ultimate authority in our daily lives, setting standards for behavior and policy or laws to influence or demand adherence to it.

Some individuals, who spend their day creating lists, may not define political correctness as a true worldview, but more of a symptom of other views such as human secularism. I chose to split this belief into a separate worldview because it has recently become a blatantly imposing building block of our culture.

PC seems to be everywhere, permeating media, politics, education, entertainment, religion and sports. Growing stronger by the day, its core beliefs are being spread, not through proselytizing, but through laws, policies and outright intimidation. One is not asked to join this church; one is coerced into becoming a member. You don't call the pizza place with your order; the pizza place sends you what they want you to eat. Lastly, you don't eat the pizza; it eats you.

One can hear the PC choir chanting praise to diversity, tolerance, gender-neutrality and entitlement while denouncing personal responsibility and traditional faith. Unfortunately, the words have been redefined to fit their scheme. For example, the meaning of tolerance has morphed into a brand of totalitarian tolerance. No longer are we simply encouraged to express a variety of views in a peaceful setting. Rather, we are being told which position is correct with little, or no, room for offering a different view. Longing to retain the votes of a fragmented majority, government officials find themselves becoming hostages to a myriad of special interest groups.

In his 1796 farewell address, our first president warned us to be wary of ignoring our faith. George Washington counseled that "reason and experience both forbid us to expect that national morality can prevail in exclusion of religious principle." Coming from the Founding Father of our country, this thought bears heavy consideration. Does dependency on our government while ignoring our creator predict moral calamity? Read the news on your tablet!

So, how does this faith focused on government stack up in the pizza test? How well does clinging to the dogma of political correctness serve your ability to make good choices?

Let's go back to the slices in our box. Menu 4 summarizes the toppings for each slice.

From a purpose standpoint, the ultimate authority of the government allows lawmakers to decide who succeeds and who fails. Government websites may not state that fact in so many terms, but in their reality, they allocate access to education and funding to support their agenda. "PC-thought" may lead you to believe you have freedom to choose a course in life, but in reality, this worldview defines the shape of the pizza box, allowing you to function only within boundaries defined by those who create the regulations.

How about standards and truth? Talk about a worldview that can give the congregation a sensation of vertigo. It may be fair to compare the realm of PC to a kaleidoscope in which every turn of the Earth on its axis brings a new view through the lens. What you see today will definitely not be what you see tomorrow. Looking for truth and consistent standards through this lens is like looking at the stars on a foggy night. The view keeps changing depending on the people currently in power.

How about guidance? Who will be there to help you? According to the wizard behind the curtain, the bulging administrative offices at the local, state and national levels can handle it. Renew your driver's license recently? Enough said.

The bottom line of the PC view finds a group of humans attempting to fulfill the role of God. Will it work? Never has and never will. History is littered with nations who have tried to make it work, many of whom have begun with the right intention for their people. But as many have said, "power corrupts and absolute power corrupts absolutely."

Personally adhering to this worldview would be disastrous. Learning to live within it is essential. It is here after all.

Pizza Palooza Rating:
Crust: Stuffed, but with the wrong ingredients; high in fat
Topping: Stifling

Essentially, a mostly empty box is delivered to your door. It may have a nice picture on the box and even retain a flavorful smell. But, the contents should head straight to the dumpster.

Biblical worldview assessment

Replacing the entire role of God with the people that God has created will breed failure. Scripture has defined an appropriate role for government. In Romans 13:1 it says, Obey the government, for God is the one who put it there. All governments have been placed in power by God. Yes, we are instructed to obey the government; however, Scripture also teaches that governments are to obey God, submitting themselves to His authority. When a conflict of who you worship arises, we are taught to put God first. Political correctness removes God, hence, it fails as a foundation for making successful choices. If you have ordered a pizza based on this belief system, call back and cancel your order.

The Bible according to PC

Back to the comparison to Proverbs 3:5-6, this view would rewrite the scriptural adage to read, "Trust in the Government with all your heart; do not depend on your own understanding. Seek the Government's will in all you do, and it will direct your paths." You may like today's answer, but how about tomorrow's?

Recommendation: Support righteous government; God has endorsed it for the good of His creation.

MENU 4

A Government-owned Franchise

The 'Big PC' Pizza

Thin Shape-Shifter Crust
Delivered by Government

THE CRUST

- Created by various governments
- Changeable at the whim of governmental bodies
- Based solely on laws created by the ruling governments
- Thin shape-shifter crust

THE SLICES

THE TOPPINGS
★ ★ ★ ★ ★

1 PURPOSE

The government decides or limits your purpose in life

2 FREE WILL

The government sets limits on your freedom to pursue
or reject that purpose
The government interprets your level of responsibility to
make good choices

3 CAPABILITY

The government limits your capability to fulfill your purpose

4 STANDARDS

The government creates and modifies standards of right
and wrong

5 TRUTH

The government defines truths and may define them
differently for various groups

6 GUIDANCE

The government provides guidance when/if it chooses

To Order   *Trust the government with all of your heart and money. Acknowledge its laws
In all of your life and it will control your life* . Proverbs 3: 5-6 *RESTATED*

EAT WELL - PLAY WELL

Call in Your Order

"Where you are in Christ is more important than where you are in life"

- Colossians 1:4-8

Combo pizzas

Life is not a clear cut black-and-white game. Nor, do any of us always choose a consistent path, call the right play or seek dependable guidance. After all, we are human. Occasionally, we will create a combo pizza topped with viewpoints from more than one of the four pizzas described above. In the real pizza world, most of us have, at some time, ordered a combo pizza, say half pepperoni and half sausage. The same approach holds true for the worldview pizza. Maybe you have tried one of the following:

- **Half Me - Half He:** I believe in looking to God for direction, but sometimes, I would rather take my own course of action. This is a very popular item on the menu.

- **Half Me - Half PC:** I believe in being part of the PC crowd except when I really want things my way.

- **Half He - Half Tree:** I believe in God, but all that stuff in Scripture doesn't fit with science.

The possible variations are seemingly endless. Even when we understand and have faith in the right principles, we tend to wander. Scripture recognizes both our propensity to get off track and the value in coming back saying, "Once you were wandering like lost sheep. But now you have turned to your Shepherd, the guardian of your souls." 1 Peter 2:25.

Major religions?

What about the other big issues on the worldview front? How

nourishing are the major religions: Islam, Buddhism and Hinduism just to name a few? And what about Atheism? Do these worldviews offer hope for making great choices?

The scope of this book does not allow an in-depth assessment of every worldview alternative. Instead, we have focused on four contemporary views that are dominating our educational system and media, hence, will continue to play mind-changing roles in the lives of young people. If you wish to pursue a further review of major religions, I suggest reading a few of the selections listed in the Going Deeper section. However, be prepared to find major deficiencies in terms of how many of those belief systems reflect reality. Some actually deny that reality even exists, crippling them as a support system for making the hard choices in a real world.

Back to football

We have visited the Pizza Palooza and built our six-slice Big View Pizza but now it's time to get back to football. As we make that transition, perhaps it would be helpful to rephrase our worldview questions with football lingo. The questions we posed in the pizza parlor may look like this in the locker room:

- Who ultimately calls the shots in your life? You? God? A coach?
- Who is on the field when you snap the ball?
- Who creates the playbook for you to follow?
- Who sets the rules of the game?
- Can you play in the position you have chosen?
- How do you define the scoreboard in your game?

Stop here for a few minutes and think through these questions and jot down your own answers. Are you comfortable with them? Do you need to make any changes in your playbook? Is your outlook based on God's viewpoint or are you peeking out from a bridge created by your own set of constructed beliefs? Do you consistently stick with the same pizza, or do you tend to order different crusts and toppings to meet the circumstances? Whatever your choice, remember, in the long run: You do what you View!

————— Read On! —————

FOUR DUDES

Worldview Matters - Coaching Matters

A businessman, a rock star, a terrorist and a football player: Four young men; four decisions; four outcomes.

On June 18, 1971, a young man followed through with a decision born out of an idea he presented in a college term paper some nine years earlier. Legend has it that his Yale economics professor graded the paper as a "C," scribbling on it that the idea had little chance of success. Not thwarted by this seemingly low assessment of him or his ideas, he moved ahead with resolve, eventually forming a company to turn his plan into reality. That man is Fred Smith. His company: Federal Express (now FedEx), which is arguably one of the most innovative and successful companies of all time.

On July 3, 1971, 15 days after Fred Smith inaugurated Federal Express, another more well-known young man also made a life-changing decision. A 1965 graduate of UCLA, he and his cohorts had already become a wildly successful rock band, idolized by a growing army of admirers. On the morning of July 3; however, success became meaningless when he was found alone, dead in a bathtub in a Paris hotel, the apparent victim of ingesting heroin. That man: Jim Morrison. The "company": The Doors, arguably one of the best rock bands in history.

While Fred Smith and Jim Morrison were individually setting the course for their lives, another young man was in the process of forming his worldview as a forerunner to several life-changing (or should I say world-changing) decisions he would make. Under the tutelage of his gym teacher in the early '70s, this teenager was being molded to create the framework for making future choices that would rock the world. He was absorbing a worldview that others wanted him to hear and, apparently, the ideas stuck. That man: Osama bin Laden.

Let's roll the clock forward now. In his book, Touchdown Alexander, star NFL running back Shaun Alexander relates how, as a high school senior in 1995, he made the decision of where to attend college and play football. As one of the premier high school players, Shaun received what seemed to be countless offers to play football from major high-profile colleges throughout the nation. But as an 18-year-old kid from Florence, Ky., with a tough decision ahead, he needed a workable approach to decision making. Shaun relates that while sitting at his desk with a stack of offers from various colleges, he would throw each offer over his left shoulder. If it landed in the wastebasket, it was rejected. If it landed on the floor, it would remain a viable choice. By this method, he narrowed his choice to three universities: Michigan, Notre Dame and Alabama. Ultimately, he chose Alabama and went on to set a whole host of records before becoming a stellar performer in the NFL.

The impact

So, what's the deal? Do worldviews matter? Does your perception of life play a role in determining the results of your choices? No doubt about it. Four decisions by four young men led to four outcomes: 1. a hugely successful business, 2. a personal tragedy, 3. the destruction of the World Trade Center and the death of thousands, and 4. a stellar NFL career and Christian witness. Each individual was surrounded by people who influenced their thinking. Each made a decision aided by a view through the lens molded by their estimation of reality. All viewpoints were real to them, but I would venture to say that you and I would not judge the outcomes to be equally desirable.

Perhaps you and I should take away from these brief examples that not only do viewpoints matter, but coaches count. How they nurture a relationship with less-experienced people can have a huge impact on their lives and, perhaps, the entire world.

A review of the Barna Group website in March 2006 reveals the following insight by this respected research organization: "Ongoing research by The Barna Group consistently demonstrates the powerful impact a person's worldview has on their life. A worldview serves as a person's decision-making filter, enabling them to make sense of the complex and huge amount of information, experiences, relationships and opportunities they face in life. By helping to clarify what a person believes to be important, true and desirable, a worldview has a dramatic influence on a person's choices in any given situation." Barna Group, 3-6-09.

Worldviews are not simply a topic for the classroom. They are a matter of the street. You do what you view!

QUICK HIT #3: DERWIN GRAY

A Change of Heart!

Venue:
TEXAS STADIUM
IRVING, TEXAS
OCTOBER 1998

In his own words, Derwin Gray describes the event that changed his worldview and his life. "My last play in the NFL was not that much different than any other play. I sprinted downfield on kickoff coverage. I collided with a blocker. I turned to the right; he turned to the left. But in the midst of this turning, my left foot got stuck in the AstroTurf. When that happened, I heard the medial collateral ligament in my left knee snap, and on the outside of that same knee, I heard the bone crack. I had been hurt before. This time; however, I knew my career was over. As I lay on my back writhing in pain, I looked up through the hole in the roof of Texas Stadium. Like an angry 5-year-old, I told God, 'Don't you know I have a dream of playing for 10 years.'"

But God had a donkey for Derwin to go get!

We all have our own dreams and Derwin had his. As he related in his book, Hero, "In the midst of my pain, God was leading me to a new and better dream ... His dream." Sprawled on his back in Texas Stadium, Derwin was in an "it's all about me" mode. God had different ideas for Derwin, though. God had a donkey for him to get; a donkey that would further His kingdom. On that fateful day, Derwin had not only a twist in his knee, but a life-changing twist in his outlook or worldview. Known to many as the Evangelism Linebacker, he currently ministers to thousands of people through a variety of venues. As an author, speaker and founder/pastor of Transformation Church in South Carolina, his change in worldview has brought glory to God and a deeper walk for multitudes.

QUICK HIT POINT:

What can we learn from Derwin's story? Should his recognition that God wanted him to play a different game provide a learning (or coaching) moment for you and me? Simple answer: Definitely! Complex answer: Sure! Derwin moved from an "all about me" to an "all about He" view on life and also from an "I'll call the plays" to a "God calls the plays" platform. In the lingo of pizza, he is adding toppings to a new crust; one that starts with God and not with man. His pregame meal fortifies him for a new game and yours can, too!

─────────── **Read On!** ───────────

PART 4
THE POWER OF THREE

The Ultimate Game-Changer

When it comes to having a "good day on the field," some stadiums are more friendly than others posing challenges from both fan noise and playing conditions. In football and in life off the field, the ultimate game changer for a team and for each of us personally is what I am calling the Power of Three. As illustrated above, the Power of Three emanates from an all-powerful God (owner) working His purpose through every player while utilizing other people (coaches) to help guide the way. One may say that God needs no one to accomplish His aims and, yes, that is true. But God, by His infinite free will, has chosen to accomplish many of His tasks through each and every one of us. Additionally, He often (and I can offer a personal "Amen" here) utilizes other people to work with us in formulating and achieving His goals. Thus, the Power of Three becomes the true game changer; a force we should adopt and teach others to employ.

In this section, we shall pursue a brief understanding of each element of this triangle plus the element of trust which binds the three in truth. Seven sections are devoted to this important topic:

- The Power of the HSML Coach
- Quick Hit #4 - Stephen
- The Power of the H3P3 Player
- Quick Hit # 5 – Rachel
- The Power of God
- The Power of Trust
- Quick Hit # 6 – Jeff Kemp

THE POWER OF THE HSML COACH

Coaching counts! In a stadium dominated by a culture of confusion, inexperienced players must rely heavily upon guidance from others. That help typically comes from those individuals who have played the game and personally experienced the good, bad and the ugly results of their own choices. We'll call those experienced people "coaches" who, if they are successful, take on a multi-faceted role as a servant, mentor, leader and yes, even a hero.

In this section, we will chat about characteristics of a coach who is effective in working with young people as they pursue a course in life. Check out the following short chapters:

- The Hero-Servant-Mentor-Leader Coach
- Coaching 101: A Job Description
- Quick Hit #4: Coach Stephen - The Legacy of a Biblical Coach

THE HSML COACH

"I can't believe God put us on this earth to be ordinary."

– Lou Holtz, former head football coach for several top universities

---

Venue:
GRAMBLING STATE UNIVERSITY
1941-1997

Growing up the son of a sharecropper, Eddie Robinson went on to become one of the best collegiate coaches of all time, posting a career record of 408 wins throughout 56 years as the head football coach of the Grambling State University Tigers. More than 200 of his players went on to careers in the NFL. Yet, those who knew him describe him as a humble man crediting his players, family and others with his achievements. "Coach Rob did a lot more for us than teach us about football," says Everson Walls, one of Grambling's stars in the NFL. "He used to come through the halls early in the morning with a cowbell, waking us up for class and church." Former Grambling quarterback and Super Bowl XXII MVP Doug Williams noted this about the man who invested his life in the success of others: "I doubt that Coach Robinson really understood his impact. I think the reason for that was the way he was brought up. He was such a humble type of individual that he didn't bask in his success; he didn't wear it on his shoulders."

233

In a world governed by short attention spans and even shorter fuses in both the media and college administrative offices, the era of 56-year coaches is rapidly becoming extinct. However, the real point and lesson for each of us to take away from Eddie Robinson's story is not his longevity, but his impact. He became involved in the lives of each member of his team, not only to make them stronger football players, but also better contributors off the field. Sure, he taught them blocking and tackling; but, he also taught them how to take a moral stand filled with truth and teeming with personal responsibility. He coupled skills with principles that you, too, can pass along to those in your sphere of life. In his own words, "Coaching is a profession of love. You can't coach people unless you love them."

In answering the question. How many people will the average person meet in his or her lifetime, popular internet sites put the number somewhere north of 10,000. So where Eddie Robinson had the opportunity to coach for 56 years, sending more than 200 players to the NFL, each of us has the opportunity to personally influence the lives of thousands of individuals. Many of those interactions will reflect brief encounters, but, undoubtedly, many others will bring the opportunity to engage at a much deeper level. For some, you will become their hero; for others, you will provide hard-learned advice; and for still others, you may simply be a friendly set of ears, always available to listen. In each case, you will have the opportunity to become a servant, meeting the specific needs of each person. Thus, you will take on the coaching role that may be considered a hero-mentor-servant-leader.

In his words, quoted at the beginning of this chapter, coach Holtz hit the nail on the head. God did not put any of us on this Earth to be ordinary. As a human, you were designed and built in God's image, full of creativity and packed with the resources to fulfill His purpose in your life. Scripture teaches that those of us with experience have not only the capacity, but also have the responsibility to assist those just entering the game.

Let's briefly take a look at the role of the hero-servant-mentor-leader coach. These attributes describe four general roles that make you relevant in the eyes of the players in your life. In a later chapter, we will chat further about a variety of specific traits of a successful coach. I'm quite sure you will be motivated when you see that many of them are your own strengths.

Part 4 - Figure 1 illustrates the four components that will make your life as a coach meaningful. Every one of us is capable of living out these elements to some degree. In God's design, we are individually and uniquely endowed with various gifts and strengths. Thus, some may be stronger in certain areas than others. Not to worry. Perfection only exists in the author of our existence, not in any of His creation. But striving to be relevant in all four of these areas is a noble goal.

Part 4 - Figure 1. The Hero-Servant-Mentor-Leader Coach
A true model for excellence

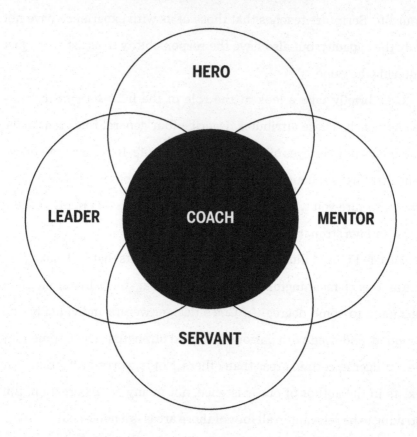

Intimidating? Unachievable? Beyond your pay grade? Is this a model that few can achieve? If you believe the self-aggrandizing pundits of today's media, maybe so. If you believe in yourself and the tenets outlined in Scripture, not so much. You and I can fulfill each of these roles and in doing so, become invaluable in the lives of others. Take a shot at the job and you may find yourself drenched in Gatorade before the season ends.

Put on your headset, grab your clipboard and let's take a quick look at the hats you will wear.

HERO-SERVANT-MENTOR-LEADER

Where have all the heroes gone?

VENUE:
CLEVELAND GLENVILLE HIGH SCHOOL
CLEVELAND, OH
EARLY 1930s

As the Great Depression of the 1930s cast a heavy shadow of gloom across the United States, a couple of kids teamed up at Cleveland's Glenville High School to write and illustrate their idea of a superhero. Little did comic book artists Jerry Siegel and Joe Shuster know when they sold the rights to Action Comics for a mere $130 that their character, Superman, would come to be recognized as the greatest superhero of all time. Volumes have been written analyzing Superman's character including the who, what and whys in their lives that resulted in Siegel and Shuster's creation of the mythical hero. Was it the Great Depression generating a need for hope? Was it the recent murder of Shuster's father during a robbery of his dry cleaning store spawning a character untouched by mere bullets? An entire historical cottage industry exists, offering various interpretations for the man in the red cape. Some have even concluded that characteristics of Superman reflected those of Moses (Siegel and Shuster were Jewish). All parties seem to agree; however, on a few key points. Superman's character exhibited a high moral posture, reflected in his stance against all types of evil. Additionally, he was able to unflinchingly withstand anything the wicked world could throw at him. Essentially, he did everything right to correct everything wrong; a true hero!

The Superman character spawned new heroes and fed early TV programming with handsome figures who claimed the moral high ground in their daily quest to set the world right. Shows such as Superman taught the young Baby Boomer generation to appreciate their roots in the USA and their foundations in Biblical morality. Having grown up toward the end of this glorious era; however, I was totally devastated (and scarred for life) when George Reeves, the early TV Superman and my hero, committed suicide. Heroes, especially Superman, weren't supposed to die by their own hand or anyone else's. Bullets are supposed to bounce off, harmlessly falling to the ground. Instead, my hero was dead and I had to learn to live with it and find another hero. I did eventually with President John F. Kennedy. There's a lesson here: You never want to be my hero.

As a young kid unknowingly formulating my own thoughts about heroes, perhaps the death of an actor and a president brought a sense of reality that even heroes can take a fall. Bullets don't always bounce off.

Many experts say people grow up with a need for heroes. They also point out that whoever someone looks to as a hero has more to do with their own needs than the accomplishments of that hero. And therein lies the good news! Heroes are out there. Or, should I say, YOU are out there. You may work the night shift at the local auto plant. You may be the single mom working three jobs to raise your kids. You may be the retired schoolteacher who mistakenly thinks your productive life is behind you. You may be in any number of situations but, quite frankly, you can be (and should be) the day-to-day hero for a member of the upcoming generation. They desperately need an example of how and how not to get the job of life done. They need to learn the realities and opportunities of life.

But what about the big heroes that parade across the sports and entertainment scene? Don't they fit the bill as examples? Unfortunately, we as a society and as individuals often interchange the terms "celebrity" and "hero." Many true heroes do attain celebrity status, but not all celebrities rate hero status. Many celebrities are falling like leaves on an October afternoon. In sports, finding a star to put on the Wheaties box is tough. In Hollywood, well what can I say? Frustrating? Of course. Sad? Always. Depressing? Sure. Unusual? Not at all. Big-time heroes can take big-time falls. And, in most cases, those individuals were never heroes from the get-go. The Athletes in Action website (2012) confirms this situation: "Many athletes and coaches, once thought to be ideal role models for today's youth, are swept up in a culture that seems to have abandoned limits and a moral compass for a 'win-at-all-cost' mentality. In the end, the sports pages are no different than the front pages of our newspapers."

So, who are the heroes? Pastor, speaker and former NFL great Derwin Gray reminds us that we are each created by the greatest of all heroes, God Himself. In his wonderfully inspiring book, Hero, Derwin suggests we should pause to reflect on the potential that God built into each of us. Derwin affirms our value when he says, "you are of incalculable worth, capable of doing things you never thought were possible because the image of the great hero is tattooed on your soul."

In the foreword to the book, Home Grown Heroes: How to Raise Courageous Kids, a true American war hero and recipient of the Congressional Medal of Honor, the late Brigadier General Joe Foss says, "America needs a new generation of heroes ... people who are ruled by a conscience that doesn't take the Ten Commandments lightly, who have a fundamental reverence for their creator, and a respect for the people and things He has created."

Scripture is replete with examples of ordinary people who have done extraordinary things. The book of Hebrews (Chapter 11) lists many of them. Check it out. Also, while you are searching Scripture for what a hero should look like, stop by Psalm 101. In eight short verses, David outlines daily goals of a hero from God's viewpoint. He offers that this person should:

- Sing praise to the Lord
- Live a blameless life
- Avoid things vile and vulgar
- Hate crooked dealings
- Reject perverse ideas
- Avoid every evil
- Reject those who slander
- Deny conceit and pride
- Protect good people
- Promote those above reproach
- Ferret out criminals

Coming from David, a man who has been described as one seeking God's heart, but who, as a human, also stumbled often, these directives should become the bumper-sticker statements of our drive through life.

You, the hero

When I say you need to be a hero in a young person's life, I don't expect bullets to bounce off your chest or for you to be featured on the cover of Sports Illustrated. So, what should that day-to-day hero image be? For our purposes, let's simply define a hero as someone who a young person can honestly say, "I want to be like you." Remember the old Nike ad that dominated TV for so long proclaiming, "I want to be like Mike." Put your name in that phrase and consider that you, too, could be a hero.

HERO-**SERVANT**-MENTOR-LEADER

Before the Passover celebration, Jesus knew that his hour had come to leave this world and return to his father. He now showed the disciples the full extent of his love. It was time for supper, and the devil had already enticed Judas, son of Simon Iscariot, to carry out his plan to betray Jesus. Jesus knew that the father had given him authority over everything and that he had come from God and would return to God. So He got up from the table, took off His robe, wrapped a towel around His waist, and poured water into a basin. Then He began to wash the disciples' feet and to wipe them with the towel He had around him.

When He came to Simon Peter, Peter said to him, "Lord, why are you going to wash my feet?" Jesus replied, "You don't understand now why I am doing it; someday you will." "No," Peter protested, "you will never wash my feet!" Jesus replied, "But if I don't wash you, you won't belong to me." Simon Peter exclaimed, "Then wash my hands and head as well, Lord, not just my feet!" Jesus replied, "A person who has bathed all over does not need to wash, except for the feet, to be entirely clean. And you are clean, but that isn't true of everyone here." For Jesus knew who would betray him. That is what he meant when he said, "Not all of you are clean."

After washing their feet, he put on his robe again and sat down and asked, "Do you understand what I was doing? You call me 'teacher' and 'Lord,' and you are right, because it is true. And since I, the Lord and teacher, have washed your feet, you ought to wash each other's feet. I have given you an example to follow. Do as I have done to you. How true it is that a servant is not greater than the master. Nor are messengers more important than the one who sends them. You know these things—now do them! That is the path of blessing." John 13: 1-17.

Planted in front of the tube for years, I have seen a lot of football coaches running the show from the sidelines. Did I ever witness one washing a player's feet? Not a chance! We have been trained to think of a coach as Mr. Tough Guy, in charge, barking orders, pacing the sidelines and calling the plays. On the other end of the spectrum, most of us picture a servant as a mild, head slightly bowed, unspoken individual who lives at the discretion of his or her master. So, how can we reconcile both characteristics in the same job description?

Perhaps this will help. Picture the creator of the universe, the leader of a group of 12 men, the teacher and the one whose very words caused the raging sea to become calm, bending before these men to wash their feet. On the night before His crucifixion, Jesus did just that. He washed the grimy, raunchy feet of the Apostles to illustrate they must become servants if they hope to have others follow them. According to Jewish law, not even slaves could be forced to perform that despicable task. So, the point is clear: If you expect someone to follow you, you need to fulfill their needs, not yours. It does not mean that you must be lower on the organization chart than the person you are serving. Many people at the top of the ladder define themselves as servants to the needs of those several rungs below. It's a way of life!

Huge point so take note: When Jesus washed their feet, he washed them all including those of Judas Iscariot who within hours would turn Him over to authorities to be crucified. As God, Jesus knew he was washing the grime off one bent on his destruction. Perhaps, Christ's action should serve as an example to all of us: You don't just serve those who like you; you serve those who need you!

To be a servant does not imply that you need to crawl on your knees as a slave. Rather, you should come to the job with a sense of humility. As author C.S. Lewis pointed out, "True humility is not thinking less of yourself; it is thinking of yourself less." So, for our purpose, let's simply define being a servant as someone who fulfills the needs of a person working out decisions in their life. You are not an overlord, imposing your own agenda. Rather, you are present to help another person fulfill their own plan.

HERO-SERVANT-**MENTOR**-LEADER

In 2003, the Indianapolis Colts posted a 12-4 season, winning the AFC South, but falling short in the AFC Championship game in New England. Not to worry though, head coach Tony Dungy was rapidly building the team that would win Super Bowl XLI in 2006. Coach Dungy, like all NFL coaches, was a busy guy, constantly in the limelight of the press and under brutal pressure to produce winning teams. But coach Dungy also had a private side. He had a view on life that went far deeper than the shallow spotlight of the sports blogs.

In April 2004, Tony took time out of his football schedule to deliver the keynote address at the Northwest Ohio Fellowship of Christian Athletes banquet. Unknown to Tony, a young man who truly hoped to attend the banquet dinner lay on the couch at home too weakened from cancer to make it. Jonathan Judge, a high school senior with maturity far beyond his years, had been fighting cancer for seven years and would succumb to the dreaded disease two months later. Following the banquet, a couple of local heroes approached Tony hoping to get an autograph they could take to Jonathan. Tony turned down the request and instead would personally deliver the autograph to him. If Jonathan could not make it to the banquet, Tony decided to take the banquet to him. He put his schedule and his private airplane on hold, jumped into a car and rode to visit the young man. No media, no cameras and no story in the following morning sports section. It would just be Tony, privately meeting with a boy who had a need.

This foray into the suburbs of Toledo, Ohio, would not advance his career nor pad his

246

bank account. It would; however, be a "do what you view" moment; a natural extension of what Tony saw as important in his life. And maybe, just maybe, this intimate setting would prepare him a bit for the loss of his own father less than two months later and the tragic loss of his own son in 2005.

This guy's heart is definitely in the right spot, operating from a position of humility, serving people with a genuine belief in the God of the Bible. Coach Dungy portrays the same characteristics whether the cameras are rolling or he is tucked away with a small group in the privacy of a home.

From being fired as coach of the Tampa Bay Buccaneers to winning the whole shebang in Super Bowl XLI; from experiencing the joys of fatherhood to attending his own son's funeral, he has experienced the ebb and flow of life. When Tony speaks, his voice echoes both credibility and reality. Experience rings clearly. Experience qualifies Tony to be a mentor.

But Tony is not alone on the roller coaster of life. If I were to personally interview you, I am certain that you, too, would bring a boatload of experiences, both inspiring and dreadful, to the locker room. We all do. And that's what qualifies us to become coaches in the lives of those still lacking the know-how.

Thinking back to those who assumed the mentoring role as my own career developed, I generally perceived them as people who knew the ropes in the organization. They had experience getting things done; they may not have been my boss. Rather, they achieved influence through their willingness to commit the time needed to pass knowledge and experience on to me. Most played the "inquisitive role" (and this is huge), not always providing a direct answer, but asking the questions which helped me get to the answer myself.

As coach Dungy wrote in his book The Mentor Leader, "It is impossible to mentor from a distance. Without engagement, you cannot lead effectively." So, if you are willing to engage someone and commit to spending a bit of time with them, you can definitely fulfill the role of mentor.

Tme Out:

Take a couple minutes to mentally list the collisions and touchdowns you have already experienced in life. What have they taught you? Would others benefit from hearing about them? Are you willing to share them?

Now, go do it!

HERO-SERVANT-MENTOR-LEADER

Sometimes one needs to look for examples. Other times, God brings them to your door.

As I sit comfortably in my office writing a chapter for Winning Choices, a familiar face is humming along with a gas-operated grass trimmer a mere 15 feet outside my office window. One of the busiest and most respected citizens of Northwest Ohio, Clint Longenecker normally supports his family as an award-winning professor at the University of Toledo's School of Business and Innovation. But, today, in 90 degree weather, Clint is spending his Friday afternoon coaching his son on the "modus operandi" of landscape maintenance.

Playing out before my very eyes is the epitome of the hero-servant-mentor-leader coach role. I could not ask for a better example of what this book hopes to teach. Clint truly understands what it means to get out of the stands and into the game.

What can we all learn from the vignette that continues to play out as I write?

You need to be there. Clint is not sitting on the lounge chair at home. He is at the office building where his son is employed teaching him both skills and attitude.

You need to be a servant. Clint understands the needs of his son as the young man struggles to develop his work ethic. Accordingly, to teach his son, Clint assumes the important role of a servant, not an overlord.

You need to be a hero. In 90-plus degree weather, Clint's son may not appreciate today's opportunity to learn, but the memory will stick. His father has just exemplified the role of an everyday hero, providing an example of doing it right.

You need to be a leader. Clint is not standing on the curb yelling instructions above the noise of the blower. He is carrying the blower, sweating shoulder-to-shoulder with his son, setting an example of how to get the job done right.

Legendary coaches whose achievements grace the hall of fame of their respective sports unquestionably serve to inspire each of us as we seek to take our own game to a new level. I believe that often the local story in our own neighborhood serves to motivate us in a more personal way. The individual whose hand we can shake, or back we can slap offers confirmation that we, too, can do what needs to be done.

Bill McCartney, former University of Colorado coach and founder of Promise Keepers, said, "All coaching is, is taking a player where he can't take himself." As I conclude this brief example, Clint and his son have completed their task and the place looks great. But someday, it will be overgrown with grass and weeds again. People will forget how well it looked on this hot, June day. But, more importantly, learning has taken place. A hero-servant-mentor-leader coach has gotten in the game. And though the grass will once again need attention, I am confident Clint's son will never forget this coaching moment. That is what getting in the game is all about.

Summing it all up

What do the coaches who have amassed tons of victories and trophies have to say about their profession? Check out the comments of several household names in Part 4 - Figure 2. Together, they are suggesting that a successful coach will create a vision for their players by listening, questioning and being an example by working hard to help them get where they can't go alone.

Just as important as what they are saying is what they are not saying. Note that none of these coaches say you have to be a brilliant strategist or have 20 years on the sidelines to be a good coach. Combined, their advice teaches us that a good coach realizes that "it's not about me." Conversely, personal success comes from working hard to help others succeed.

If, for some strange reason, you doubt your abilities and need to affirm your qualifications for being an example to others, check out the Quick Hit on coach Stephen later in this section. Actually, even if you are comfortable with yourself, still check out how he influenced history.

Are these coaches right? Do they offer good advice? Probably so, but if we need a more qualified opinion, perhaps we should look to the greatest coach of all time, Jesus Christ. His team, mainly a group of uneducated fishermen, went from bumbling through life to turning a world upside down through the power of the Holy Spirit. As their leader, Christ taught them the basics of becoming a true leader and a successful coach. For example, in the gospel of Matthew, we find Christ telling His disciples, "You know that in this world kings are tyrants, and officials lord over the people beneath them. But among you it should be quite different. Whoever wants to be a leader among you must be your servant, and whoever wants to be first must become your slave. For even I, the Son of Man, came here not to be served, but to serve others, and to give my life as a ransom for many." Matthew 20: 25-28.

Just prior to ascending to His father, Christ gave the team final instructions on coaching (aka The Great Commission). In Mark 16:15, He told them "to go into all the world and preach the Good News to everyone." In the totally unauthorized football version of the Bible, one would find that same verse telling us to "get in the game and make winning choices."

Let's finish our discussion by revisiting the 56-year coach Eddie Robinson. The impact of great coaches can be measured, not in their popularity or fame, but in their impact on the lives of those they mold. Here again Coach Robinson fits the bill, symbolizing the type of individual needed on the streets today. "Leadership, like coaching," coach Robinson said, "is fighting for the hearts and souls of men and getting them to believe in you."

Coach Eddie Robinson had his head and heart in the right place! So can you!

Part 4 - Figure 2. Coaches on Coaching

Ara Parseghian ...

"A good coach will make his players see what they can be rather than what they are."

John Madden ...

"Coaches have to watch for what they don't want to see and listen to what they don't want to hear."

Joe Gibbs ...

"You and I are the players, God's our head coach, and we're all playing the biggest game of all."

Phil Dixon...

"Probably my best quality as a coach is that I ask a lot of challenging questions and let the person come up with the answer."

Lou Holtz ...

"I won't accept anything less than the best a player's capable of doing, and he has the right to expect the best that I can do for him."

Vince Lombardi ...

"Leaders aren't born they are made. And they are made just like anything else, through hard work. And that's the price we'll have to pay to achieve that goal, or any goal."

Tony Dungy ...

"For some reason the football coach of a major college program is seen as one of the leaders of the campus. And some way we have to let our young people know that that leader can look like anyone."

Tom Landry ...

"Leadership is a matter of having people look at you and gain confidence, seeing how you react. If you're in control, they're in control."

Game Winning Point: "Coaching is a profession of love. You can't coach people unless you love them." -- Coach Eddie Robinson

Game Changing Verse: "Fix your thoughts on what is true, honorable and right." Philippians 4:8.

PLAYBOOK TIPS

- Focus on excellence and fundamentals.

- Expect 100 percent; give 100 percent.

- Seek to encourage; seek to not discourage.

Read On!

COACHING 101
A JOB DESCRIPTION

"I've always tried to coach people the way I would like to be coached; positively and encouragingly rather than with criticism and fear ... I've tried to be as fair as possible."

– Tony Dungy

Many NFL owners would probably say that the job description for a head coach includes only three points: 1. Win 2. Win and 3. Win. The oft-quoted NFL coach Vince Lombardi shored up that idea proclaiming, "If winning isn't everything, why do they keep score?" Macho thinking aside; however, a coach's job, just like all jobs, spans a variety of tasks. Throughout my own career, I have worked in multiple jobs supported by a plethora of job descriptions. Only a few of the many of the job descriptions actually reflected what I was expected to do. If that has been your experience, too, then you may be tempted to skip this section and move on. Don't!

Job Description

What should one look for on the resume of a hero-servant-mentor-leader coach? If you were charged with writing a job description, what duties would you include in the required competencies column?

On and off the field, coaches come in a variety of sizes and styles.

Disciplinarians, tacticians, communicators and other descriptions typically roll off the lips of the media in describing the guy or gal on the sidelines. Although we should recognize that coaching is not a one-size-fits-all proposition, there are several aspects that appear common among successful leaders whether operating on the football field, in the family room or on the street corner. Let's take a look at a few specifics. There may be more, but the following eight fill out a job description rather well.

1. Teach fundamentals to inexperienced players

As former Stanford standout Craig Awbrey said after the Angel Tree Football Clinic, never teach advanced techniques to inexperienced players. They will fail and be discouraged. Despite having a closet full of t-shirts and trophies doled out merely for participation, inexperienced players need to learn the principles and practices of the game. This holds true in football and in life. Good coaching early in life develops a winning mindset while curtailing bad habits. Back to coach Lombardi's wisdom: "Winning is a habit; unfortunately, so is losing." Ask any truly successful professional on or off the field. They will tell you that nailing down the fundamentals early in life, typically with the aid of a mentor, is critical to lifelong success regardless of your line of work.

2. Remind experienced players of those same principles and basics

Locker rooms should be furnished with high chairs. Although I will not reveal names (to protect the innocent and the guilty), one leading NFL coach said he often pictures his players in high chairs, acting as babies, constantly needing to be reminded of the most basic aspects of the game. That may be a stretch; it may not be. Real champions will tell you that they continually practice the basics to ensure that those fundamentals literally become an inherent part of their makeup and character. In the heat of action, "you do what you view" so, in the off hours, coaches become reinforcers, driving principles and practices deeper into the character of each player.

3. Help players formulate a game plan

As author and speaker Zig Ziglar said, "You were born to win, but to be a winner, you must plan to win, prepare to win and expect to win." Scripture takes it a step higher, indicating that "without a vision, the people perish," Proverbs 29:18. Ultimately, the team executes individual plays, but the coach creates the overall game plan.

Good coaches have been shaped by personal experience on the field. Most have enjoyed both the thrill of victory and the pain of defeat. They have learned how to take a hit and get back up. They have learned that winning and losing are both fleeting. To become champions, players need to learn what works and what doesn't in a variety of game situations. Here is where the mentor aspect of the coach rises to the occasion, providing direction based on experience.

4. Channel emotion into powerful action – motivate and discipline

Emotion wins; emotion loses. At one end of the spectrum, uncontrolled emotion leads to unsportsmanlike conduct. Repeated over and over, uncontrolled emotion adds a big "L" to the win/loss column. At the other end, lethargy may not draw a penalty flag, but it also doesn't put points on the scoreboard. The end result is the same: a big fat "L." As we all realize, but often don't wish to admit, we live in a world dominated by emotion. From family relations to buying habits, our passions drive our decisions.

In addition to smarts and a good set of hands, we need a high level of commitment (aka emotion) to achieve results. Coming from the heart, emotion produces huge amounts of energy. Every good coach knows how to fire up his or her team while simultaneously instilling the discipline to keep that passion channeled toward victory. Remember, atomic energy harnessed produces electricity to light your home; unharnessed it produces a bomb that can destroy it.

5. Provide clarity; manage time; monitor progress

When talking about monitoring progress, former Cincinnati Bengals coach Bruce Coslet can get right to the point. Following a disappointing loss, he summed up the team's performance saying, "We can't run. We can't pass. We can't stop the run. We can't stop the pass. We can't kick. Other than that, we're just not a very good football team right now."

In your world, when the game is tight, who or what does a player see when he looks to the sidelines for help? When the game is on the line and their face reflects a what-do-I-do-now-coach attitude, do they see you or do they see a sideline of confusion? Are you there to provide clarity or are you distracted by some other aspect of the game? Are you building their confidence or letting them flounder in uncertainty as they try to figure out the next move?

Experience breeds a sense of timing and progress. Inexperience lacks both. Hence, a perceptive coach is able to keep the team moving forward, knowing deadlines and recognizing challenges and opportunities posed by the ticking clock. Calling a timeout when needed to get attention or provide direction also falls upon the experienced leader. Hopefully, the words of Coach Lombardi, "We didn't lose, we just ran out of time," don't ring true on a consistent basis.

This trait proves to be pivotal in getting the job done consistently. Recall the earlier discussion of how an accountability partner breeds a higher rate of success. The simple presence of a committed coach prevents the team from procrastinating as the game unfolds.

6. Celebrate the wins and learn from the losses

"Success is not forever and failure isn't fatal," observed legendary Miami Dolphins head coach Don Shula. No one, and I mean no one, wins every game. Though we can't come out on top in every endeavor, we can learn from each and every choice that we make.

We have all grown up with the admonition to learn from our mistakes. But, as adults, do we have the guts to honestly look in the mirror? Do we spend more time justifying than rectifying? As a side note, I wonder why our parents didn't tell us to learn from our successes. A first class coach takes the time to delve into the good, the bad and the ugly. Without doing so, the past typically foretells the future.

7. Create an atmosphere of respect and dialogue

This is huge! Respect and communication define the hero-servant-mentor Coach. Face it, the players get it. They learn skills, develop confidence and play with a higher level of commitment when they value the relationship with their coach. As Craig Awbrey explained earlier, screaming is a thing of the past. In fact, his coach, Bill Walsh, incorporated humor to imbed many of his ideas with the team. Creating a relationship of respect focuses on setting an example worth admiring (hero) and communicating with the players in ways that meet their needs (servant and mentor). Sincerity and humility should be foremost in this effort.

8. Power up the spiritual side of the game

The heart of the problem is always a problem of the heart. Simply a play on words? Or, a meaningful assessment of life on the street? I would go with the latter. Too often, coaches concentrate on the head and the hands, ignoring the heart. But, to continue the play on words, the heart of the matter goes deeper than the heart. Consider the power resident in our spiritual relationship with God. As 2 Corinthians 3:5 reminds us, "Our only power and success come from God."

As we have related several times, Winning Choices is fueled by a trust in and acknowledgement of the God of the Bible. Unfortunately, most of us tend to forget that reality when we are winning the game. It's only when we are behind on the scoreboard and the clock has emerged as our enemy that we are inclined to call a timeout and get our act focused with God's help. Don't go there. Rely on the power of God (that He offers freely) from the get-go and your win-loss record will improve dramatically.

Coach to your strengths

The idea of playing to your strengths is as old as the game itself and the same advice holds true for coaching. Do what you do best! It's not always an easy approach as we often tend to mimic the styles of those we admire even when their natural mannerisms differ significantly from ours. For those of you old enough to picture Super Bowl winning coach John Madden and NFL coach Tom Landry, think of their antics (or lack of them) on the sidelines. Madden roamed about, waving and shouting like a madman. Landry stood poised quietly with a rolled up "something or other" in his hand. Both coached well. Both won games. Both knew and employed their strengths to get the job done.

Attempting to lead through weakness doesn't work for an NFL coach. It won't work for you and it doesn't work for me. If you are able to reach out to those you serve at the street level where they live and work, speak their language and recognize that neither you nor they are perfect, you can get the job done.

While we're considering coaching attributes, let's check in with a guy who has spent time on the field. Known to many as the "Evangelism linebacker", Derwin Gray achieved a career as an outstanding safety in the NFL. After six seasons, God had a different plan for his life (More on Derwin's story later). Now, as lead pastor of the Transformation Church near Charlotte, N.C., Derwin coaches people in their walk with God. I asked him to list the top five traits that he hopes to see in a successful coach. Derwin offered the following thoughts:

- The coach must have character that demands imitation.
- The coach must have battle scars from life.
- The coach must have knowledge and experience that players want to integrate into their lives.
- The players must know the coach loves them and believes in them.
- The coach must be humble enough to learn from the players.

LIFE ACCORDING TO RICK
God has a job for each of us

In this section, we've chatted about the hero-servant-mentor-leader style of coaching, plus walked through a series of what can be termed job responsibilities. But, if we had to get to the heart of the matter, what would we find as practical advice for getting the job done?

To answer this question, I checked in with Rick Isaiah, vice president of the Fellowship of Christian Athletes, for his thoughts. As a former standout receiver at the University of Toledo and having spent time in a similar role with the Cincinnati Bengals, Rick understands how coaches can influence their players.

Rick's thoughts: Values Matter! Relationships matter!

Right up front, Rick insightfully points out that successful coaching hinges on developing influential relationships with those they lead. He laid claim to the adage: "Rules minus Relationships equals Rebellion" as a fundamental principle that every one of us should understand and follow. "What I have learned," Rick said, "is that without an authentic, trust-filled relationship, it is difficult for those whom we are leading to fulfill their full potential. And, in fact, the absence of that relationship can lead to full rebellion. No one wins in this case."

Rick related that his high school wide receivers coach proved instrumental in creating his path to a meaningful life. Recognizing Rick's talent, the coach developed a mentoring relationship that led to a football scholarship at the University of Toledo. Financially unable to pay for his own trip through college, this scholarship opened the door to a life of opportunities. Now as a senior leader and coach in an organization that impacts thousands of young people, Rick knows what works and what doesn't. So, I thought I would simply ask him.

My questions to Rick:

1. Is there a tried and true coaching formula for encouraging young people to adopt the team's values?

Rick: There is a lot to be said for the "different strokes for different folks" maxim when working with young people. Most are still working through their worldview and bring different family histories and personalities to the locker room. At FCA, we understand that coaches need to be flexible in how they teach and mentor kids, but insist that their approaches are founded in the Word of God. As an organization, we have adopted four foundational values that permeate all that we do. We attempt to instill integrity, serving, teamwork and excellence as defined by Scripture in all activities (Note: Check them out in Part 4 - Figure 3). If we can see these four attributes consistently reflected both on and off the field in the lives of those we serve, we consider that we have succeeded as an organization. We firmly believe that these values are not taught, but caught. That is, they are imbedded through the development of meaningful relationships, not simply through lectures.

2. Based on your experience, would you share a few tips that coaches can consider in making the FCA values (or any values) stick in the lives of the young people who they mentor?

Rick: Here are a few suggestions that work for me:

Authenticity - Lead by example. Young people are watching your integrity. Don't ask them to follow values that you don't follow yourself.

Goal Setting - Set individual goals and follow up. Inexperienced people need help staying on track and are often reticent to set challenging goals for themselves.

Goal Accomplishment - Create avenues to success as a team and as an individual. Everyone, especially those just getting started, does better if they understand the roadmap to success. A lack of direction often leads to costly mistakes.

Accountability - Create a means of checking up. Either a coach-to-player or a buddy system will help keep behavior in line with personal goals. There is a reason that teams have captains. Team members/peers can often be more effective than others because they are all part of a common effort. Plus, let's face it, to young people, older people can't relate to their situation.

Prayer - Seek God's voice through joint prayer. God should be our ultimate guide, so speaking with and listening to Him should be priority No. 1.

Personal Growth - Spend time in scripture discussing each value. The four FCA values can be found in the lives of people throughout the Bible. Discussing a Biblical story is often the best way to illustrate the good, bad and ugly of adhering to or ignoring God's direction for our lives.

Transparency - Discuss how each individual has been challenged in the four values. Every individual faces different challenges each and every day. Chatting about them as a group often leads to solutions that an individual immersed in the situation might miss.

So there is life according to Rick. As we concluded our discussion, he was quick to warn me that his thoughts are simply his thoughts, thus, should not be considered the "coaching Bible." He reiterated the need to be totally dependent on Christ as we work with others.

Rick also noted that these four values span the spectrum of life. They are not limited to the athletic field, nor to any specific group. Any age, gender, race, nationality or economic status faces the same challenges and opportunities. Every coach willing to get in the game and make winning choices can teach powerful principles that will guide their players for the rest of their lives.

A practical point of caution

Typically, the word caution does not show up in describing a coach. However, a point of warning does need to be inserted, especially in today's world. Whether coaching on or off the field, the job can eat up the clock. As former coach Don Shula's wife Dorothy once expressed, "I'm fairly confident that if I died tomorrow, Don would find a way to preserve me until the season was over and he had time for a nice funeral."

While I had Rick's attention, I asked him about the issue of burnout. In his role with FCA, he devotes significant time to developing and managing the coaches in that successful endeavor.

He says as a coach in athletics or as a mentor off the field, overloading your schedule is a dangerous lifestyle. Unfortunately, it is the path many have chosen; some not even realizing the depth of it or how to get out of it. We advise them to schedule time to simply shut down, balancing their life, taking time to stay engaged with their family. Although it's easier to preach than to practice, we continually remind our coaches to employ quality time, avoiding mixing work with family life.

The point: You need to manage your life. Just remember, a burned out coach is of no use to anyone.

Fear Not

And finally ... Fear not! Being a successful coach requires compassion and commitment; not a resume filled with victories, nor a house packed with trophies.

If you feel a bit reticent to jump in the game, consider this piece of trivia: Tom Landry, Chuck Noll, Bill Walsh and Jimmy Johnson accounted for 11 of the 19 Super Bowl victories from 1974 to 1993. They also share the distinction of having the worst first season records of head coaches in NFL history. Never give up! Never!

Game Winning Point: "If anything goes bad, I did it. If anything goes semi-good, we did it. If anything goes really good, then you did it." -- Bear Bryant

Game Winning Verse: "And the servant of the Lord must not strive; but be gentle unto all men, apt to teach, patient." 2 Timothy 2:24.

Read On!

Part 4 - Figure 3. FCA VALUES
(as stated on the FCA official website)

Integrity

We will demonstrate Christ-like wholeness, privately and publicly.

"Honesty guides good people; dishonesty destroys treacherous people." Proverbs 11:3

Serving

We will model Jesus' example of serving.

"Do you understand what I was doing? You call me 'Teacher' and 'Lord,' and you are right, because that's what I am. And since I, your Lord and teacher, have washed your feet, you ought to wash each other's feet." John 13:12-14.

Teamwork

We will express our unity in Christ in all our relationships.

"Is there any encouragement from belonging to Christ? Any comfort from his love? Any fellowship together in the spirit? Are your hearts tender and compassionate? Then make me truly happy by agreeing wholeheartedly with each other, loving one another, and working together with one mind and purpose. Don't be selfish; don't try to impress others. Be humble, thinking of others as better than yourselves. Don't look out only for your own interests, but take an interest in others, too." Philippians 2:1-4.

Excellence

We will honor and glorify God in all we do.

"Work willingly at whatever you do, as though you were working for the Lord rather than for people. Remember that the Lord will give you an inheritance as your reward, and that the master you are serving is Christ." Colossians 3:23-24.

QUICK HIT #4: COACH STEPHEN

The Legacy of a Biblical Coach

Stephen is the man! No doubt about it! He neither touched a football nor ate a pizza, but wow, did he provide an example of the impact one may have on another's life. We're talking about the Biblical Stephen, an individual unknown to many, but whose dedication and commitment has left his mark on history even into the 21st century.

Stephen, like most of us, was just an ordinary guy with an allegiance to an extraordinary God. Much of what we know of him can be found in the Bible, specifically, the book of Acts. The sixth and seventh chapter of that documentary of the early church describes this young man as a guy who knew his stuff and was loyal to His Lord. When the apostles in the growing church of Jerusalem found it tough to keep track of day-to-day activities, they appointed several men to look after those obligations. Scripture records Stephen as the first chosen for that responsibility. As a "man committed to God" he served in that capacity while expanding his influence by unabashedly declaring the gospel.

But God had a different idea. He had a donkey for Stephen to find and a job for him to do.

An HSML coach

Undeniably, Stephen had been fulfilling the servant and leader aspects of being a hero-servant-mentor-leader, or HSML, coach as he helped manage the needs of the church. But soon, he would fulfill the hero and mentor qualities in a very special way. In response to his preaching and that of others, the church was rapidly expanding, creating phenomenal displeasure among Jewish religious leaders. Displeasure turned to anger and anger to wrath. In a fit of rage, the leaders stoned Stephen, making him the first martyr of the young church. In our day in which

273

everyone wants to go to heaven, but no one wants to die, we may find his death to be a tragic loss. For him, to die for His savior was an honor that became a rallying point for the blossoming church.

How does his death relate to being a hero or mentor? True, many coaches today are "stoned" by the sports media, but how did the act of literally being stoned to death make Stephen a coach? Easy answer: one member of the "audience" --Saul of Tarsus!

Most readers dwell on his stoning, but may miss the point that Stephen set an example (a coach if you will) to the man who would later take the church throughout the gentile world. Stephen probably did not realize the impact he had on one member of Jerusalem's synagogue, that man being Saul. Later called Paul, most scholars agree he was a big-time member of the synagogue where Stephen debated with Jewish leaders. Acts 7 records how those leaders were unable to match Stephen's arguments about Christ's redemptive act, resorting eventually to false witnesses to build a case against him. Paul, a very intelligent man, was probably in the midst of this debate, either participating in the deliberation or observing it. And as Stephen met His death at the hands of those same Jews, scripture indicates that Paul, again, was present watching Stephen's ultimate commitment to His Lord.

As the legendary football coaches have taught us, setting an example is a huge part of the leadership surrounding the role of a coach. Good coaches leave a mark on their players.

Undoubtedly, Stephen's commitment to Christ truly left a "coach's mark" on Paul. Eventually, that mark would bear fruit as Paul became the most influential church leader in spreading the gospel to the gentile

274

world. To be fair, history also describes Paul's conversion through his encounter with Christ on the road to Damascus. God and God alone can change lives. But, He often uses others (in this case Stephen) to pave the way.

The point: If you have doubts that you, perhaps just an ordinary person, cannot have an extraordinary impact on the life of another, spend a few minutes in the shoes of Stephen. Unknown to him, he influenced the man who would influence the world. History and culture would never be the same.

THE POWER OF
THE H3P3 PLAYER

Winning Choices focuses on coaches and providing ideas and tools to help others make better choices. So you may look at this section in a couple ways. First, you may read it as background information to share with those you mentor. Or second, since we are not only coaches, but also players in our own lives, you may look at this section as a means of improving your own game.

Throughout the next few pages, we check out the characteristics of a player who produces winning results. In football, every player, not just the quarterback, is making choices constantly as each play unfolds. The same situation holds true off the field. In some situations, you or I may play a leadership role calling the shots while in other situations, we may contribute in some other fashion. But ultimately, each of us will have to step up to take ownership of our own choices and live with the results of our actions.

As you coach others, be aware that many individuals are reticent to play in a leadership role, preferring instead to assume a less demanding responsibility. Part of our job as mentors is to help them realize they need to learn to take ownership of the drive and be accountable for the outcome of their choices. More on that topic in the following two chapters:

- Becoming an H3P3 Player
- An H3P3 Workout

BEING AN H3P3 PLAYER

Winners play the game with their head, heart and hands

Winners play, play well and play well with others

"Football is a game played with arms, legs and shoulders but mostly from the neck up."

– Knute Rockne, former football coach at the University of Notre Dame

"Courage, sacrifice, determination, commitment, toughness, heart, talent, guts. That's what little girls are made of; the heck with sugar and spice."

– Bethany Hamilton, American professional surfer and author of Soul Surfer

---

P3 - PLAYS WELL WITH OTHERS

VENUE:
ANGEL TREE CLINIC
STANFORD UNIVERSITY
PALO ALTO, CALIF.
AUGUST 2013

Known as one of the game's most iconic coaches, few people have a resume approaching that of coach Willie Shaw. Following a rewarding college career at the University of New Mexico, coach Shaw spent a lifetime helping young men learn the principles and attitudes for becoming a winner. During a career spanning 32 years, he played an integral part on the coaching staff of 14 NFL and college teams. Under his guidance, a host of players learned how to become hall of famers both on and off the field.

As the Angel Tree Clinic discussed earlier turned from one-on-one coaching to a group setting, coach Shaw was given the microphone with an opportunity to teach yet another group of young people the key aspects of life. His message:

You are always part of a team

He explained to the kids (and the rest of us) that throughout life, each of us will continually be a part of several teams including endeavors in athletics, careers and more importantly a variety of family units. Learning to be a successful team member, coach Shaw explained, plays a huge role in your personal level of achievement. He relayed that during his career, he had worked with a whole host of extremely talented athletes. Some of those athletes, however, struggled to become team players, often stumbling over their own egos. On the other hand, less-talented players who learned how to work together brought more success to the team and ultimately to themselves.

Five hundred people sat listening quietly to coach Shaw's advice. Their silence spoke loudly. His message was hitting home. So what do each of us have to do to be a team member? As coach explained, first we need to put the team's goals ahead of our personal ones. We need to understand our needs and skills, but, equally important, we need to understand the needs and skills of others on our team. Whether on the football field, on the job, in the neighborhood or in the family, each person on the team brings a unique set of experiences and skills to the game. We need to recognize those differences and respect them as we work together to win.

Being part of an athletic team is not a foreign concept to most of us. However, seeing your entire life play out as a member of various teams may be a new way of viewing your world. But, if you think about it, coach Shaw's observations are dead on. Very little activity in our modern world happens in isolation. Most of our day-to-day activity depends on successfully interacting with a variety of people who, like coach Shaw said, bring different responsibilities, talents and experience to the table. So let's grab on to coach Shaw's thoughts and lay out three qualifications any successful decision-maker must consistently exhibit.

It all started in kindergarten

For those of us who graduated from kindergarten before the age of political correctness, we attended school under the watchful eye of a teacher armed with a pen and a report card. At the least indication of trouble, he or she was able to jot a negative comment in the category titled, "plays well with others" and fire it off to our parents for corrective action. As life progressed into elementary school, that highly feared document, the report card, grew in length adding categories for attendance and skills in the 3R's. Thus was born the 3P measurement of success that followed us into adulthood. The 3P's: Plays (shows up), plays well (can add up a column of numbers) and plays well with others (stays out of trouble on the playground) became our lifelong measurement of success. If you think I'm wrong about this, take a quick look at the performance review system that you currently labor under. You will quickly discover vestiges of the 3P's.

The good news: The teachers of yesterday were right. The 3P's make a lot of sense. Much more so than today's PC view which allows little Johnny to do whatever he wants to do, knowing full and well he will advance to the next grade sporting a T-shirt for participation (or not).

The 3P approach defines an easy-to-understand path to success. Every person who hopes to have a winning season in life must 1. Play, 2. Play well and 3. Play well with others. In other words, show up, bring some skills and utilize them in conjunction with others who are doing the same to get the job done. Fall short on any one of the three and the entire house collapses on your head. It sounds simple and it is simple.

Part 4 - Figure 4 illustrates these three traits. Without a boatload of imagination, one can visualize how this approach can apply literally to any "game" on or off the field. Let's expand a bit on each aspect.

Plays

Woody Allen, actor, director and observer of life, has said, "Eighty percent of success is showing up." Although meant to lend a touch of humor, that statement contains a bucket of truth for you and me as players.

We really do need to show up! Most do, but many do not. Showing up physically while leaving your brain at home doesn't count. The big decisions of life await you; but observing from the sidelines while others call the shots does not get the job done. Avoiding decisions does not win ballgames. "Whatever" should not be your battle cry! Procrastination should not be your core competency. Taking yourself out of the game by not getting in the game yields nothing. Unless you want others to make your choices for you, you need to be in the game, ready to play.

Plays Well

A winner plays well. "Always learning; Always improving" should be written on your wall.

If you check out the football hall of fame or in life, you will note one common characteristic. Each and every hall of famer played well on a consistent basis throughout an extended career. There is no room on the wall for one -game winners or one season players. Mediocrity may get you in the game, but your win-loss record will reflect your attitude and skills. A great attitude combined with good skills produces results. A lack of either sends you to the locker room, not the trophy room.

As coach Lombardi said, "If you're not fired with enthusiasm, you'll be fired with enthusiasm."

Plays Well with Others

A winner plays well with others. "Team rah! Team rah! Rah, rah, team rah!"

Egos aside, if you ask any truly great player, he or she will acknowledge the contribution that a team makes in his or her personal success story.

Very few, if any, great things on the field are accomplished alone. Life is truly a team sport. You may be the one responsible for snapping the ball, but you won't get into the end zone without other players, coaches, trainers, etc.

Champions appreciate others (especially the God who gave them their talents) and are able to leverage the total team's capacity to achieve both short and long term goals. On the other hand, those unable to work with the team typically find themselves on the bench as the first step in being off the team.

part 4 - Figure 4. Traits of a Winning Player
PLAYS

- Comes ready to play.

- Has a personal game plan.

- Has a solid set of basic principles.

- Has a solid skill base.

PLAYS WELL

- Plays with poise and enthusiasm.

- Creates and maintains focus and momentum.

- Can take a hit.

- Manages the clock.

- Continually Improves skills.

PLAYS WELL WITH OTHERS

- Engages coach and team.

- Embraces spiritual guidance.

- Takes ownership of the drive.

- Communicates above the roar of the crowd.

Time Out

OK, coach, here is where the challenges come for you. Take a few minutes to mentally compare the three aspects discussed above with the list of attributes of the players in the 21st century stadium. We discussed them earlier but for reference, I have listed them below. How do each of these attributes affect the individual's ability to play, play well and play well with others?

He or she is probably ...

- experiencing a more secularized education with multiple worldviews.

- experiencing information overload.

- more politically correct.

- taking on the appearance of being more environmentally conscious.

- searching for a heroes but finding few.

- fascinated with sports and entertainment.

Additionally, he or she may be ...

- experiencing shortfalls in life skills.

- dropping out of organized religion.

- experiencing a high level of anxiety.

- the product of a tough family life.

Obviously, each of the statements above reflects a generalization that may or may not reflect the attitude of the individuals who you mentor. But, they do serve as a checklist to help you fine-tune your approach to working with an individual. For example, someone experiencing a high level of anxiety may find it tough to play with poise and enthusiasm. Or, an individual from a tough family background may struggle to simply show up for the next event. You and I, the experienced ones, need to remain both observant and flexible to understand the needs of those we serve and adapt our own approach to help them succeed.

H3 - PLAYING WITH YOUR HEAD, HEART AND HANDS

The three P's work well in defining a successful player. If you would prefer another approach to ensuring you are playing your best game, let's chat about the H3 half of the "H3P3" player. H3 simply offers a bit of a twist to the old head, heart and hands storyline.

VENUE:
TUNNELS BEACH
KAUAI, HAWAII
OCTOBER 2003

On the morning of Oct. 31, 2003, the shark struck. Teenage surfer Bethany Hamilton was enjoying what she did best when a 14-foot tiger shark attacked in what could have easily been a fatal assault. Had two other surfers not come to her aid, she may have bled to death right there in the water. Through the grace of God and the fast action of a couple friends, Bethany survived, but lost an arm in the ordeal.

For most surfers, the loss of an arm would end their dream. Not for Bethany. "I don't need easy. I just need possible," she exclaimed. A year later, she proved that declaration to be true as she shocked the California crowds by winning a national amateur championship. Since then, she has racked up multiple victories in the super-talented pro circuit proving she has the heart to be a winner and do the impossible.

In the movie, Soul Surfer, which highlights her story, Bethany said, "I don't really want people looking to me for inspiration. I just want to be a sign along the way that points toward heaven."

Now that's what I call a great quarterback who knows what the game is about!

So, how did Bethany do it? In a sport that requires tremendous balance, Bethany dug deep into her soul finding the strength through her faith in God coupled with her conviction to achieve the seemingly impossible. It's hard for anyone to imagine what goes on in the mind of a champion, especially one who overcomes huge obstacles to get there. I will not even attempt to understand her psyche, but will offer an observation as one watching the action from "far down the beach." In making her comeback, I believe Bethany demonstrated the very qualities of an H3 player. She engaged her mental, spiritual and physical assets to realize her comeback. And the good news: you can also call on that same combination of resources to outfox the sharks in your life.

On Being H3 – Playing a three-dimensional game

How much dog do you have in the game? Or put another way, as two-time Heisman winner Archie Griffin said, "It's not the size of the dog in the fight, but the size of the fight in the dog."

Take a minute to think about any great player, or, maybe, your favorite, in any sport. Ask yourself, "What sets them apart?" Now, consider your answer in terms of "H3." Do they avoid mental errors? Do they know the rules and tactics of the game? Do they exhibit outstanding physical talent and physical toughness? Do they come to the game ready to play with passion and pump up the rest of the team? In other words, do they excel through, not just one asset, but a combo of head, heart and hands, and do so on a consistent basis? There are a lot of questions but one answer: Sure they do.

So often, we hear sports announcers proclaim "she really brings a passion to her game" or, conversely, "that his heart doesn't seem to be in the game today." Or affirm, "She has definitely gotten into her opponent's head in this match." Sports announcers love to fill air time debating the mind, the heart and the physical peculiarities of every player. For one, it makes the broadcast more entertaining. But, more importantly, it reflects reality.

Games are won by a combo of smarts, passion and physical prowess. But, what if I have all of the smarts and skills to play, but leave my heart in the locker room? More than likely, if your heart is in the locker room, your backside will be on the bench. Scripture emphasizes the importance of the heart, cautioning us in Proverbs 4:23, "Above all else, guard your heart, for it affects everything you do." As Keith Sholl, former pastor of the church I attend reminded us, "At the heart of every problem is a problem of the heart."

Championship play demands championship players. That axiom holds true both on and off the field. Take the passion out and mediocrity reigns. But what if my heart is engaged, but my brain rests quietly on the sidelines? That's not good. The old graveyards out west are packed with young gunslingers who shot from the hip without mentally sizing up their opponents. When God designed man in His image, part of that likeness related to the ability to think. That likeness was not an afterthought, nor do we have the right to ignore it to the point of mental atrophy. God made us complete in Him. As such, He expects us to adopt that fullness in how we play the game. His design may be illustrated as follows:

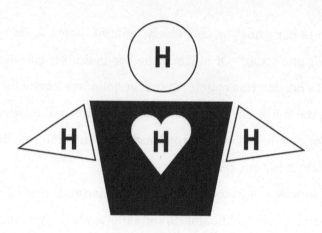

Only Head + Heart = No action

Only Head + Hands = No passion

Only Heart +Hands = No consistency

But H+H+H = Creativity, Flexibility, Success

Tme Out:

Spend a couple minutes thinking about the H3 idea, answering the following questions:

1. The last time I made a decision, did I bring all three of these qualities to the table?

2. What quality (intellect, emotions or physical capabilities) usually dominates my actions? Does it get you where you need to go?

Bethany understood that getting there may not be easy. As coach Bear Bryant once put it, "There's a lot of blood, sweat and guts between dreams and success." Depending on your pursuits, they may be easier or tougher than what Bethany faced. But, in the end, if you employ your brain, your heart and your hands, you will have a great shot at being a winner.

So there you have it. An H3P3 player--utilizing a combo of head, heart and hands to play, play well and play well with others! A simple approach to becoming a winner? Sure! But what thoughts might we pursue on the discipline required to get there? Check out the H3P3 Player Workout in the next chapter.

Game Winning Point: Synergy is a good thing. "True humility is not thinking less of yourself; it is thinking of yourself less." C. S. Lewis

Game Winning Verse: "Love the Lord your God with all your heart, all your soul, all your strength and all your mind." Luke 10:27.

PLAYBOOK TIPS

■ Talk to yourself. Remind yourself during a game to use all 3H's.

■ Know when to lead; when to follow. Do both appropriately.

Read On!

H3P3 WORKOUT
Taking your game to a new level

Strengthen your head, heart and hands. That is, strengthen your mind, your emotions and your physical condition. Check out the following workout cards for areas of focus.

Spend time in the weight room

Strengthen your mind, your soul and your body. Live a healthy lifestyle as it makes a huge difference in whatever you do. God created you in His image and consequently, we have an obligation to care for that creation as well as possible. Regularly schedule time to lift a few pounds; lift (and open) a Bible; plus pick up a new skill. As the end zone banner at Stanford says:

"YOU ARE GETTING BETTER OR YOU ARE GETTING WORSE. YOU NEVER STAY THE SAME!"

So growing or atrophy remains our only options. Choose wisely. A few related verses to consider:

"So, whether you eat or drink, or whatever you do, do all to the glory of God." **1 Corinthians 10:31**

"For I can do everything with the help of Christ who gives me the strength I need." **Philippians 4:13.**

Spend time in the "wait" room

Reflect and wait on God. His timing is not always our timing. Maturity and experience will bear out to the truth behind the need to be on His schedule. Make sure you go with the flow, but make sure the flow is God's flow, not yours. A point of caution: do not confuse waiting with procrastination. Waiting is holding your position until the right time to act; procrastination is standing idly by when the time for action has arrived and gone. Scripture to ponder:

"I waited patiently for the Lord to help me, and he turned to me and heard my cry." **Psalm 40:1.**

"Wait for the Lord; be strong, and let your heart take courage; wait for the Lord! **Psalm 27:14**

"Be still and know that I am God!" **Psalm 46:10.**

"He gives power to those who are tired and worn out; he offers strength to the weak. Even youths will become exhausted, and young men will give up. 31 But those who wait on the Lord will find new strength. They will fly high on wings like eagles. They will run and not grow weary. They will walk and not faint." **Isaiah 40: 29-31.**

Pump up the prayer

Pump up the iron? We all get that idea. But, pump up the prayer? What are we talking about here? Simple. If we adhere to Proverbs 3:5-6, the key verse ofWinning Choices, we need to keep the line open with our creator. Just as pumping the iron molds our bodies, pumping up the level of prayer brings us closer spiritually to the one who will lead us through life's many decisions. But, what does pumping it up entail? Some thoughts from Scripture:

"Don't worry about anything; instead, pray about everything." **Philippians 4:6.**

"Pray without ceasing." **1 Thessalonians 5:17.**

Does this mean we should don sackcloth and sit in ashes 24/7? Not a chance. Essentially, it means you never hang up on God. Instead, you are continually open to His influence and direction. Christ offered an example of this. He was a man of action who remained open to contact with His father. Often, he would steal away into a quiet place, spending time alone in prayer. Most of the time he was on the move, accomplishing His purpose on Earth. Many theologians believe that "pray without ceasing" truly teaches that we should lead our lives in a way that we are always open to the influence of God. Prayer is a two-way thing, so if we can't pray, then shut off the phone. Just like many do with their cell phones, we should continually stay tuned into God's communication.

Spend time in the playbook

Connect with God in the Bible to develop your mind. God has provided wisdom to guide our lives. As mentioned above, spend time daily listening to that wisdom by searching for a particular issue upon which you need guidance or simply enjoying the benefits and peace of generally reading through its pages.

Scripture says:

"All Scripture is inspired by God and is useful to teach us what is true and to make us realize what is wrong in our lives. It straightens us out and teaches us to do what is right. It is God's way of preparing us in every way, fully equipped for every good thing God wants us to do." **2 Timothy 3: 16-17.**

"For the word of God is full of living power. It is sharper than the sharpest knife, cutting deep into our innermost thoughts and desires. It exposes us for what we really are." **Hebrews 4:12.**

Hang out with the right people

Sit down and think about friends, coaches and teammates in your life. Decide that you will hang out with the right people; those who create a positive influence on your life. Avoid the bad seeds. Realize that God places wise people in our paths to help guide us.

"In the multitude of counselors there is safety." **Prov. 24:6b.**

"Plans fail for lack of counsel, but with many advisers they succeed." **Proverbs 15:22.**

"Two people can accomplish more than twice as much as one; they get a better return for their labor. If one person falls, the other can reach out and help. But people who are alone when they fall are in real trouble." **Ecclesiastes 4: 9-10.**

"For where two or three gather together because they are mine, * I am there among them." **Matthew 18:20.**

"Whoever walks with the wise will become wise; whoever walks with fools will suffer harm." **Proverbs 13:20.**

"... bad company corrupts good character." **1 Corinthians 15:33.**

Get a checkup!

Check out your skill set from an H3P3 perspective. God has a purpose for each of us and provides the skill set to accomplish it. So, if you are trying to determine God's will for you, look at your skills from a head, heart and hands perspective. That is, do you have the mental, physical and emotional talents to be successful in the endeavor that you believe is God's purpose for you? The skill set may not be a slam dunk (to switch sports analogies). Faith becomes part of the equation. Moses did not think he had the skills to lead the people out of Egypt. But, in faith, He followed God's will.

"There are different ways God works in our lives, but it is the same God who does the work through all of us." 1 **Corinthians 12:6.**

"God has given gifts to each of you from his great variety of spiritual gifts. Manage them well so that God's generosity can flow through you." **1 Peter 4:10.**

Read On!

QUICK HIT #5: RACHEL

Rachel's prayer:
"God take the broken pieces
of my life and make
something beautiful."

Earlier, we witnessed God's power in the life of surfer Bethany Hamilton. What, you may ask, does a surfing story have to do with me? I have never been on a surfboard nor have I even seen a shark beyond the local aquarium exhibit. I'm not a world class surfer; in fact, I'm not a world class anything. I'm just little ol' me working my way through the opportunities and challenges of life. So, let's leave the waves behind and bring the story a bit closer to home. Let's spend a moment in the life of another hero. Let's spend a moment in the life of Rachel.

Rachel's story

This is Rachel's story ... not one of an individual overcoming the ravages of poverty or a broken home. No, Rachel enjoyed the benefits of being raised by two solid Christian parents who would accompany her on her journey. Rachel's story is one of descending into the depths of personal pain and rising from those depths a changed, beautiful example of God's grace.

Raised in southeast Michigan, Rachel spent her childhood not on the beaches of the world, but in the typical activities of everyday America. At the young age of 12, with all of the exciting teen years lying just ahead, she was focused on many of the same things as most kids. But God had a different idea. He had a donkey for Rachel to find and a job for her to do! Similar to those disciples who were sent to get a donkey for Christ's triumphal entry to Jerusalem, Rachel was sent on a journey to grow God's kingdom.

Though not yet a teen, Rachel was diagnosed with CRPS, or complex regional pain syndrome, which is a chronic, severe pain condition that can incapacitate even the toughest person. Throughout this book, we have heard from football guys who would tell you that good players learn to keep pushing through a wall of pain. Rachel has never suited up for football, but the wall of pain she encountered would have ended the career of any one of these players. She personally compares the pain level to that of pouring gasoline on her skin and lighting it. Physicians typically rank the excruciating pain of CRPS at or near the top of any condition encountered by a human.

Heading down - Rising up

Pain can drive any one of us into areas we thought we would never go. In Rachel's case, the relentless torment drove her into the world of anorexia, spiritually doubting the God that she once trusted. At 15, she was told she would die if she did not seek help immediately. After five months of therapy in an Arizona clinic, Rachel conquered the eating disorder, but the unyielding pain was now leading to a growing sense of depression. But, God knew all about that and he was on the move.

At 16, Rachel entered the Nashville Mercy Ministries treatment center, telling God that "this is it. If you don't move, I'm done with life." Rachel believed she was ready to die -- life just seemed too hard. Eight months later, emerging as what she describes as a new person, Rachel's trust in God had returned. Throughout her stay, she said that God had shown her He was there in some very big ways.

Free of pain, Rachel was ready to head off to college. Unfortunately, her challenges were not done. Spraining her ankle the night before classes were to begin led to a return of CRPS, followed by two years on crutches and yet another problem, lymphoedema. The swollen leg subsequently became infected. Doctors told her that amputation was the only solution. But, this time, rather than doubting God, she approached Him with what I will term Rachel's prayer:

"God take the broken pieces of my life and make something beautiful."

Rachel describes the day she received a prosthetic leg and began to walk free of pain, as "one of the happiest days of my life." Since then, Rachel has participated in several races and has teamed up with Bethany Hamilton to learn to surf. She has finished her degree and, most importantly, has joined her heart with her boyfriend Mark in the bond of marriage! Yes, God did have a donkey for Rachel to go get! He has changed her life, providing a true channel of opportunity to grow His kingdom. Oh, by the way, Rachel and Mark ran down the aisle at the end of their wedding ceremony!

Rachel and Bethany share a truly common bond that should encourage each of us to face life in an extraordinary fashion. Both have endured extreme pain, yet, both have experienced the abiding love of God. Both bring to life a true faith that transcends their pain and suffering. Both have learned that God can be trusted. Though circumstances are, humanly overwhelming, His grace is truly much more awesome. Yes, Bethany and Rachel have both confirmed that our loving God can heal us in ways that honest doctors can only describe as true miracles.

Mom and Dad

Rachel's parents have spent challenging minutes, hours, days and months accompanying Rachel on her journey. So, I asked them, "What one piece of advice would you pass along to those helping others who face huge challenges?" Here's what they said:

Heather: Surround yourself with people who will support you. Don't go it alone! Take one day, one minute at a time, and trust that God really does have it under control. It won't always seem like it, but that is when you put your faith into action. Finally, allow yourself to grieve, feel sad, angry, etc. Those are all normal emotions, even for Christians. It doesn't mean you are lacking faith; it means you are human. "It is well with my soul, but not with my circumstances."

Kirk: Be honest. Be honest about your needs. Be honest about your limitations. Be honest with God...and remember He's God and you're not! Pride does tremendous damage, especially in the midst of life's storms. I often seize control when I should "let go and let God." I'm prone to not ask for help when others want to lend a hand. I can deny the depth of the pain rather than acknowledging reality. In addition, know it is in the midst of storms that you discover the difference between your true and fair-weather friends.

Great advice from great people. Take time to reread their comments, adding their practical counsel to your own personal toolkit.

Now, to wrap up our discussion, let's return to Rachel for a final comment that should bring a smile to our face and joy to our heart. In concluding a great video discussion of her journey, Rachel said, "One day, when I get to heaven and meet Jesus, I am going to thank God for being faithful and for catching me. Then, I am going to say, "Let's go have a race so we can run!"

Wow!

QUICK HIT POINT: So, where does that leave you and me? Or, as Rachel's father, pastor Kirk often says when concluding a sermon, "So what?" What can each of us take away from Rachel's story?" To answer that question let's return to Rachel for her wisdom:

"God can be trusted. Our God is a big God; Even though it's hard to trust when things are dark and seemingly hopeless, there's always hope. Nothing is impossible for him. Your story is not over yet. Turn to Him for strength. Through faith you will find hope."

Want to hear more from Rachel? Check out her blog:
https://myelephantsintheroom.wordpress.com/2014/12/07/why-i-am-grateful-for-my-amputation/

Read On!

THE POWER OF GOD
The Owner of All Things

"I am the Alpha and the Omega—the beginning and the end,"
says the Lord God. "I am the one who is, who always was, and
who is still to come, the Almighty One."

– Revelation 1:8

Psalm 24 begins with a powerful, foundational statement about God: "The earth is the Lord's, and everything in it, the world, and all who live in it." Winning Choices is not a text on theology. Volumes exist that appropriately address the magnificence and power of God so my comments will be very limited. As the owner of our franchise (and all else); however, perhaps it is appropriate to simply list a few of the limitless actions ascribed to God in the Bible. As Matthew 19:26 says, "With God, all things are possible." So, when it comes to helping each of us make better choices, no other owner comes close. He has assured us of His availability, 24/7. Plus, He can empathize with our own weaknesses because "He was tempted in all ways that we are, yet did not give in to those enticements." Hebrews 4:15.

Check out the following list of what God has done and will do as the owner of the universe. Every action can be supported by multiple verses although I have only provided one.

He has created all things ... speaking them into existence

"For when he spoke, the world began! It appeared at his command." **Psalm 33:9.**

He has conquered death

"For our perishable earthly bodies must be transformed into heavenly bodies that will never die. When this happens—when our perishable earthly bodies have been transformed into heavenly bodies that will never die—then at last the Scriptures

310

will come true: 'Death is swallowed up in victory. O death, where is your victory? O death, where is your sting?'" **1 Corinthians 15:53-55.**

He manages the day-to-day existence of His creation

"He (Christ) existed before everything else began, and he holds all creation together." **Colossians 1:17.**

He creates storms; He calms storms

"When he woke up, he rebuked the wind and said to the water, 'Quiet down!' Suddenly the wind stopped, and there was a great calm. And he asked them, 'Why are you so afraid? Do you still not have faith in me?'" **Mark 4: 39-40.**

He has provided a way to eternal salvation

"For if you confess with your mouth that Jesus is Lord and believe in your heart that God raised him from the dead, you will be saved." **Romans 10:9.**

He changes hearts

"And I will give you a new heart with new and right desires, and I will put a new spirit in you. I will take out your stony heart of sin and give you a new, obedient heart." **Ezekiel 36:26.**

He offers to direct lives

"Trust in the Lord with all your heart; do not depend on your own understanding. Seek his will in all you do, and he will direct your paths." **Proverbs 3:5-6.**

He judges evil

"I said in my heart, God will judge the righteous and the wicked, for there is a time for every matter and for every work." Ecclesiastes 3:17.

He will come again to set up His eternal kingdom

"Then the sign of the Son of Man will appear in heaven, and then all the tribes of the earth will mourn, and they will see the Son of Man coming in the clouds of heaven, with power and great glory." Matthew 24:30.

──────────── Read On! ────────────

THE POWER OF TRUST

Trust first in God and then those He brings into your life

Think about it, you and I place our trust in a wide-range of people and situations. From the day we first peered as newborns into our mother's eyes, each of us has developed varying degrees of trust with individuals, families, organizations and yes, even with things. A continued fulfillment of expectations fortifies our level of trust while disappointment weakens that same degree of confidence. Most of us understand the ebb and flow, accepting changes as part of the struggle of life itself.

The glue in our franchise

Hanging with our franchise analogy, perhaps it would be valid to think of trust as the glue that bonds various parts of the organization together. As such, the glue can adhere well or not. Many of us have enjoyed being part of a group in which team members displayed an open sense of trust. A lack of hidden agendas led to camaraderie and fulfillment. On the other hand, nearly everyone has also been part of an organization where the commodity of trust was in short supply. Lack of honesty, communication and/or commitment had, to some degree, become endemic to a breakdown in confidence among the team. Ask yourself, how well did the group perform? High turnover? Poor quality? Low morale? No doubt about it, a loss of trust leads to a basket full of problems. A football franchise, similar to any organization, is strong when an element of trust exists among all members including players, coaches and owners. A breakdown in trust typically leads to a collapse of performance by both individuals and the organization in its entirety. A winning season can suddenly collapse when the positive energy created by trust evaporates.

Thus, as we continue to compare our own world to that of a franchise, we are obligated to scrutinize the level of trust between ourselves as coaches or players and with the owner, in this case, God. Being fallen sinners, none of us are capable of absolute trust. However, our owner, the God of the Bible, exhibits trust as part of His very nature. Hence, by definition and in reality, for a perfect God, trust is absolute, unwavering, 100 percent dependable. Thus, when He instructs us to trust in Him, there is no implication His trust must be earned. It is simply there. One, who by nature cannot lie nor mislead, cannot, by that same nature, break any bond of trust.

Accordingly, as we search for guidance in calling the right plays in life, our attention should focus first on God and then on those whom He places in our lives. Priority 1 should be to seek His guidance in a decision, followed by asking Him to place the right people in our lives to make it happen. Unfortunately, in a world bent on self-sufficiency, placing God at the head of the line happens infrequently, even among those who should know better. Check out the following venue.

VENUE:
STATE OF ISRAEL
1970's

The words of Golda Meir, former prime minister of Israel: "Trust yourself. Create the kind of self that you will be happy to live with all of your life."

The words of God, creator of Israel (and all things including Golda):"Trust in the Lord with all of your heart and lean not on your own understanding; In all your ways, acknowledge Him and He will direct your paths." Proverbs 3: 5-6.

Poor Golda, she should have known better. Growing up in the Jewish faith, the words of Proverbs have undoubtedly echoed through her mind. But, hearing is one thing and believing it is totally different. Fortunately, you and I have the opportunity to do both.

As we dig into the discussion of decision-making and discover the basics of worldviews, these totally contradictory statements highlight a critical point. Trust either begins with God or trust begins with us. Golda starts with self. God starts with God. Each of us must decide who is right. Do we start with man's words or do we begin with God's words? And, does it make a difference? Hint: Yes, it does. It makes a huge difference.

The infamous T-formation

In the early days of football, the offense would often line up in what came to be known as a T-formation. Dating back to 1882, this offensive formation has been attributed to none other than Walter Camp, the father of American football. As the play unfolds, three running backs would line up in a row about five yards behind the quarterback and a running play would ensue. Spectators would witness the old three-yards-and-a-cloud-of-dust play over and over. In today's wild passing game, however, the T-formation has pretty much gone the route of leather helmets.

But, in your game, the T-formation applies today as much as it did in 1882. Your T-formation (aka trust-formation) either lines up with God or finds you standing alone in the backfield. Your choice will prove to be a key part in your playbook. Trusting in God leads to victory; trusting in yourself (without God) leads to disaster. Because trust is so fundamental, Proverbs 3:5-6 was selected to be theme verse of this book. Let me repeat it: "Trust in the Lord with all of your heart and lean not on your own understanding; In all your ways, acknowledge Him and He will direct your paths."

Scripture teaches that with God, trust is a little bit more "trustworthy." In fact, it's a lot more trustworthy. What God says He is going to do, He does. Both His nature as God and thousands of years of experience have proven that to be true.

So, what does this theme verse really declare? Why should our playbook include it on every page? Let's break the verse into four parts. Each is vital to the entire verse, plus, each component will fulfill a specific purpose as you learn to make winning decisions.

1. Trust in the Lord with all of your heart

What do these nine one-syllable words really say? Essentially, trust bonds us to someone in a way that we will rely on them or have confidence in them. When that someone is the Lord, the relationship becomes total. But, how much should we trust Him? What does it say? Sometimes or just a bit? No, it emphatically affirms, "With all of your heart!" It's not simply a mind thing. Trust in God goes deeper into your emotions and your soul finding its way to the surface as a deep conviction.

2. Lean not on your own understanding

Do these words imply that we lack a brain? Not at all. They confirm reality. God has given each of us intelligence, plus He often places others in our lives who build on that intelligence. When reality strikes, we all learn that we are human, capable of limited understanding. On the other hand, God's creation and His scriptures testify to His knowledge, allowing us to lean on the wall of His wisdom, a much more solid structure.

3. In all your ways, acknowledge Him

No mincing of words arises in this short phrase. The words "all,", "your" and "Him" are rather straightforward. "Acknowledge" may be a bit more open for discussion. Think of it as not only recognizing His total wisdom, but also as submitting to His authority in each of our lives. By acknowledging Him, we are handing over to Him the things we may typically wish to control. When done consistently, acknowledging becomes a very freeing exercise.

4. And He will direct your paths

What's the key word in this part of the verse? Try "will." Note that this verse does not say "may" or "might" or "should." Simply put, the verse shouts "WILL." I find that simplicity to be very comforting in the game of life. He knows us. He knows our strengths and our weaknesses and will utilize each of those attributes to fulfill His purpose.

Although beginning each day with trust sounds appealing, actually doing so may offer more of a challenge. Our propensity to call the shots often trumps our will to yield. Author, theologian and preacher Charles Swindoll offers his comments saying, "We must cease striving and trust God to provide what He thinks is best and in whatever time

He chooses to make it available. But this kind of trusting doesn't come naturally. It's a spiritual crisis of the will in which we must choose to exercise faith."

Trusting your team ...

Beyond trusting God, does trust play a role on a football team or any other endeavor in life? According to Fran Tarkenton, legendary Vikings quarterback, trust is a key ingredient to winning. In his blog, In the Huddle with Fran Tarkenton (Jan. 29, 2015), he offers the following comment: "... The foundation for all those great teams has to be trust. Trust and relationships, getting people with different backgrounds and different skill sets to trust one another and play as one. When everyone on a team is connected and trusting one another, then you can win. When you don't have those relationships, teams fall apart. Some people chase their own selfish objectives, and others find their skills and abilities wasted and ignored. To win, you have to get every man on the team contributing everything he can."

When God sends any of us onto the field, He willingly provides both a set of winning plays and a capable team. We are not alone out there. God places people in our lives who have the experience and knowledge to help us accomplish the purpose that He lays out for us. When you line up to take the snap, make sure you are in a T-formation, or better yet, a trust-formation.

Game Winning Point: Prioritize your trust, first in God and then in those he brings into your life.

Game Changing Verse: "Trust in the Lord with all of your heart and lean not on your own understanding; In all your ways, acknowledge Him and He will direct your paths." Proverbs 3: 5-6.

PLAYBOOK TIPS

- Reduce stress through trust; God takes on the load.
- Verbally acknowledge God in your daily life and see. It refreshes the lips.
- Memorize Proverbs 3:5-6 including it in your daily playbook.

Read On!

QUICK HIT #6:
THE JEFF KEMP JOURNEY

A game-changer faces
a game-changer

VENUE:
FRONT PORCH
JEFF KEMP HOME
1992

As a 10-year veteran NFL quarterback, Jeff Kemp understood the thrill of a game-changing play. Little did he realize the power of a game-changing play that lay ahead as he pondered life on his front porch, having just been cut by the Philadelphia Eagles. The Power of Three was just about to shape his life and send him down a new road of serving thousands of people like you and me. Let's check out his own words:

I got cut in 1992 after I'd had a really good season with the Eagles. I came home to Seattle. For four weeks, no team would pick me up. In the fourth week of the season, the Seahawks had a quarterback get hurt. We thought, "This is great." I called the coach of the Seahawks Tom Flores. I said, "Coach, I'm in town. I'm in shape. I'm ready. Please sign me." It was a voicemail and I hung up. Then, he called me back on my voicemail machine and said, "Hey, I heard you got cut. Sorry about that, but we're not going to sign you. We're going to sign someone else," that I'd never heard of—another blow to my ego, but this is God working.

When I got that call and heard that message, I just didn't have any of my great Christian maturity or faith left. The bottom dropped out. I went out to the front porch of my house. I was so broken and so mad and so frustrated that I wasn't going to get to play football that season; and my career was ending. "I can't believe it's this bad!" I was feeling yucky and rotten. I was mad at God. I wasn't going to pray and I told Him.

But I'm married. So, I'm not just myself. I'm a team. I'm sitting there in my pity party when my wife Stacy comes out. She is compassionate toward me. She goes, "Oh, Jeff, I can't imagine how much this hurts; but I've just got to remind you. We've been through some tough things, and God has always had a good purpose. He's always opening another door. He's always taught us something and had something good ahead of us." I looked at her, and I said, "I know that! I just can't believe that it's finishing like this. I just want to finish football with some dignity!"

Well, there are two sides to love, and Stacy's good at both sides. She started kicking in the tougher side of love, and she did it so delicately that it impacted me like a sledge hammer. She said, "You know, as I recall, Jesus led a perfect life. Then, when He left this world, He didn't receive any dignity. Maybe you need to let go of that desire." Here's what happened in that moment. My very worst moment of my life—granted, no one had died of cancer, I hadn't lost my wife, or a child, or something more precious to me— but losing my career hurt. I had the worst moment of my life converted to the greatest moment of my life in a matter of seconds.

Jeff went on to relay that he had grown up in a competitive family which often included a mix of a conditional performance and reward culture. There was enough of that mixed in me that I kind of viewed God as a formula thing: I please Him, He helps me. We work together,'" etc., etc. I didn't have a passionate love affair with Jesus. All of a sudden, I started to cry. I felt a love with Jesus—a love from Jesus, a love for Him. That was because I was in such a blitz—losing my security of my career—that which I had been treasuring. All of a sudden, it put my true treasure on Jesus. It was a blitz that opened my eyes to that."

Before the Mannings became popular as father-son NFL quarterback traditions, a pair of Kemps earned that honor. As the first ever father-son duo, Jeff Kemp and his father, Jack, became standout quarterbacks in the NFL. The son of a statesman, politician and family man, Jeff led what some writers may term, a storybook life. Following a great college experience at Dartmouth, Jeff went on to rack up wins for 10 years in the NFL. So, sitting on the porch, knowing his career was probably over, he reacted as most of us would. He was dejected.

But God had a different plan. God was on the move. He was about to send Jeff, like the disciple we discussed earlier, to find a donkey; a donkey to fulfill the purpose of the king of kings. God was molding a game-changer on the field to become a game-changer in marriages. From facing the blitz on Sundays, Jeff was being prepared to help families face their own blitz 24/7.

The Power of Three on the move

Earlier, we outlined what I call "the Power of Three" -- God, the coach and the quarterback -- relating how an all-powerful God often utilizes other humans to coach someone through the issues they face. Here we have a prime example of that powerful team in action. Jeff would rather refer to their marriage as a team. For now, let's just consider Stacy to be his coach; someone God would use to intervene in Jeff's life, establishing the perspective of reality and pumping him up for the game ahead. As Jeff points out, Stacy provided the sledgehammer to set the baseline of reality of the situation; then followed up with the reminder that God always had a good purpose for their life. She advised him to drop the dignity deal and get on with life. She grabbed him by the face mask to get his attention focused on the game.

God, the real game-changer, was about to alter Jeff's game in ways he could probably not imagine. Right there on his front porch, broken and facing a personal blitz, Jeff's eyes and heart were opened to the love of Christ. The veil of apprehension was lifted. The seeds of change were planted by the Lord and watered by Jeff's tears. While Jeff was able to impact a lot of people during his football career, his service since then has been an amazing game-changer in an area where game-changing needs to happen. In a day when the scoreboard reflects that it's 4th and long for the institution of marriage, Jeff has entered the game to change the score. Want to learn more about this dynamic guy's journey? Check out Jeff's recently released book, Facing the Blitz, to learn how you, too, can outplay the linebackers or challenges in your own life.

As with the other individuals we have discussed, Jeff followed God's request to "go get a donkey" that He will utilize to multiply His kingdom.

The Quick-Hit Point: When life seems to throw a game-ending play at you, pay attention, as God may be opening an unbelievable door for you to accomplish His purposes. This is summarized best by the prophet Jeremiah: "For I know the plans I have for you," declares the Lord, "plans to prosper you and not to harm you, plans to give you hope and a future." Jeremiah 29:11.

———— Read On! ————

Part 5
THE POWER
OF THE TWO MINUTE DRILL

Reality ... There is a right way to do

OK, now it's time to start moving the chains. We've chatted about the "right way to VIEW," pointing out that a solid worldview is the foundation to a truly successful decision. Now, let's take up the discussion of the "right way to DO." In other words, let's talk about getting the job done. We will, of course, turn to the world of football to learn a surefire approach to success.

Choose your idiom ... shoot from the hip; play fast and loose; act first, think later ... all reckless approaches to life. Most of us would refuse to admit that these idioms describe how we manage our calendar. If asked, most would probably insist we think first, take aim and play fast, but not loose. Well most of us are wrong.

Successful football teams; however, thrive on the ability to act fast and efficiently when time is short and the game is on the line. Utilizing a preplanned package of plays, they run a series of downs typically called a two-minute drill or a no-huddle offense. In doing so, they maximize their own talents, attack their opponent's weaknesses and minimize the time required to call the plays. Doing so requires extreme focus, urgency and energy. But in the end, their efforts often clinch the game's winning score.

Are you ready to become the coach of dynamic decision-makers? In the upcoming chapters, you will learn the seven key steps that championship football teams employ to be consistent winners. Their success can be your success. In a style similar to winning NFL teams, you and those you coach can also develop a "second nature" approach to implementation. If you do, you will be ready when game day arrives... You, too, will win.

And, lest you think we left God behind and are talking pure football, after you read this portion of the book, check out the parallels to a Biblical TMD in Figure TMD 3. I'm not saying the words "two-minute drill" can be found in the Bible nor that all football teams follow a scriptural route to success. Read the comparison. Then, call it as you see it. What we are talking about here has roots in ancient principles that have proven time and time again lead to success.

Before we get into the seven specific elements, let's wind the clock back in time to what many consider to be the best two-minute drill in NFL history. In that infamous 15-down, 98-yard drive, a bunch of plays came together as planned while others didn't work at all. The play-by-play summary serves as a lesson to all of us.

Part 5 breaks down like this:

The DRIVE

Two-Minute Drill – Part 1

Making the Decision

TMD One – Set meaningful decision goals

TMD Two – Identify players and matchups

TMD Three – Create extreme focus

TMD Four – Develop a winning game plan

Two-Minute Drill – Part 2

Managing the Decision

TMD Five – Execute: Snap the ball

TMD Six – Build momentum, move the chains, manage time and adapt

TMD Seven – Succeed, get in the red zone, score and win!

The Big D – Discernment

"The Drive" revisited

——————— Read On! ———————

THE DRIVE

"Gentleman, this is a football,"

– Vince Lombardi, as he focused his team

In football circles, it has become known simply as "The Drive." In the NFL record book, it shows up as the 1987 AFC Championship game between the Cleveland Browns and the Denver Broncos. On a cold, overcast, dreary day in Cleveland, Denver quarterback John Elway engineered a 98-yard fourth-quarter drive that helped put his Broncos in Super Bowl XXI. "The Drive" was the perfect illustration of an effective hurry-up offense or two-minute drill utilized when the team is down and its back is against the wall. "The Drive" also helped propel John Elway's name into the stratosphere with the legends of the NFL.

With his offense struggling for most of the game and his team down 20-13, Elway took control in what many describe as one of the greatest winning drives in the history of the NFL. The Browns had scored late in the game to go up by a touchdown. All of the momentum now favored Cleveland. The Broncos return team fumbled the ensuing kickoff, recovering the ball on their own 2-yard line. This set up the Denver offense to start play with terrible field position against a tough Browns defense. The turn of events suddenly allowed Cleveland fans to imagine their team playing in their very first Super Bowl. Unfortunately for them, John Elway and the Broncos saw it differently.

Getting the job done

As the clock wound down to 5:32 left to play on that frozen afternoon in Cleveland, the focus was all about getting the job done. No one cared about team ratings, future draft picks or post-game press conferences. Two teams of dirty, cold, tired men faced each other in an epic battle to determine who would advance toward the Super Bowl and who would hang up their pads until next season. In the remaining few minutes, all of their skills, training and attitude (plus perhaps a few lucky bounces) would decide the outcome. Every coach and player on the field understood the rules and principles of the game. Now, 'knowing' had to take a backseat to 'doing'.

The same situation faced by Denver and Cleveland emerges in your life each and every day. In pursuing choices, it is one thing to acknowledge and adhere to the right set of foundational principles. It is quite another to actually make it happen. In an earlier discussion, we learned the importance of a solid foundation or worldview. Now, we need to chat about a process or set of tools to actually convert an idea into a decision and manage it to a successful conclusion. The Broncos didn't march 98 yards and score against a skilled Browns defense by chance. For them, victory flowed from a sense of determination; a desire to get the job done. That same spirit of determination can also propel you to victory.

The two-minute drill

The heat of battle is no time to invent; it is a time to implement. Winning NFL teams already have plans in their playbook to handle a variety of situations as the clock approaches zero, playing conditions change and opportunities or challenges unfold.

In football circles, these plans are known as a two-minute drill or a no-huddle offense. Teams practice an array of two-minute drill plays throughout the season until they become second nature. When game day arrives, they are ready. Cincinnati Bengals head coach Marvin Lewis explains it this way: "On my team, we dedicate a key segment of our Thursday practices to the mechanics of two-minute drills that we hope we will not have to use against our next opponent. We take great care in preparing our team for the contingency and necessity of having to run a two-minute drill, if that is what it will take to win. Long hours of planning and practicing are devoted to this preparation, which is a real priority for my team."

As you will see, the steps and discipline of a two-minute drill (let's call it a TMD) can become a great template for you to use in both making and implementing any decision. Offering a disciplined checklist to ensure you don't miss anything along the way, the TMD approach utilizes the right people by employing their skills in a focused manner to get the job done. Little time is wasted as players and coaches alike pursue the ultimate goal. You will also find that these same principles apply, not only in a crisis mode, but in the normal course of planning and implementing any decision.

"The Drive"

Before we jump into the fray; however, let's do a quick exercise that will help you see the benefits of learning theses skills. Let's learn from the legend himself, John Elway, as he managed "The Drive" on that cold day in Cleveland. Figure TMD 1 describes the play-by-play rendition of the final minutes of the game. Take some time to read it and jot down your observations of what went right and wrong and how those situations may apply as we learn to get the job done. After you complete this mini exercise, you can read my observations at the end of this section. Huge point: Every play does not work as planned. But winners, despite adversity, know how to suck it up and keep the ball moving to achieve their goals.

In the end, the Denver Broncos won. Was their victory a result of being more prepared for the challenges of the last few minutes than the Browns? Sports enthusiasts can take sides, offering a ball bag full of reasons why their team either won or lost. Few will challenge the thought that being prepared will give any team an advantage in a close game.

As legendary Alabama football coach Bear Bryant put it, "In life, you'll have your back up against the wall many times, you might as well get used to it." He also taught us to prepare for these tough times explaining, "It's not the will to win, but the will to prepare to win that makes the difference." You, the coach, are the key to making that preparation a reality.

So coach, are you ready to get at it?

—————— Read On! ——————

Figure TMD 1 - The DRIVE
AFC Championship Game
January 1987

Clock at start of drive: 5:32   Clock at end of drive: 00:37

Play-by-Play

1. First down and 10, Denver 2-yard line. Sammy Winder 5-yard pass from Elway.

2. Second down and 5, Denver 7-yard line. Winder 3-yard run.

3. Third down and 2, Denver 10-yard line. Winder 2-yard run.

4. First down and 10, Denver 12-yard line. Winder 3-yard run.

5. Second down and 7, Denver 15-yard line. Elway 11-yard run.

6. First down and 10, Denver 26-yard line. Steve Sewell 22-yard pass from Elway.

7. First down and 10, Denver 48-yard line. Steve Watson 12-yard pass from Elway.

8. First down and 10, Cleveland 40-yard line (1:59 remaining). Incomplete pass by Elway

9. Second down and 10, Cleveland 40-yard line (1:52 remaining). Dave Puzzuoli sack of Elway 8-yard loss.

10. Third down and 18, Cleveland 48-yard line (1:47 remaining). Mark Jackson 20-yard pass from Elway.

11. First down and 10, Cleveland 28-yard line (1:19 remaining). Incomplete pass by Elway.

12. Second down and 10, Cleveland 28-yard line (1:10 remaining). Steve Sewell 14-yard pass from Elway.

13. First down and 10, Cleveland 14-yard line (:57 remaining). Incomplete pass by Elway.

14. Second down and 10, Cleveland 14-yard line (:42 remaining). John Elway 9-yard run (scramble).

15. Third down and 1, Cleveland 5-yard line (:39 remaining). Mark Jackson 5 yard pass from Elway - touchdown.

Your observations on what went right and what went wrong:

TWO-MINUTE DRILL PART 1
MAKING THE DECISION

"You were born to win, but to be a winner, you must plan to win, prepare to win, and expect to win."

– Zig Ziglar, American author and motivational speaker

As this chapter unfolds, we will discuss four steps that are critical to making a winning choice.

1. Set meaningful decision goals. If you don't know specifically what you are trying to accomplish, there is little chance of getting it done. In a football game, knowing where you are on the field and where you have to go is a bit easier than in the game of life.

2. Identify players and matchups. Getting the right players on the field and knowing the environment in which you will be playing is critical. This area is one that many people miss, often forming a team that is incapable of getting the job done. Skills, experience, knowledge, commitment and availability are all critical elements to examine when selecting the right players.

3. Create extreme focus. Focus, not obsession, ensures that that everyone knows their role and contributes in concert as a team. Lack of focus leads to fumbles, broken plays, excessive use of time and other not-so-good outcomes. Winning teams are focused teams. On the other hand, obsession leads to indecision. You need to strike the right balance.

4. Develop a winning game plan. If you don't plan to win, then plan to lose. A game plan adds structure to the decision, minimizing oversights and other "why didn't we think of that" outcomes. Having a Plan B (and maybe C, D and E) may also help get you into the end zone.

Think about these four areas for a moment before we delve into them a bit deeper. Sound simple? Seem obvious? Yes on both counts. Then again, think of a project or task you were part of at some point in your life. Do you recall other seemingly intelligent, highly skilled (and paid) team members making comments such as:

- We have no idea where we're trying to go.
- We definitely have the wrong people on this project.
- No one seems interested in getting the job done.
- We need to quit shooting from the hip.

Sure you do. We all do. Reality is not always pretty. More often than any of us wish to admit, in the rush to finish, we fail to plan. We fail to spend appropriate resources on these four critical elements.

Finally, before we expand on each element, let's tie these thoughts into our football comparison. If these four steps in the process were superfluous, NFL teams would not spend millions to hire scouts, coaches or other staff people to attend to them. They would simply hire players and tell them to get out there and play. Would that produce a winning season? Probably not. How about off the field? For you and those you mentor, the challenges you will encounter are much more difficult than those faced by teams in a typical Sunday football game. Life is much less defined than football. The game seems endless; the issues boundless. So, coach, you need to prep them. You need to arm them with these tools lest they fall prey to a stubborn defense.

TMD STEP 1
SET MEANINGFUL DECISION GOALS

Where are we at; where do we want to be?

"Face reality as it is, not as it was, or as you wish it to be."

– Jack Welch, former chairman and CEO of General Electric

VENUE:
SAINTS VS. LIONS
NOVEMBER 1970

The kick heard 'round the world: On a November Sunday in 1970, the New Orleans Saints and the Detroit Lions were locked in a low-scoring battle. As the game wound to a finish, Detroit kicked an 18-yard field goal to take a 17-16 lead with a mere 11 seconds remaining on the clock. New Orleans' hopes for a huge kickoff return failed and with 2 seconds remaining and the Saints found themselves on their own 37 yard line, 63 long yards away from victory. But on that day, Tom Dempsey trotted onto the field to attempt to pull off what most coaches, players and spectators would consider to be impossible … a 63-yard field goal. However, on that fall day, "impossible" was pushed out a bit further as Dempsey split the uprights to win the game. His record has been tied since then, but he will go into the record books a winner, having taken his game to a new level to achieve his goal.

Looking back to Tom Dempsey's winning kick, the decision to go for it seemed like the right thing to do. But had his kick fallen short, the sports writers would have been unanimously frothing at the mouth, criticizing the coach's bad call. That's life in professional sports. But consider what may have gone on in the decision to try the kick. First, the clock had only two ticks (or one play) remaining. Second, the Saints needed a score (but not a touchdown) to win. Third, the coach knew Dempsey had the capability to get it there. So, packaging all parameters into the decision, did the coach make a reasonable decision? Looks like he did (easy to say afterward). Had the ball been on their own 10-yard line instead of the 37, would that decision have made sense? Can anyone, including Tom Dempsey kick a 90-yard field goal? Would sending him out there to try be a case of not making a reasonable decision goal? Definitely (at least until some young stud actually does it and proves me wrong).

In our world, individuals and mentors should draw two points from this brief example. First, you must know the outcome (goal) you expect from this decision. In this case, a 3-point field goal would do the trick; no touchdown is necessary. Second, and very importantly, you must understand your field position as it relates to your goal. Given this field position coupled with the skills of your team, do you stand a chance of making it happen? In football, this is relatively apparent. Coaches know what is in the realm of possibility. In the game of life, knowing the real score and judging where you are at in relation to where you plan to be is not quite as easy. As a coach, you add immeasurable value in helping a player sort through the noise of the stadium to create reasonable, meaningful goals. You can both temper truly unreasonable efforts, or stretch the vision of an overly conservative player.

As Jack Welch, former CEO of General Electric, once put it, "Face reality as it is, not as it was or as you wish it to be." Reality is out there. Sometimes, it appears as an opportunity just waiting for us to grab. And, yes, sometimes it just plain sucks! Either way, we must learn to both define it and utilize its underlying truth as we make plans for the future. We must understand where we are on the field of life and utilize that starting point to define individual expectations. Every successful two-minute drill begins with the question of "where are we?" followed by "where do we need to go?" Only then can the team create a plan for getting there.

If Jack Welch doesn't fit your profile of an adviser, then let's turn to Scripture. You may have heard individuals claim power through the verse, "With God all things are possible." Matthew 19:26. True. But, the entire verse reads, "With man, this is impossible, but with God, all things are possible." The God of scripture is all powerful and can achieve through us, or without us, whatever He chooses. The verse does not mean we can selfishly pursue our own desires and expect to find success. The real power comes from being in His will. Then, and only then, can we "achieve the impossible."

Thoughts from God's playbook on knowing the real core and setting goals

Check out Genesis 41. In that passage, we discover a defining moment in the life of Joseph, one of the first quarterbacks recorded in Scripture. At the outset of this chapter, we find Joseph to be a simple servant of the captain of the guard. By the end of the chapter, he was second in command (the pharaoh was still the top dog) throughout all of Egypt. Why? First, despite being in a foreign, pagan land, Joseph demonstrated an allegiance to and trust in his creator, the God of Israel. Secondly, God blessed him with various skills. In addition, to being able to interpret pharaoh's dream (which landed him the job), Joseph also utilized his planning, goal setting and management skills to prepare the kingdom for a time of severe famine. Joseph told the pharaoh they were to face seven years of plenty followed by seven years of severe famine. He truly knew the score and was able to develop a plan, get the right players on the field to execute the proper plays. The result: when famine came, they were prepared for it. Joseph knew the importance of 1. A good plan and 2. An unwavering trust in God. What a great model for each of us to follow!!

Game Winning Point: Reality is real, not just someone's opinion!

Game Changing Verse: "Without a vision, the people will perish. " Proverbs 29:18

PLAYBOOK TIPS

■ Simplicity works. Only pursue enough details to get the job done.

■ Create specific outcomes.

■ Ensure all players understand the goal.

TMD STEP 2
IDENTIFY PLAYERS AND MATCHUPS

Who needs to be on the field to get us where we want to be?

Genesis 3: "Now the serpent was more crafty than any of the wild animals the LORD God had made. He said to the woman, "Did God really say, 'You must not eat from any tree in the garden'?" The woman said to the serpent, "We may eat fruit from the trees in the garden, but God did say, 'You must not eat fruit from the tree that is in the middle of the garden, and you must not touch it, or you will die.' "You will not surely die," the serpent said to the woman. "For God knows that when you eat of it your eyes will be opened, and you will be like God, knowing good and evil." When the woman saw that the fruit of the tree was good for food and pleasing to the eye, and also desirable for gaining wisdom, she took some and ate it. She also gave some to her husband, who was with her, and he ate it. Then the eyes of both of them were opened, and they realized they were naked; so they sewed fig leaves together and made coverings for themselves."

Talk about an all-around bad situation! The matchups were ugly. A strong defense (serpent) overpowered a weak offense (Adam and Eve) who left the critical member of the team (God) on the sidelines. This historical account from Genesis, familiar to kids everywhere, offers significant advice not only as a Sunday school lesson for children, but as a life lesson for adults. Definitely on the record books as the first major decision faced by humans, it cautions all descendants of this first couple to be sure to include God on your team. Obviously, Adam and Eve were no match for Satan. And the young couple's failure to round out their decision team led to disaster personally and vicariously for all generations.

On a bit of a less significant stage, let's return to the realm of football. Ask the offensive or defensive coordinator on any football team and they will tell you that one of their biggest fears is having the wrong players on the field to handle the situation. Failure to match up with the opponent's speed, size or skills can be downright embarrassing and costly. For each of us working through life's choices, this element of a TMD is huge! Often, it is the area woefully ignored by coaches and players alike, whether experienced professionals or rank amateurs. Getting the right players into a decision and ensuring that everyone understands the objectives and skills of the competition is vital. Egos get in the way at this point. Arrogance often replaces confidence as individuals skilled in one area fail to realize their deficiencies in other areas.

One size does not fit all

Does the following bumper sticker ring a bell? "If you are not part of the solution, you are part of the problem." Though a bit overused, the catchy phrase contains a lot of truth. Getting the wrong people, too many or, as in most cases, the same people on the field for every play often leads to a pitiful outcome. Your buddies may be your buddies, but having them as your only source of help in cases where they lack experience can prove devastating. Leroy Hoard, a former running back for the Cleveland

Browns, reportedly once told one of his coaches, "Coach, if you need one yard, I'll get you three. If you need five yards, I'll get you three." Consistent as he may be, by his own admission, Hoard would not always get the job done. The takeaway: Be selective in who is on the field at any point in time. God has given each of us various skills and winning depends on involving the right people at the right time.

Who was that masked man?

Before the NFL's Dallas Cowboys existed, the TV cowboys sought to maintain law and order in their fictional land. Much of the early days of television was devoted to the shoot 'em up tales of cowboy villains and heroes. None was more famous than the Lone Ranger. The sole survivor of an attack on a band of Texas Rangers, the Lone Ranger was nursed back to health by Tonto, his Indian cohort. Then, hidden behind a lame mask, he single-handedly conquered injustice throughout the west.

Sometimes we tend to make choices as Lone Rangers by riding into battle alone. Unfortunately, that approach tends to breed failure. Good decisions on major issues, more often than not, require advice, counsel, technical help, support and other activities that you alone cannot provide. Ask any world-class quarterback. Despite their egos, they will admit they can't win alone. Former NFL quarterback Jeff Kemp acknowledged, "A quarterback can't complete a pass without a lot of help from his teammates. He can't even start the play until the ball is snapped to him." Face it, the right players MUST be on the field to orchestrate a winning drive. The rest of the team truly IS important. The same holds true for making winning choices in the game of life. You HAVE to get the right players on the field. You CANNOT go it alone.

Listen up – or don't

Listening to the right people is important. Also, not listening to the wrong people is as equally important. A classmate who tries to steer you into a certain school because they have great parties or have a winning record in sports may sound cool but, in the end, may not be the right ticket. In a digital world overflowing with every type of resource imaginable, our access to good information seems unlimited. Unfortunately, the same holds true for useless trivia or blatantly destructive information. Discernment becomes a game-winning competency. Being able to consistently grab a hold of helpful ideas while discarding the debris spells the difference between a winning season and one we would hope to forget. Discernment only comes from experience, thus, the need for a coach to be advising, mentoring and leading.

Remember the Power of Three

On a final note, including God on your team is a must! Having dropped the ball several times in my own life, I can attest that the word "perfect" is not found in my personal performance review. Similarly, I would speculate that the people you will encounter in your stadium, or on your team, suffer from similar dilemmas. None of us are perfect; we all tend to fumble more than we should. Adam and Eve's gaffe in the garden should teach us one thing: Never, never, never exclude God from a decision. It didn't work for them; hasn't worked for me; won't work for you.

A popular bumper sticker from the past proclaimed, "God is my co-pilot." It sounds divinely righteous, but perhaps you should consider changing seats. I may be crazy, but God should be the captain of the plane while you and I are the co-pilots. Try it. Let Him call the plays.

Thoughts from God's Playbook on having the right players on the field

In Ecclesiastes 4:9-12, Solomon says, "Two people can accomplish more than twice as much as one; they get a better return for their labor. If one person falls, the other can reach out and help. But people who are alone when they fall are in real trouble. And on a cold night, two under the same blanket can gain warmth from each other. But how can one be warm alone? A person standing alone can be attacked and defeated, but two can stand back-to-back and conquer. Three are even better, for a triple-braided cord is not easily broken."

The point: Being a Lone Ranger didn't work back then and it won't work now!

Game Winning Point: Know yourself, know your team, know your opponent.

Game Changing Verse: "Two people can accomplish more than twice as much as one." Eccl 4:9

PLAYBOOK TIPS

- ALWAYS include God on your team.
- Avoid having the same ol' buddies on the team simply because they are buddies.
- Go for experience and knowledge where needed.
- Know the strengths and weaknesses of other players and build them into your plan.
- Listen and observe people for clues that support a winning plan.

How do we get everyone's attention on the game?

"Be still enough to listen; be wise enough to act."

– Pastor Larry Carey

VENUE:
RAIDERS VS. CHARGERS
San Diego Stadium
September, 1978

Known in football lore as the Holy Roller, the 1978 Oakland Raiders knocked off the San Diego Chargers with a play that helped rewrite the rulebook. Down by six points with 10 seconds remaining, Raiders quarterback Ken Stabler appeared to be trapped and going down at the Chargers 15-yard line. To keep the play and game alive, Stabler fumbled the ball forward hoping that other Raiders players in the area would be able to move it forward. In the scramble, the ball was batted about until finally, Oakland player Dave Casper pounced on it in the end zone, tying the game. The extra point kick sealed the deal, adding a "W" to the season record. At the time, intentionally fumbling forward was considered to be a forward (incomplete) pass, but the refs ruled the fumble was not intentional.

When asked, Raiders coach John Madden, never at a loss for words, commented, "It was one of those things that maybe you can't do that, but the rules say you can do that, so you can do that, and if you don't want to do that, then go change the rule." And that they did! Following the 1978 season, the NFL rewrote the rule providing that in the last two minutes of the game, only the player who fumbled the ball could recover and advance it.

Is the Oakland Raiders story an example of extreme focus? Sounds like it to me. With the game on the line and the defense on his back, Stabler was able to remain mentally and physically focused on the goal, sorting rapidly through options and taking the only action that he thought would work. Fortunately it did, or else we might be using this as an example of a lack of focus.

Check out any successful football team in the midst of a two-minute drill. You will witness the importance of being truly focused. Every player knows their role, knows where to be at any point in the play and maintains an awareness of their surroundings. Without focus, the plays break down, progress stops and the team chalks up a loss. Now, flip the remote back to the channel playing in your life. The same deal holds true. Stay focused or lose! Concentrate on what counts; don't waste resources or time doing things that don't. In business, there is no value in working hard if it doesn't increase productivity in some way, shape or form. That effort needs to be applied to the right task or it's meaningless. The same philosophy can be used in life. Focus on what you need to do to meet your goals and put forth your best effort to be ready to perform at the appropriate time.

Pump it up

Focus is more than assuming an eastern yoga pretzel pose while staring at a spot on the wall. Focus involves the concentration of all pertinent resources on the task at hand. Teams focus, armies focus, businesses focus and, yes, each of us also needs to focus on the task at hand. In addition to your own eyes, ears and mind, focus may include other people, information, money, etc. Essentially, getting focused is a priority thing. If the decision you face is more important than anything else you have going on, then you may wish to forget about downloading 50 songs onto your smartphone, choosing instead to pump up your level of attention to the things that will get the job done.

Chill out

In Psalm 46 we are advised "to be quiet and know that I am God." As you work through a decision, perhaps you will need to temporarily turn off the electronic gear, get out of the blogosphere and find a quiet place to seek the Lord's input. Even Christ got away from the crowds and His disciples periodically to be alone in prayer. In Psalm 145:18, David tells us, "The Lord is close to all who call on Him." So, don't be shy about taking time to be alone to seek His advice. Great people throughout the ages have done so. Do you have a place you can be quiet and not distracted by all of the stuff that gets in the way? Where is it? Go there and as a member of the Power of Three team and get alone with your creator.

Take charge

Hall of Famer and former Dallas Cowboys quarterback Troy Aikman said, "The toughest part of playing quarterback is the amount of information that must be processed in mere seconds while all hell is breaking loose around him." In a situation where the game rides on every play, being focused is critical. For you, and those you influence, that same level of attention is important. Watch any successful NFL quarterback as they step to the line for a play. The quarterback is continually communicating with the team, observing defensive formations and calling audible changes when appropriate. Good quarterbacks recognize that while each member of the team is highly skilled, it's up to him to make sure the team stays focused and moves in unison. Remember when you step onto the field in a leadership role, you are responsible for ensuring that everyone focuses on the task at hand. If you plan to win, you cannot sit back and simply hope that everyone is on target. Leadership rides on your shoulders. You must be out in front, mentally and physically keeping a pulse on the overall process of getting things done.

Also, be aware that there will be a lot of noise in your stadium. Be ready for distractions, cheers and perhaps even belligerent boos. Noise comes with the territory in a culture of confusion. Big time quarterbacks can handle it; so must you. Learn to focus mentally, spiritually and physically and you will successfully play above the roar of the crowd.

Thoughts from God's playbook on focus

Teaching the Twelve Apostles to focus on eternal priorities consumed a major portion of time for the Lord. Despite being in the presence of the one who created the universe and performed countless miracles before their eyes, his inner group repeatedly exhibited a tendency to major on minors. Consumed by a concern for daily necessities, they spent more time worrying about their own pecking order in the kingdom than building it. So, if you find yourself struggling to grab the attention of players, consider the frustration that must have enveloped the dynamics of that group 2,000 years ago. Christ continued to focus the team through lessons, stories and examples. Feel free to emulate His style and despite frustration, develop your trust in God's ultimate plan.

Game Winning Point: Focus clarifies, obsession kills!

Obsession is the overkill side of focus. One can obsess over a decision, never moving to the next step of preparing a game plan or executing it. The road of life is littered with alternatives and choices that never came to be. You don't want to be in that position. Part of maintaining a healthy focus is confidence. If you are confident in your ability to collect information and process what it means, you're less likely to obsess or agonize about a decision. You have confidence in yourself to make the right call. And if it turns out you made the wrong decision, you have the strength to accept that you made a mistake and the confidence that you'll learn and fare better the next time.

Game Changing Verse: "Wherever your treasure is, there also will be your heart and thoughts." Luke 12:34.

PLAYBOOK TIPS

- Decide up front that you will focus on the game (Not after you choke the first three plays).
- Be vigilant to a loss of focus of other team members. Refocus!
- Do NOT obsess!

What do we need to do to make it happen?

"Have a plan. Follow the plan, and you'll be surprised how successful you can be. Most people don't have a plan. That's why it's is easy to beat most folks."

-Paul "Bear" Bryant, legendary Alabama head coach

VENUE:
WHEREVER YOU READ
AUTHOR PAT KIRWAN

Below is an excerpt from Pat Kirwan's book, "Take Your Eye Off the Ball: How to Watch Football by Knowing Where to Look" (Triumph Books/NFL Publishing).

A coach's master playbook can contain about 1,000 plays -- pretty much anything he would ever consider calling in a game. Every bomb, blitz and blocking scheme is in there somewhere, along with every gadget play and goal-line scenario. And every call has its roots somewhere in that all-encompassing bible, which every coach is forever adding to and carrying with him from job to job.

The best coaches pare down their game plans more than most fans realize, but not at the risk of making themselves predictable. There is great potential for coaches to become overwhelmed by too much information -- the classic case of paralysis by analysis. If he's not careful, a coach will wind up preparing a little for everything he could possibly face rather than learning his opponent's true tendencies and preparing to take away the things his foe does best. For the most part, if a coach hasn't seen an opponent do something in its last four games, he's not going to practice against it.

I'm not suggesting a game plan should be simple. It needs to be smart, and it needs to generate matchup advantages against a particular opponent. That is the name of the game in the NFL -- matchups.

It's important for a coach to pinpoint the plays he's most likely to use so that he doesn't waste valuable practice time working on something that won't pay off in the upcoming game (plus, players absolutely hate practicing things that they never use). Come game day, it's not what the coach knows that matters, it's what the players know. Or as Marty Schottenheimer used to say, "When you're in trouble, think players, not plays."

Wow. This excerpt reveals a lot of good advice for each of us as we seek ways to be a catalyst in the lives of others. While NFL coaches garner huge paychecks to come up with hundreds of plays, you, perhaps as a volunteer, can still follow their lead. Remember, your primary job assignment is to provide clarity in a culture of confusion.

What makes up a good game plan?

Goal-based: As my friend and co-author Tim Stansfield is fond of saying, "If it doesn't get the job done, it's not worth doing." It's as simple as that. What you are doing here is not an academic exercise. It's all about getting to where you need to be, regardless of the challenges. Keep the goal in mind.

Simple: Speaking of simple, this is huge when working with players who are new to the game. Just as a football coach pares down a daunting playbook into a reasonable game plan, you need to employ "simple" as you work with others to create a plan that works. But, and this is a big but, while simple is good, oversimplifying may breed disaster. For example, if the decision relates to finding a college that meets the needs of a young person, you should spend a bit of time outlining those needs. Are there financial limitations? Are their grades good enough? Is the college's reputation OK? Will the curriculum work? Simply concluding that "if it was good enough for your brother, it's good enough for you," is not an example of simplification rather an illustration of abdication. Perhaps the rule should be that your game plan should not be any more complicated than necessary to get the job done. But don't think that simple is a stroll down easy street. As Apple founder Steve Jobs put it, "Simple can be harder than complex: You have to work hard to get your thinking clean; to make it simple. But it's worth it in the end because once you get there, you can move mountains."

Clear: "Specific" might be a better word to use here. Any plan, especially one that involves individuals lacking experience, needs to assign specific tasks and timing for all players. False starts in a culture of confusion often result from an "I didn't know I was supposed to do that!" situation.

Flexible: Oh by the way, you better think about a plan B. Whether in sports, career, marriage or any of the other fine activities of life, the original plan seldom makes it through untouched. The outcome may be the same, but how you get there may be significantly different. Learn the skills of flexibility and you will be far ahead of the rest of the crowd. Need a few practical thoughts? Reread Janna Bowman's Plan B comments in the Angel Tree Section.

Thoughts from God's playbook on having a game plan

Approaching 9 feet tall, the Philistine giant Goliath cast a long, scary shadow, terrifying anyone in his path. Anyone, that is, except David, the shepherd boy. David was set on taking the big guy down and he had a plan. As a shepherd alone on the hillside, he had already faced and conquered giants in the form of wolves and other wild animals. His skills were honed while protecting his flock. He was ready for Goliath. He had a game plan, plus the faith and the tools to pull it off. And, as they say, the rest is history.

As a final point in developing a game plan, remember to embrace God. Through prayer, we should align our game plan, or will, with God's game plan, not the other way around. God's game plan is perfect ours, not so much.

Game Winning Point: Plan to win; or plan to fail.

Game Changing Verse: "Wise people plan before they act." Proverbs 13:16.

—————————— Read On! ——————————

TWO MINUTE DRILL PART 2
MANAGING THE DECISION

"Plans are only good intentions unless they immediately degenerate into hard work."

- Peter Drucker, author and educator

Every successful effort begins with an idea coupled with a plan. But every successful effort is, in the end, truly successful only when fueled by disciplined execution coupled with enduring momentum. Earlier we discussed preparation. Now, we will chat about the steps essential to getting the ball into the end zone and successfully achieving your goal.

Speaking at a seminar in Toledo, Ohio, author and management guru John Maxwell resolutely stated that much has been written about decision making, but woefully little has been articulated about decision management. He was affirming that the world is inundated with ideas on making plans, but no one seems too interested in the process of making them reality. The second phase of the two-minute drill addresses the areas of shortfall John Maxwell has described: getting the job done.

Many head coaching careers have come crashing to the ground due to this same dilemma. Creating a game plan is one thing. Making it happen is another. Same goes for life. Deciding you want to study biochemical engineering at Johns Hopkins University in Maryland is one thing; actually getting accepted, enrolling and attending class is quite another.

Throughout the next few pages we'll chat about the second half of a two-minute drill, the three critical elements of converting good ideas into reality and making dreams come true.

5. Execute. If you don't snap the ball, you can never win the game. This may seem obvious, but hordes of people create elaborate plans for their life, but never take step one toward making them a reality.

6. Build momentum: Move the chains, manage time and adapt. Momentum takes that initial spark of energy and converts it into the inertia required to keep things moving in the right direction at the right speed. In the book The Time Trap: The Classic Book on Time Management, authors Alec Mackenzie and Pat Nickerson point out, "A goal without a deadline is a dream." How true this is.

7. Get into the red zone, score and win. How many times have you witnessed a game in which a team can move the ball up and down the field but could never get it across the goal? Playing well is a fine attribute. Finishing well demands you take it up a notch.

TMD STEP 5
SNAP THE BALL

How do we launch this effort?

"Do or do not, there is no try."

- Yoda from Star Wars

VENUE:
MEADOWLANDS STADIUM
EAST RUTHERFORD, N.J.
NOVEMBER 1978

As one of the most respected and productive running backs of all time, Larry Czonka epitomized the role of tough guy with Pro Bowl honors, Super Bowl wins and, in 1987, induction into the Pro Football Hall of Fame. Czonka spent most of his career grinding out yards for the Miami Dolphins, but for two seasons, he wore a New York Giants jersey. On a November day in 1978, he was part of a play that, unfortunately for New York, became known as the Miracle at the Meadowlands. Leading the Philadelphia Eagles 17-12, New York, with only 31 seconds on the clock, needed to simply take a knee, run out the clock and head for the locker room victorious. Instead, offensive coordinator Bob Gibson called "65 Power-Up," a play in which Czonka would take a handoff and carry it up the middle. Following what appeared to be an early snap, Giants quarterback Joe Pisarcik attempted to hand off the ball to Czonka. The handoff was botched, striking the fullback on his hip and bouncing free. Eagles cornerback Herman Edwards grabbed it on the first bounce, returning the ball 26 yards for the

373

winning touchdown. That wasn't an "All-Pro" execution day for Czonka. On the other hand, the following morning, an execution did take place. Offensive coordinator Bob Gibson was fired, never to coach again.

A quick aside: During the early years of the Tampa Bay Buccaneers, the team struggled to win even a game, finishing its first season 0-14. Following one particular game during those early struggles, legendary coach John McKay was asked what he thought of his team's execution. In response, he quipped, "I'm all for it."

Execution is thrilling. Bad execution is disastrous. Ask the 1978 New York Giants team.

In the first four steps of the two-minute drill, we spent time planning, getting the team together, getting focused and developing a plan to win. All of those activities are hugely important. But each essentially happens in a safe environment.

Now things are going to change. The shelter of the locker room, the safety of the sidelines or the calm in the huddle are history. Now, the 300 pound smelly linemen are poised, ready to fly across the scrimmage line and put your team into a world of serious hurt. This is the spot on the field where your skills, your commitment and your faith converge. This is the starting point where ideas become reality; where dreams become authentic. The opportunity is great. But your team does need to do one thing. Snap the ball!

A clean or successful snap to start a play in football offers up a comprehensive lesson plan for life. Think about what happens. First, the right players are on the field equipped properly to do the job. Each knows the plan of action and their role in it. They know where to be on the field and remain poised in place until the quarterback starts the play. Then, they move in unison to make it happen, knowing full well that they may have to alter their course to achieve the best results. And, finally, only the whistle stops them from playing. No one moves early. No one moves late. No one, except the quarterback, changes the play. That's a pretty good way to get any project started. It sounds like it makes sense for you and your quarterback to do the same thing. But, what's the big deal? We all know we need to snap the ball to get the play moving. We see it happen time and time again in every game we watch. Maybe in football that is obvious. But in real life, not so much.

The numbers tell a different story. Based on some figures, it is estimated that as many as 95 percent of the population is prone to procrastination. Among them, perhaps 20 percent are chronic procrastinators. Sounds incredible. But haven't we all been there before? We get an idea; we think about how to pull it off; we talk with our buddies about it; and then ... nothing happens! Why? What happened or, better yet, what didn't happen? Is it really procrastination? Or perhaps it is a lack of time or resources. Maybe it's the fear of exposure or the fear of failure. Our reasons are countless. The result is the same. Nothing good begins when nothing begins. Proverbs 26:13 tells us that the lazy person is full of excuses. I have mine. What are yours?

An unknown author once said, "The sooner I fall behind, the more time I have to catch up." It's natural. We all tend to push decisions to the back burner for a whole host of reasons. When the game is on the line (aka a major decision) that behavior is unacceptable. That's why the discipline of a two-minute drill combined with a strong support team and faith in God are important. You CAN make it happen ... on time! Coach, please stress to your quarterbacks they truly must be the leaders on the field. In the end, getting the job done depends on them. The good news is they CAN do it! With a good game plan, and the right people on the team, each of them should be quite confident to step up to the line, call the play and get the ball moving down the field to victory.

Thoughts from God's playbook on execution

Procrastination is not a modern phenomenon. In the Old Testament book of Joshua Chapter 18, Joshua, the man chosen to lead Israel after Moses, asks the leaders of several of the tribes why they are sitting down on the job of taking the land that God had earlier promised to them. As their leader, he took control, sending map makers to layout the land in preparation for dividing it up among the tribes. On a final note, be sure to emphasize that execution is not simply activity. In the Miracle at the Meadowlands, the Giants displayed a lot of activity. Everyone was in motion, doing something; but, unfortunately for them, most of them were doing the wrong thing. Successful execution includes performing the right set of tasks, at the right time and in unison with the rest of the squad. In this final play of the game, the Giants failed on all counts. That does not have to be the story in the games you coach.

Game Winning Point: You can't score a touchdown until you snap the ball. Execute!!

Game Changing Verse: "Look carefully then how you walk, not as unwise, but as wise, making the best use of the time." Ephesians 5:15.

PLAYBOOK TIPS

- Ensure the quarterback takes responsibility to call the signals.
- Make sure that all players understand their roles.

How do we keep the ball moving?

"We can't run. We can't pass. We can't stop the run. We can't stop the pass. We can't kick. Other than that, we're just not a very good football team right now."

- Bruce Coslet, former NFL player and coach

VENUE: SAN FRANCISCO STADIUM
SAN FRANCISCO
OCT. 24, 1964

Momentum counts! ... Oops!

Former NFL Pro Bowl defensive end Jim Marshall provides a great example of personal momentum. As a member of the famous "Purple People Eaters," along with Alan Page, Gary Larsen and Carl Eller, Marshall is credited with 127 sacks and 30 fumble recoveries. He played in four Super Bowls, plus held the record for consecutive starts (270 games) until longtime Green Bay Packers quarterback Brett Favre surpassed him in 2010 with 297 starts. Quite the career momentum.

But on Oct. 25, 1964, in a game against the San Francisco 49ers, momentum took an ugly turn. FYI: When scientists discuss momentum, they incorporate two parameters: velocity and direction. Sports announcers, on the other hand, employ a much more liberal definition, using the word to describe the conduct of play of the team that is presently taking the other team to the cleaners.

One could validly say that stopping the momentum of the other team fits in the job description of the defense. Creating turnovers fits the bill. In that game for the record books, Marshall recovered a 49ers fumble and ran 66 yards into the end zone, throwing the ball out of bounds in celebration. In terms of the two parameters of momentum, he nailed the velocity part of the definition as he rumbled down the field, but as far as the direction, well, what could one say. Unfortunately, he ran the wrong way. The result was a two point safety for San Francisco. Undeterred, later in that same game, Marshall sacked the 49ers quarterback, forcing a fumble. Teammate Carl Eller scooped up the ball, returning it to the right end zone for the winning score.

For decades to follow, sportswriters would tag the wrong-way play as one of the most embarrassing events in professional sports.

"Momentum." Sportscasters and physicists love the word. Those who pack the airwaves with descriptive adjectives employ it incessantly to describe the flow of the game, filling airtime with endless dialogue praising the team currently dominating play. But there is more to the idea of momentum than simply a trash talk tool for broadcasters. Momentum in the world of football (and in your world) is critical to long-term success. Usually, two-minute drills are not one-play events. Statistics (football feasts on them) consistently prove that the majority of football scoring drives typically entail more than 10 snaps. How about with you and the people you coach? Same deal? Of course. Accomplishments of any magnitude in life normally require more than a single step. Very few things neatly fit into a solitary action. You will need to help people learn how to move the chains by keeping the momentum in their favor.

Be aggressive!

Great achievements entail risks. Whether in a marriage, a career, in college or some other endeavor, not all things are certain. As baseball great Yogi Berra once said, "It's tough to make predictions, especially about the future." Act decisively. Don't be afraid to take those risks, just be aware of them and manage yourself accordingly.

Avoid stupid!

How often have we seen what appeared to be a well-managed, winning drive late in the game turn into a disaster because of one critical error? On and off the field, this often happens when the team falls behind their plan, forcing them to scramble in an effort to make up for earlier shortfalls. For example, when penalties put a team into a "4th and 25" situation, they may panic and try some weird play that has little chance of succeeding. And, often, they succeed at not succeeding, sending them into the locker room with a loss.

Manage time!

As the leader, it's up to you to know the sequence of the plays or steps to achieve your goal. Also, you are responsible for managing the clock. In football, this involves the use of plays that consume little time, plus getting out of bounds to stop the clock. In your world, clock management entails keeping on the timeline that you have created in your game plan. Speaking of time, you also need to know when to call a timeout. If things don't seem right, they probably aren't. You may need to pause and regroup with your team to keep the chains moving.

Tim Grunhard, center for the San Francisco 49ers, earned his living standing in front of Joe Montana. Grunhard once explained that Montana's superiority came not only from his physical skills, but from his ability to think three or four plays ahead during a two-minute drill. Joe was able to keep the chains moving, always having a Plan B in his head. Take note and think like Joe!

Thoughts from God's playbook on momentum

In fulfilling His purpose, God always has and always will provide the fuel and strength necessary to keep the chains moving. In Job 17:9, Scripture reinforces this truth stating, "The righteous keep moving forward, and those with clean hands become stronger and stronger." If we are in His will, His strength will replace our weakness; His wisdom, our folly. In his letter to the Philippians verse 3:14, the apostle Paul provides insight saying, "but one thing I do, forgetting those things which are behind and reaching forward to those things which are ahead, I press toward the goal ..." Avoiding the temptation to dwell on the past, he realized the importance of momentum in achieving the goals that Christ had laid before him.

As one of the best defensive ends of all time, Jim Marshall exhibited his prowess throughout a 19-year career in the NFL. In a punishing sport such as football, staying on top of your game requires momentum and that inner desire to move forward. Many will remember him for that one mistake. But obviously, as a great player, Marshall was able to put that embarrassing event aside and continue to take his game to a new level. You will face challenges and like everyone else, occasionally head in the wrong direction in whatever you do. But you, too, can recover and rebuild the momentum in your life. That choice lies deep within you.

Game Winning Point: Take time to manage time.

Game Changing Verse: "There is a time for everything, a season for every activity under heaven." Eccl 3:1.

PLAYBOOK TIPS

- Know your field position and be aware of the clock.
- If necessary, modify your plan, not your goal.
- Avoid useless activity.

TMD STEP 7
SCORE AND WIN!

How do we complete the effort and ensure victory?

"When you win, nothing hurts."

-Joe Namath, former NFL quarterback

Dash Right 93 Berlin
VENUE:
UNIVERSITY OF KENTUCKY
KENTUCKY VS. LOUISIANA STATE UNIVERSITY
NOV. 9, 2002

As the Kentucky Wildcats took the field that day, they were considered a huge underdog to the reigning SEC champion LSU Tigers. But, ahead by as many as 13 points, Kentucky's day looked promising to fans. With 15 seconds left on the clock and the game now tied, Kentucky opted to kick a 29-yard field goal. The kick cleared the uprights giving them a 3-point lead with only 11 seconds remaining. But as Kentucky was about to find out, 11 seconds is a long time.

A long kickoff pinned the Tigers on their own 9 yard line. One short pass play later, they were stopped on their own 26, with 2 seconds now on the clock. The final play: Dash Right 93 Berlin was called. Quarterback Marcus Randall was considered to be a fine player, but lacked the arm to throw 70-plus yards into the end zone. Confident (or should we say overly confident) Kentucky players doused head coach Guy Morriss with Gatorade ahead of the final snap. As the play unfolded, Randall heaved the ball as far as he could, but it completed its arc 25 yards short of the goal. Fans stormed the field, climbing the goal posts to celebrate the upset.

But wait a minute. Somewhere between the 30 and 25 yard lines, a Kentucky player deflected the pass. His effort proved fatal as the ball bounced off his hands and into the arms of LSU's Devery Henderson. Henderson, avoiding a shoestring tackle, sprinted across the goal for the winning score.

Amazingly, confused fans continued to mob the field celebrating what they would soon find to be an incredible turn of events. Dubbed the Bluegrass Miracle, the play would go into history books as an example of simply not putting the victory to bed. Even LSU head coach Nick Saban, exhibited a bit of empathy for the Wildcats during the post-game press conference. Celebrating, but not gloating, Saban said, "I don't know what to say; I feel bad for Kentucky's players. But, this is a big moment for us and I'm happy as heck for our team." Coach Saban chose the right time to celebrate … after the win!

One universal principle in both football and life: No one scores a touchdown without getting the ball into the end zone. Superhuman effort, fancy plays, teamwork and other clichés that fill the sports pages are truly meaningless without that one simple reality. You must finish the drive and get the ball across the goal line. You must implement your decision and drive it to a conclusion. Not doing so on the field or in your world results, not necessarily in failure, but in a lack of getting the job done.

Your game can reach new heights by paying attention to three critical points as you close in on your goal.

1. Play gets tougher in the red zone.

For readers not familiar with the term, the "red zone" is the area of the field between your opponent's 20 yard line and the goal. The entire shape of the field changes as 22 players bunch into a smaller area. Passing speed, accuracy and simple brute force become the name of the game. Both teams know that every inch counts. In your game, deadlines may grow shorter and the number of activities that must be coordinated and happen concurrently may expand. Having helped plan my daughters' weddings, I can attest to that. Fortunately, for me, my wife took on the brunt of the workload as the day and hour approached.

2. Make sure you actually won.

Dash 93 Right Berlin (aka The Bluegrass Miracle) was the final play in one of the most exciting finishes in college football. University of Kentucky players and fans alike have undoubtedly relived the final seconds countless times, attempting to alter the outcome. These wild, final few ticks on the clock can teach us all a lesson about finishing the game before celebrating the victory. As Yogi Berra said, "It ain't over till it's over."

Were the UK fans and even the team a bit premature in their celebration? Obviously so. In your world, it may be a bit tougher to know when you have won the game. Here's a thought: Make sure you define winning when you set up your game plan. Doing so will help you determine if you actually crossed the goal line. For example, if your goal is to get a job with the local hospital, make sure you actually HAVE the job before you stop pushing forward. Enjoying a successful interview is rewarding, but until you accept an offer and show up for work, you don't really have the job.

3. Celebrate, don't gloat.

Celebration of a victory is a good thing. Make sure you (and those who helped you) whoop it up after a successful effort. After all, you and your team have been busting your butts to get the job done. Be careful about overdoing it. Coach Tom Osborne may have been at the bottom end of the celebration spectrum. He said, "I celebrate a victory when I start walking off the field. By the time I get to the locker room, I'm done." You may wish to go a bit further than Coach Osborne. Suggestion: Don't gloat! There is a difference between celebrating and rubbing it in the face of others not so fortunate. For starters, gloating is not a sign of maturity. Plus, from a practical standpoint, there is a good possibility that you may be on the field again competing with the same people. No need to provide them with news clippings for the locker room.

Thoughts from God's playbook on accomplishment

In today's culture of confusion, true accomplishment often finds detractors, claiming that achievement proceeds from greed or other evil desires of the heart. What does God say? Right out of the blocks, in the first chapter of Genesis, God describes His own accomplishments of creation as being good. In fact, he uses that adjective eight times to stress the beauty of His work during that first week of time

Later, in the book of Ecclesiastes, God establishes a practical rule for all of us, teaching that "Two people can accomplish more than twice as much as one; they get a better return for their labor." Winning can be found throughout God's playbook. Those who seek His will, find a way to win.

Coming back to Earth for a final comment, coach Vince Lombardi laid out the challenge saying, "The price of success is hard work, dedication to the job at hand, and the determination that whether we win or lose, we have applied the best of ourselves to the task at hand." Great advice, coach!

Game Winning Point: When calling signals, look in every direction, especially UP!

Game Changing Verse: "Commit your work to the Lord and you will succeed." Proverbs 16:3.

PLAYBOOK TIPS

- Avoid losing energy or focus as the goal gets closer.
- Make sure you won before you celebrate.
- Do NOT gloat. It could come back to haunt you!

Read On!

THE BIG D - DISCERNMENT

"Put on all of God's armor so that you will be able to stand firm against all strategies and tricks of the Devil."

-Ephesians 6:11

While under house arrest in Rome, the apostle Paul wrote to those Christians living in Ephesus advising them to field a strong defense against the powers of Satan. In verses 10-17 of that letter, he essentially coached us on how to suit up for the game.

"Be strong in the Lord and in his mighty power. Put on all of God's armor so that you will be able to stand firm against all strategies of the devil. For we are not fighting against flesh-and-blood enemies, but against evil rulers and authorities of the unseen world, against mighty powers in this dark world, and against evil spirits in the heavenly places. Therefore, put on every piece of God's armor so you will be able to resist the enemy in the time of evil. Then after the battle you will still be standing firm. Stand your ground, putting on the belt of truth and the body armor of God's righteousness. For shoes, put on the peace that comes from the Good News so that you will be fully prepared. In addition to all of these, hold up the shield of faith to stop the fiery arrows of the devil. Put on salvation as your helmet, and take the sword of the Spirit, which is the word of God." Ephesians 6: 10-17.

Former Miami Dolphins quarterback Dan Marino once said, "There is no defense against a perfect pass. I can throw the perfect pass." He was quite the humble man wasn't he? Despite his multitude of passing records, Dan was intercepted 252 times throughout his 16-year NFL career. He, like all other quarterbacks, found out that defensive squads are made up of a lot of tough and talented dudes. Legends are built around them. The Steel Curtain, the Fearsome Foursome, the Doomsday Defense, the Purple People Eaters, the Monsters of the Midway and the Legion of Boom all bring to mind renowned nicknames for stalwart defenses that wreaked havoc on the offense.

Throughout the book, we have been focusing on the offensive side of the ball as we learned key elements of a two-minute drill. We can't leave the topic without chatting briefly about the value of a good defense. Think about it. Which cliché should we believe: "Offense wins games; Defense wins championships" or "The best defense is a good offense"? Sports pundits have debated the topic far beyond the realm of necessity. One thing has rung true throughout the past 50 years. Teams lacking a strong defensive squad seldom take home a Super Bowl ring.

In our real world, a strong defense is also a must if we hope to play a good game. The apostle Paul summed up the situation in the scripture highlighted above. The evil one definitely has you, me and everyone who tries to walk a life of faith in his sights. In sports, trash talk is employed to get into the heads of the opposition, forcing them to lose focus and make mistakes. Guess what? Satan also employs trash talk to get into our heads in an attempt to get us off target. Think back to our discussion about the encounter of Eve with Satan. Early in the game, employing that first bit of trash talk, Satan challenged the authenticity of what God had told her, filling her mind with doubt. And what followed that initial Garden of Eden trash talk? Adam and Eve fumbled the ball big time. It happened to them; it can happen to you.

The Big D ... discernment

In football, defensive formations change depending on the situation and the strengths of both teams. Configurations like the 4-3, the nickel, and the zone blitz ring familiar to players and fans alike. In our game, an appropriate name for a winning defensive formation is the Discernment Defense (aka The Big D). Defined as "seeing things from

God's perspective and acting in accordance with His will," discernment endows each of us with a game-changing skill.

Discernment allows us to sort through the myriad of options and the trash talk in a culture of confusion, choosing the appropriate action. Discernment permits us to respond instead of react. It wraps our emotions with controls, avoiding the penalty flag during a heated game.

The Big D is more than knowledge. It encompasses the fear and knowledge of the Lord, wisdom, understanding, good judgment, discipline and obedience. Discernment originates in the heart, but employs our mind. It helps us recognize God's priorities for us as we manage decisions. Sounds rather tough, doesn't it? Like many other aspects of life, our ability to sift through the situations we face will improve with practice or deteriorate with neglect.

Great NFL linebackers aren't great simply because they are big. Speed, endurance, plus the ability to read the offense and anticipate plays, are key to getting the job done. While many of these traits appear to be innate qualities of the individual athlete, coaching plays a huge role in learning and development. In our world, inexperienced players need the ongoing involvement of a mentor and coach to help separate the chaff from the wheat. Once again, coach, we find that you can play an instrumental role in the life of another.

The Big D from God's perspective

Scripture tells us that we play in a rugged league. In 1 Peter 5:8, we are cautioned to "Stay alert! Watch out for your great enemy, the devil. He prowls around like a roaring lion, looking for someone to devour."

In other words, learn to observe and discern everything around you. Lions don't give their prey a lot of time to react. Roaring is followed very quickly by chewing.

Need more advice from Scripture on the importance of discernment? Check out these verses noting that the word wisdom may be used interchangeably with discernment:

"Getting wisdom is the most important thing you can do. And whatever you do, get good judgment." Proverbs 4:7.

"Solid food is for those who are mature, who have trained themselves to recognize the difference between right and wrong and then do what is right." Hebrews 5:14.

"If you need wisdom - if you want to know what God wants you to do- ask Him and He will gladly tell you. He will not resent your asking." James 1:5.

"Intelligent people are always open to new ideas. In fact, they look for them." Proverbs 18:15.

A few practical tips

From a practical standpoint, how can we improve our defensive game in the midst of a culture of confusion? Here are a few suggestions. Read them and then try adding others to customize the list to your stadium.

- **Call a timeout.** Sometimes you need to slow down, pray and think about the next steps before the next play begins.
- **Be aware of your environment.** If things around you don't seem right, they probably aren't.
- **Listen to that "voice within."** God designed each of us with a conscience for a reason.

- **Listen to multiple, trustworthy advisers.** No one person knows everything about everything.

- **Be aware of God's voice.** He may speak to you through Scripture, prayer or nature.

- **Double (or triple check) info found on internet.** A lot of good and bad stuff floats around in cyberspace. Research several sources when facing critical choices.

- **Get your act together early.** Avoid starting the day in chaos. It will typically go downhill quickly.

- **Remember who owns the team.** God is there 24/7 to help you. Always has been; always will be.

So, there you have it. Utilize your offensive skills to move the ball, but master appropriate defensive formations to ensure victory.

Game Winning Point: Keep your eye on the ball and your heart on God!

Game Changing Verse: "Fear of the Lord is the beginning of wisdom." Proverbs 9:10.

PLAYBOOK TIPS

- Anticipate the next play, every play.
- Conserve your energy, it may be a long game!
- Learn to work as a defensive team!

————— Read On! —————

"THE DRIVE" REVISITED

Seven TMD elements:
Born in the locker room; honed
on the practice field; executed
on game day!

In summary, to get from point A to point B, from where you are to where you want to be, you need to become adept at the following:

Making the Decision

Set meaningful decision goals.
Identify players and matchups.
Create extreme focus.
Develop a winning game plan.

Managing the Decision

Execute.
Move the chains, manage time and adapt to change.
Get into the red zone, score and win.

If you follow this approach, will you win every time? No. Will you win more often than if you don't adhere to these key elements? Most definitely.

So, as a tune up to imbed these ideas, let's revisit "The Drive." Spend a few minutes reading through the play-by-play again. Try to identify areas where the Broncos exhibited strengths and areas in which they were perhaps not as prepared as they should have been. Some have said that when John Elway would take the field for a final drive, fear could be seen in the eyes of the defense. They knew he was capable of winning any game time after time. Plus, they knew that he and the team had prepared for this moment.

Part 5 - Figure 1 lists each of the 15 plays of the drive. My observations and comments by Elway following the game are also listed. What do you think? What would you, as coach, tell your quarterback before play one, after play nine and after play 15?

"The Drive" consumed approximately five minutes of clock time. The drives you face may last a lifetime. How you plan and execute will make a huge difference. In fact, there IS a RIGHT way to do!

Also, as I noted earlier, the steps of a TMD have a valid comparison in Scripture. Check out the parallels in Figure 2.

Part 5 - Figure 1. The DRIVE
AFC Championship Game
January 1987

Clock at start of drive: 5:32   Clock at end of drive: 00:37

Play-by-Play

1. First down and 10, Denver 2-yard line. Sammy Winder 5-yard pass from Elway.

2. Second down and 5, Denver 7-yard line. Winder 3-yard run.

3. Third down and 2, Denver 10-yard line. Winder 2-yard run.

4. First down and 10, Denver 12-yard line. Winder 3-yard run.

5. Second down and 7, Denver 15-yard line. Elway 11-yard run.

6. First down and 10, Denver 26-yard line. Steve Sewell 22-yard pass from Elway.

7. First down and 10, Denver 48-yard line. Steve Watson 12-yard pass from Elway.

8. First down and 10, Cleveland 40-yard line (1:59 remaining). Incomplete pass by Elway

9. Second down and 10, Cleveland 40-yard line (1:52 remaining). Dave Puzzuoli sack of Elway 8-yard loss.

10. Third down and 18, Cleveland 48-yard line (1:47 remaining). Mark Jackson 20-yard pass from Elway.

11. First down and 10, Cleveland 28-yard line (1:19 remaining). Incomplete pass by Elway.

12. Second down and 10, Cleveland 28-yard line (1:10 remaining). Steve Sewell 14-yard pass from Elway.

13. First down and 10, Cleveland 14-yard line (:57 remaining). Incomplete pass by Elway.

14. Second down and 10, Cleveland 14-yard line (:42 remaining). John Elway 9-yard run (scramble).

15. Third down and 1, Cleveland 5-yard line (:39 remaining). Mark Jackson 5 yard pass from Elway - touchdown.

My observations

- You often start out "in a hole"

- Winning is usually not a one-step event

- Some of your actions may fail, but you need to persevere

- Knowing what to do helps

- Having a skilled team helps – you can't do it alone

- Winning is a disciplined process

- You can move fast if you have the skills and discipline

- Practice helps

- You must learn how to mange your time

- Individual successes build confidence

John Elway's You Tube Comments

- The initial fumble (Starting point) was a bad break

- What we needed was total concentration

- I got as far as I could on each play

- Time was a factor

- Each time we moved the ball we became more confident

- We took the crowd out of the game

Part 5 - Figure 2. The Two-Minute Drill & Scripture

From Football	From Scripture
Make the Decision	
1 Set meaningful decision goals	Where there is no vision, the people perish. - Proverbs (29:18) I (Paul) run straight to the goal with purpose in every step. 1 Cor 9;26
2 Identify players & match ups	God has given each of us the ability to do certain things well. Romans 12:6 We work together as partners who belong to God. 1 Cor 3:9 Two people can accomplish more than twice as much as one. Eccl 4:9
3 Create extreme focus	Let your eyes look directly forward, and your gaze be straight before you. Proverbs 4:25 Set your minds on things that are above, not on things that are on earth. Col 3:2
4 Develop a winning game plan	Wise people think before they act; fools don't and even brag about it! Proverbs 13:16 The plans of the diligent lead surely to abundance, but everyone who is hasty comes only to poverty. Proverbs 21:5

Part 5 - Figure 2. The Two-Minute Drill & Scripture

From Football

Manage the Decision

From Scripture

From Football	From Scripture
5 Execute and manage time	The point is this: whoever sows sparingly will also reap sparingly, and whoever sows bountifully will also reap bountifully. 2 Cor 9:6 Look carefully then how you walk, not as unwise but as wise, making the best use of the time... Ephesians 5:15
6 Move the chains & adapt to change	Walk in wisdom toward outsiders, making the best use of the time. Col 4:5 Zeal without knowledge is not good; a person who moves too quicklymay go the wrong way. Proverbs 19:2
7 Get in the red zone, score and WIN	The righteous will move onward and forward, and those with pure hearts will become stronger and stronger. Job 17:9 Commit your work to the Lord and you will succeed. Proverbs 16:3 Two people can accomplish more than twice as much as one. Eccl 4:9

Read On!

Part 6
POST GAME

A time for thanks and reflection

The game is in the record books. Now what do we do? Celebrate a victory? Mourn a loss? Yes! But as any coach who sports a winning record will tell you, the game lives on. As legendary NFL coach Tom Landry put it, "When you want to win a game, you have to teach. When you lose a game, you have to learn." Hence, activity does not stop with the final tick of the clock. In this closing section, we will learn how to keep your game at the winning level.

Scripture teaches us that win or lose, we should be thankful for all that we do in God's will and should periodically stop to reflect on our lives. Football takes the reflection idea to a more in-depth level, filming every second of the game, then poring over those films to digest the good, bad and ugly. But undoubtedly, the most important point of reflection is where our life stands in relation to Christ.

In four brief chapters, we will examine the post-game activities, plus chat about how to become a Hall of Famer from God's standpoint:

- **Thanksgiving** - Take a knee
- **Reflection** - Check out the game films
- **Game Day Advice** - For football and life
- **Salvation** - On becoming a hall of famer

Read On!

THANKSGIVING
TAKE A KNEE

The proper response
in triumph or defeat

"And you will always give thanks for everything to God the Father in the name of our Lord Jesus Christ."

- Ephesians 5:20

In preparing this manuscript, I had the honor to chat with Dave Bratton, former pro staff liaison for Athletes in Action and chaplain for the New York Giants. He relayed the following account of the creation of the prayer circles that currently follow most NFL games.

VENUE:
CANDLESTICK PARK
SAN FRANCISCO
MONDAY NIGHT FOOTBALL
DEC. 3, 1990

The world of football was looking forward to this Monday night matchup of the New York Giants and the San Francisco 49ers, both sporting 10-1 records for the season. A few weeks prior to the game, Pat Ritchie, chaplain for the 49ers, called Dave Bratton, his peer in New York, suggesting they use this much-anticipated venue to spotlight the strong Christian presence throughout the league. Soliciting thoughts from players on the Giants team, Bratton came up with an idea from tight end Howard Cross. Throughout his college days at Alabama, Cross had participated in a pre-game joint prayer with the opposing team. He suggested adopting that ritual as a means of honoring God. Bratton jumped on the thought suggesting to implement the prayer activity as a post-game event. Dave told me that head coach Bill Parcells would have killed him if he suggested anything that would interfere with pre-game focus.

Pat Ritchie agreed to have players from both teams meet on the 40-yard line following the final tick on the clock. The December 3 game itself was a hard-fought contest with San Francisco coming out on top 7-3. As the game ended, Bratton and Ritchie both observed a large gathering midfield. Elation was followed quickly by dejection as they realized a fight had broken out. Dave relayed that the facts were a bit murky, but he believes the brawl started when 49ers cornerback Ronnie Lott threw a punch at the Giants quarterback Phil Simms.

Much less noticeable was a smaller group of players forming up on the 40-yard line. It was then the post-game prayer circle was born. Players were jointly taking a knee, not to end a play, but to give thanks to their creator. Throughout the course of the season, certain members of the press accused the players of taking advantage of the audience to sell their religious beliefs.

The NFL jumped into the fray declaring they would enforce the anti-fraternization rule requiring players to be off the field within two minutes of the game's end. Several players, facing significant fines, agreed to defy the clause to honor their God in prayer. In the end, the NFL never enforced the rule. The ritual quickly spread throughout the league, into the college scene and eventually, to a multitude of high schools throughout the land.

The first point: God has a way of leveraging what we believe to be relatively insignificant deeds. As we have discussed, no deed is insignificant if God wants it to be done to share His glory and expand His kingdom. Using our metaphor, both chaplains had a donkey to get for use by their Savior. They obeyed His request; He accomplished His goal.

This story, however, illustrates another point. We should be thankful to God at all times. When two groups of players meet after each game, one group has won and the other has lost. One met their goal; the other fell short. But, if we are following God's will for our life, Scripture teaches us to be thankful regardless of the outcome. In the New Testament book of 1 Thessalonians verse 5:18 we find the apostle Paul saying, "No matter what happens, always be thankful, for this is God's will for you who belong to Christ Jesus." Not always simple to do, nor easy to understand, but thankfulness should be our way of life.

Almost every Christian can relate a story of how a seeming disaster or failure morphed into a victory for the Lord. If you want to read some good football stuff, learning how failure can lead to triumph, check out NFL coach Les Steckel's book, One Yard Short: Turning Your Defeats Into Victories. The storyline focuses on Super Bowl XXXIV. On the final play of that game, the Tennessee Titans, who had been rolling toward the end zone, were stopped just one yard short of scoring the tying touchdown. Coach Steckel illustrates how that loss actually led to spiritual victories in his life and in those he touches on a daily basis. He went on to become the CEO of the Fellowship of Christian Athletes, playing a key role in thousands of young people as they develop spiritually.

Curious about the details, I asked Dave Bratton about the mechanics and content of a typical post-game prayer huddle. As expected, he responded that there is no cut-and-dry approach. In most cases, he said the home team selects a leader who will start the brief session with a prayer. Then, participation becomes freewheeling input from any of the players. Most of the prayers center on thanking God for safety throughout the game, plus healing for any player injured during the contest. Dave also indicated that often the group would offer thanks for the opportunity to play at the professional level, allowing them to pray for and be witnesses to those in the stands or on TV.

If Scripture teaches us to be thankful and if extra-large humans (win or lose) can take a knee bowing their heads under the scrutiny of thousands of fans, then who are we to wimp out. Give thanks! It's a great habit for developing a great life.

Game Winning Point: Give thanks and trust God to use our victories and defeats for His glory.

Game Changing Verse: "Give thanks to the Lord and proclaim his greatness. Let the whole world know what he has done." 1 Chronicles 16:8.

PLAYBOOK TIPS

- Ask those who participated in your activity to join you in prayer.
- Go to prayer shortly after the end of your journey; procrastinating never works.
- Ask God to help you treat success and failure with the same level of gratitude (tough assignment).

Read On!

REFLECTION - CHECK OUT THE GAME FILMS

What did we learn from this initiative?

"When you want to win a game, you have to teach. When you lose a game, you have to learn."

- Tom Landry, head coach Dallas Cowboys

Excerpt from U.S. Army guide to after-action reviews

Modern combat is complex and demanding. To fight and win, we must train our soldiers during peacetime to successfully execute their wartime missions. We must use every training opportunity to improve soldier, leader and unit task performance. To improve their individual and collective-task performances to meet or exceed the Army standard, soldiers and leaders must know and understand what happened or did not happen during every training event.

After-action reviews (AARs) help provide soldiers and units feedback on mission and task performances in training and in combat. After-action reviews identify how to correct deficiencies, sustain strengths and focus on performance of specific mission essential tasks list (METL) training objectives.

Football teams do it. Combat units do it. Businesses do it. Even God did it. And so should you. Reflect on what has just transpired. The outcome of your decision may be what you want it to be, but, regardless of the result, you should spend appropriate time not dwelling or obsessing, but learning and hopefully celebrating.

On the Eighth Day

So, what did God do on the eighth day? Scripture tells us that God created all things in six days and rested on the seventh (providing a guideline for a week). But, what did He do on the following Monday? Look at game films about creation. Plan His next initiative? Get ready for the fall? Have a Monday staff meeting?

Are these absurd questions? Probably so for God because He is God. He is unbounded by time or circumstance. Actually, God reviewed His game films at the end of each of the six days of creation, announcing that what He had done was "good." But for us mere mortal creatures, what do we do when the job is done? Do we reflect briefly on the victory or learn from the loss in preparation for the next game? Or do we simply wipe the whole matter from our memory? Let's chat briefly about the idea of checking out the game films.

Wusses need not apply! It takes a tough player to knock heads on the football field. It takes an even tougher individual to sit through the game films, seeing how they contributed to the prior game's plays. Mental toughness is often more rare than physical prowess. Guess what? The same holds true in your world. Looking back at what you did well and what could have been done differently demands discipline and a mental toughness.

A few key points may help you reflect:

1. Involve the Team

Personal reflection adds value. Playwright James Levin offered the following advice: "Follow effective action with quiet reflection. From the quiet reflection will come even more effective action." But most athletes review game films as a team and, yes, Scripture supports that approach, too. The feedback of those who lived through each play with you can make it a learning (or a laughing) experience. Scripture advises us to engage others in our post-game analysis. Psalm 37:30 declares, "The godly offer good counsel; they know what is right from wrong." And we find that "Intelligent people are open to new ideas. In fact, they look for them." Proverbs 18:15. Great advice!

And finally, do not feel obligated to make the post-game discussion an overly formal event. Chatting over a pizza should do the trick.

2. Check out the good, the bad and the ugly

Talking up the great successes that happened on the way to victory makes for a good post-game event.. But, what if things didn't go well? In fact, what if it was an outright disaster? Man up (or woman up) and face reality. As the former CEO of General Electric Jack Welch advised, "Face reality as it is, not as it was or as you want it to be."

One reality that all humans, even multi-million dollar athletes face: No one wins every game. That's not how life works. Losing does not make you a loser. As golf champion Greg Norman said after a tough loss, "I am a winner, I just didn't win today." Think about and store that comment on the back burner of your brain. Coaches, be sure to share Norman's advice with your players on a regular basis. The thought may come in handy as you work your way through those times when, not only didn't you win, but 14th place would have been nice.

3. Keep doing, stop doing, start doing

Want to play better next game? Try this little technique that can be a big help. As you chat about what's going on, take a few notes. Specifically, jot down your points in three categories: 1. Keep doing; 2. Start doing; and 3. Stop doing. This simple approach forces you to recall what worked (keep doing); what you should have done, but didn't (start doing); and what you did, but should have left out of the game (stop doing). Keep it simple. But keep it! This exercise is not meant to be a thesis, but if done properly, can be a short summary to help you lay out your next game plan.

Just remember, smart people watch game films. Give it a try and prepare to win again!

Thoughts from God's playbook on reflection

Psalm 46:10 advises we should take time to be still and ponder God. Doing so pays off handsomely in many ways. Periodically pushing away from the crowded plate of daily demands allows us to reset our priorities. Doing so helps ensure that our current life supports our long-term purpose. As an added benefit, pursuing periodic quiet times tends to lower stress, thereby, improving overall health. Meditation also allows us to add spiritual fruit to our crowded plate as described in Galatians 5:22: But the Holy Spirit produces this kind of fruit in our lives: love, joy, peace, patience, kindness, goodness, faithfulness, gentleness and self-control."

Game Winning Point: Play well, rest well.

Game Changing Verse: "Be still and know that I'm God." Psalm 46:10.

PLAYBOOK TIPS

- Be brutally honest in your assessment - it may prove key to the next game.
- Acknowledge and thank those were part of your success.

Read On!

GAME DAY ADVICE

25 thoughts to improve your game both on and off the field

"Fools think they need no advice, but the wise listen to others."

- Psalm 12:15"

Throughout our discussion, you have heard from several former NFL and college football players who are now helping the upcoming generation seek ways to make sound choices in life. In this brief chapter, I have captured their football advice on taking your game to a higher level, plus my extrapolation of their advice into life. You may find their thoughts applicable to situations you face as you help others better their walk. Listed in no particular order, you will find the thoughts from the following people. Not listed are the multitude or organizations that benefit from the talents of these servants.

Brian Allen	Running Back - Colts Businessman
Bill Anderson	Running Back - Stanford VP, Children of Grace
Gill Byrd	Safety - Chargers Coach
John Choma	Lineman - 49er's President, The Leadership Huddle
Rick Isaiah	Reciever - Bengals Fellowship of Christian Athletes
Jeff Kemp	QB - Eagles, Seahawks, Rams VP, Family Life
Craig Awbrey	Nose guard - Stanford President, Awbrey Development Group
John Cato	Linebacker - Cal Businessman
Derwin Gray	Safety - Panthers, Colts Pastor (Transformation Church), Speaker, Author
Ron Johnson	Reciever - Eagles VP, Boys & Girls Club, Monterey Ca.
David Shaw	Linebacker - Cal Businessman
Willie Shaw	Cornerback - New Mexico Former NFL Coach (retired)

SPEED UP! (Choma)

FOOTBALL: Football is an explosive sport. You need to position yourself in the right stance to act quickly.

LIFE: Life is moving at an ever-increasing speed. You must learn to think first and act quickly. Procrastination can kill your efforts.

SLOW DOWN! (Isaiah)

FOOTBALL: Coaching can be an all-consuming job, detracting from family and other priorities. Coaches must "schedule" downtime and take it to ensure a balanced life.

LIFE: Big decisions often require a huge investment of time. You and the team need to create downtime to ensure your performance does not deteriorate because of exhaustion. Schedule points in a project where the team can reflect on progress while refreshing mentally and physically.

THINK! (Choma)

FOOTBALL: Every play requires a multitude of choices by each player. Those who can think quickly (almost instinctively) before they act have a distinct advantage.

LIFE: In a fast-paced world, we often feel the need to act before thinking. Not a good idea! Need to continually develop reasoning skills to improve accuracy and outcome.

PLAY THE BALL! (Johnson)

FOOTBALL: As a receiver, always focus on the front of the ball as you flex your pattern to catch it.

LIFE: Learn the key items to monitor as you make and implement a decision. Watching them and adjusting your game to accommodate a change in playing conditions will lead to success

HOLD ON! (Allen)

FOOTBALL: Tuck the ball away when in enemy territory. A fumble hurts the entire team.

LIFE: Know your role and learn the fundamentals of achieving it successfully. Otherwise, you may drop the ball, causing the entire team to lose.

PROTECT THE BALL! (Kemp)

FOOTBALL: As a quarterback, you will be handing off or throwing the ball. Develop proper form and discipline to guard against turnovers.

LIFE: In football, the ball represents the valuable commodity utilized to play the game. In life, that valuable entity may be your integrity, your spouse, your career, etc. Develop discipline to protect what you value.

KEEP YOUR EYES DOWN FIELD! (Kemp)

FOOTBALL: In a game where passing has become the norm, a quarterback must develop the discipline to continually watch for opportunities down field as a play unfolds. The door opens and closes quickly as the defense adjusts.

LIFE: When making a decision, incorporate a decision-horizon commensurate with the anticipated length of the choice. Career, marriage, education and other life-long decisions require you to keep your eyes down field, making adjustments as life unfolds.

KNOW YOUR ROLE! (Willie Shaw)

FOOTBALL: Each position on the field demands different skills. In some, you lead; in others, you react. All are important for the team to succeed.

LIFE: Each of our lives plays out as a member of a variety of teams. We must learn teaming skills including when to step up as a leader and when to let others take the lead. In any role, be prepared to come ready to play at the top of your game.

CONSTANTLY LEARN! (Byrd)

FOOTBALL: The competition continually invents new offenses and defenses. As an opposing player, you must always be ready to learn how to handle changes thrown at you by the other team.

LIFE: Here, each of us must continue to observe the world around us and flex our game (within sound principles) to respond to changing conditions. Changes in technology, alone, demands for us to proactively learn new tools and techniques to accomplish our mission.

GET THE BALL OFF ON TIME! (Kemp)

FOOTBALL: Indecision normally results in a lot of bad things. From missed scoring opportunities to being sacked for a loss, not getting the ball off on time creates havoc for the team.

LIFE: Every choice entails a timetable (some written; some implied). Failing to act with the appropriate tempo will cause false starts, restarts, wasted activity, poor results, etc. Time is a hugely important commodity. Use it wisely!

AIM FOR A ONE-FOOT DIAMETER TARGET! (Kemp)

FOOTBALL: Precision counts! It can spell the difference between a score and an interception. It also helps your team do its job better.

LIFE: Details in most efforts are critical; however, so is simplicity. Include enough details to accomplish the task, but not so much that would paralyze the efforts.

FOCUS BEFORE GAME! (David Shaw)

FOOTBALL: In many instances, pressure and noise demands a player establishes focus a couple days before the actual game. In doing so, it imbeds the specifics related to that game, enhancing execution amid the chaos.

LIFE: Thinking ahead in any complex activity helps you anticipate and often resolve issues before they occur. Do not confuse focus with obsessing. The latter can lead to mental paralysis.

BE ALERT! (Anderson)

FOOTBALL: Playing conditions in stadiums are constantly changing. Weather, turf conditions, fan noise and other challenges demand a need to always be observant and adapt quickly.

LIFE: Circumstances are always fluid in life. Friendships rise and fall. Economic challenges appear. Health concerns arise. Being alert to discern changes as they appear on the horizon will enable you to adapt earlier and faster.

ADDRESS EMOTIONAL DEJECTION! (Cato)

FOOTBALL: Despairing about bad play, mounting losses or whatever the issue is can mentally freeze a player's ability to function. Learn to recognize this in yourself and others and confront the issue head on, seeking counsel from the coaching staff.

LIFE: Make sure you talk it up while pursuing a major decision. Avoid trying to achieve it alone. Advice from others can help avoid a personal mental funk.

CREATE A FIRM FOUNDATION WITH BALANCE AND AGILITY! (Choma)

FOOTBALL: For a lineman, proper stance is the starting point to success. Have a firm foundation, but be agile and light on your feet to ensure that you gain the physical advantage

LIFE: Ensure you have firm principles that do not change. Be tactically agile to handle changes in circumstances. Avoid the "we've-always-done-it-this-way" syndrome.

STRENGTHEN SKILLS! (Gray)

FOOTBALL: Your opponent is always improving; hence, if you don't, you lose.

LIFE: Your ultimate opponent, Satan, continually throws new challenges your way. Only by strengthening your skills through Christ can you continue to repel his advance.

PROTECT FIELD POSITION! (Kemp)

FOOTBALL: Do not get tackled in the backfield! Losing ground complicates play and takes away momentum.

LIFE: As decisions move forward, monitor progress to avoid obstacles that can require you to restart or repeat steps already taken. Team morale and momentum suffers when ground is lost, especially, if lost due to mistakes.

EXHIBIT CHARACTER! (Gray)

FOOTBALL: Good coaches earn respect from their players; and players from their coaches. Respect exudes from an excellent character.

LIFE: People will follow you if they observe a trustworthy character. Building it takes time; losing it can happen in a heartbeat.

AVOID REPEATED MISTAKES! (Cato)

FOOTBALL: Obviously, mistakes happen. Failure to learn from them and avoid repeating them is a cardinal sin.

LIFE: Same idea here. Make it a habit to reflect (not dwell) on recent mistakes, making a mental note of how you can avoid them again. You may want to do this with another player or coach to depersonalize the feedback.

BE HUMBLE! (Gray)

FOOTBALL: A coach must be humble enough to learn from the team. He is not all-knowing about the game.

LIFE: Avoid a know-it-all attitude. Face reality that you don't know it all. You need to seek and accept advice of qualified people in your life.

KNOW YOURSELF! (Gray)

FOOTBALL: A good player continually seeks to understand their own strengths and weaknesses, learning to play to their own strengths

LIFE: Understand your strengths and weaknesses. Seek to augment the team to fill in where you are weak. Don't spend all of your time attempting to fix your weaknesses. Play to your strengths.

OWN THE DRIVE! (Awbrey)

FOOTBALL: A winning quarterback (and the rest of the team) takes responsibility for working together to win.

LIFE: Rewards and responsibility must be in balance. If you are the prime beneficiary of a decision, then you must step up to have the prime responsibility for seeing it through successfully.

LEARN TO SACRIFICE! (Choma)

FOOTBALL: A successful lineman knows when to lay it all on the line, expending himself entirely, even though glory may come to another member of the team.

LIFE: Learn to be a sacrificial team member, willing to work hard to see another succeed. Ultimately, all glory should go to God.

AVOID OVERLY COMPLEX PLAY! (Awbrey)

FOOTBALL: Many coaches build too much complexity into the playbook for inexperienced players. Typically, that leads to turnovers as the team struggles to play as a unit. If you cannot repeat a play successfully in practice, never try it in a game.

LIFE: Occam's Razor is a popular theory which asserts that no activity should be more complex than required to be achieved successfully. As in football, complexity can lead to confusion and a breakdown in momentum. Keep that in mind.

KNOW THE DEFINING POINT IN A GAME! (David Shaw)

FOOTBALL: Every game has a defining point that establishes the momentum and ultimate outcome of the game.

LIFE: Every project or decision also has a point that projects success or failure. Be observant to note it and take appropriate action.

——————— Read On! ———————

SALVATION - ON BECOMING A HALL-OF-FAMER

A personal eternal decision

"Believe on the Lord Jesus Christ and you will be saved."

- Acts 16:31

Listen up! Here's the ticket: If you want to be in the Hall of Fame, there's only one way to get there. Check it out in this brief chapter.

In Your Face - The Big Decision!!

> # JOHN 3:16

Millions of viewers have seen end zone signs proclaiming John 3:16 during almost every football broadcast throughout the season. Surely, some of those watching can recite the words; a few may even know what they mean. For some, it may be a distraction, but for others, that brief moment may have been their first step toward salvation. Typically visible during extra point attempts, one may conclude that the more touchdowns scored, the more God's word is proclaimed. One may even step out on the limb and conclude that God likes a high-scoring brand of offense.

In your face (and mine)!

Throughout Winning Choices, we have spent time looking at the reality of making choices in today's world. Every day, we each make hundreds of routine decisions and periodically, we make those decisions that hover at the life changing end of the spectrum. There is one decision that each of us faces at some point in our lives that far exceeds all of the others. When measured against other choices we make, you may agree it is off the charts. That decision relates to our personal response to the reality of Jesus Christ. It is THE decision with eternal consequences.

As my pastor, Keith Sholl, once said, "Christ is the reality that creates all other realities."

OK, at this point you may be saying that I am getting a bit personal. Sure, throughout this book, we have discussed the worldview presented by Scripture, but what gives me the right to be in your face? Why should I close this book discussing such a delicate and private topic? The simple answer: You need to hear it and I need to hear it! How we respond to Jesus Christ is the ultimate choice of all time. Each of us can decide to spend eternity as a hall-of-famer on God's team or as an outcast. Truly, the choice IS ours. Let's chat, briefly, about this opportunity.

Christ came into the world to save sinners - you and me – ("This is a true saying, and everyone should believe it: Christ Jesus came into the world to save sinners." 1 Timothy 1:15). If we admit we ARE sinners and accept His gift of salvation, we will become members of His team for eternity ("Now repent of your sins and turn to God, so that your sins may be wiped away." Acts 3:19). He gave His life on our behalf and rose from the grave conquering death for all time. In speaking to the apostle Thomas, Christ laid out the playbook saying, "I am the way, the truth and the life. No one comes to the father except through me." John 14:6. What does that mean to us? Essentially, Christ is telling us that no one can get to heaven except through Him. He is saying that He alone provides the path (the way). Simply put, He meant that if we believe He died and rose from death on our behalf and if we freely accept His death and resurrection as our way of salvation, then truly we will be saved and spend eternity with God.

Pumping iron

If I'm good and try to do the right thing, won't God let me into heaven when I die? Sounds like a good approach unless you really think about it. How good is good? How much trying is enough? How much do I have to do to make the team? Or, what bad thing can get me cut from the roster? Working one's way to heaven just doesn't work. Scripture points out that to be accepted and enter the presence of a perfect God, we would each have to be perfect in our own lives. I'm not sure that I can even define perfection let alone BE perfect. Face it, as Scripture says, "we all have sinned and come short of the glory of God," Romans 3:23. In the book of Ephesians, Paul explains we cannot pump iron (work out) to achieve salvation. Ephesians 2:8-9 assures us that "God saved you by his special favor when you believed. And you can't take credit for this; it is a gift from God. Salvation is not a reward for the good things we have done, so none of us can boast about it."

Ticket prices soar

On Jan. 15, 1967, in a game loaded with household names and future hall of famers, the Green Bay Packers defeated the Kansas City Chiefs in Super Bowl I. The price of admission: $6, $8 or $12. Pricing has changed a bit since the good old days. Recent games reflect a face value of $800 to $1,200, often topping $3,000 on the secondary market for a 50-yard line seat. It's not your typical "family-of-four" Sunday outing. Looking at it another way, you may be talking more than $1,000 per hour of entertainment. A bit on the high side.

What would you expect to pay for a 50-yard line ticket to a game that lasts eternally (there is no clock in heaven)? The answer: For you, it's free; for God, it was the price of His son's death on the cross. Your ticket has already been bought at a very high price. He offers it to you if only you will ask.

A salvation two-minute drill

Throughout the book, we have been talking football, specifically developing ideas based on a two-minute drill. At the risk of sounding a bit irreverent, perhaps, looking at the topic of salvation incorporating the elements of that no-huddle offense would offer another way to have it sink in. At getinthegame.org or winningchoices.net , you will find a summary of the points of salvation using a "Here's the Ticket" format. Review it, follow it, share it!

Allow me to finish our dialogue by capturing the wisdom of one of the NFL's greatest coaches, Joe Gibbs:

> "You and I are players, God's our coach, and we're playing the biggest game of all. We have a loving God that made us. We need to get on His team. It says in His word, there's only one way to Him and that's through Jesus Christ"

——————— Read On! ———————

BACK IN THE LOCKER ROOM

"Be on your guard; stand firm in the faith; be courageous; be strong. Do everything in love."

– 1 Corinthians 16:13-14

This book will end where it began: the locker room. Throughout Winning Choices, we met a host of individuals who have sought out the donkey that God wanted to utilize for His purpose. We also addressed the first question of all time, posed by Satan as Adam and Eve faced a decision:

Did God really say? ...

The answer is "yes." Throughout our discussion, we discovered that God really did say a lot about making sound choices and helping others to do the same. We found that He expects each of us to lead through the 'Power of Three' as heroes, servants and mentors for generations to come.

In the same portion of Scripture, we also read about God's question directed at Adam and Eve but applicable to each of us. He asked:

Where are you?

That is the question we each must answer as this book concludes. Where are we in relation to God? First, from an eternal perspective, and then from a day-to-day standpoint, we each must reflect on what donkey God expects us to retrieve. What activity should we pursue to fulfill His purpose? What relationship does He want us to build with others to further His kingdom? Let's turn to legendary Washington Redskins coach Joe Gibbs for a final thought:

"The further you go in life, the more you realize what you're going to leave this Earth. It's not going to be, 'It was a great platform. It was great to win the Super Bowl,' but really and truly what you're going to leave on this Earth is the influence on others."

So who within your stadium can benefit from your willingness to coach? Who can find hope and achieve it through your influence? Who will happily drench you in Gatorade? Only you can answer these questions when you make a point to get in the game and make WINNING CHOICES!

May the Lord bless you in ways that will continually amaze you!

GOING DEEP

Champions continually grow their game

"Learning is the only thing the mind never exhausts, never fears and never regrets."

– Leonardo da Vinci

"But in your hearts revere Christ as Lord. Always be prepared to give an answer to everyone who asks you to give the reason for the hope that you have."

– 1 Peter 3:15 (NLT)

A typical NFL wide receiver runs a 40-yard dash in less than 4.5 seconds. This blazing speed is often utilized in a deep passing route that catches a defense off balance. The resulting quick score quickly changes the momentum of an entire game.

While few of us can "go deep" at that speed, all of us can "think deep" in the realm of learning and knowledge. Bookstores, libraries and the internet are packed with in-depth resources that can assist in your journey to help others. Please check out a sampling of the offerings related to the general topics addressed Winning Choices.

Written Materials

Worldviews:

Why You Think the Way You Do: The Story of Western Worldviews from Rome to Home
Glenn S. Sunshine

Comparing Christianity with World Religions: The Spirit of Truth and the Spirit of Error
Steven Cory and Dillon Burroughs

Think Biblically!: Recovering a Christian Worldview
John MacArthur and Pat Enis

How Now Shall We Live?
Charles Colson and Nancy Pearcey

Christianity and God:

20 Compelling Evidences that God Exists: Discover Why Believing in God Makes So Much Sense

Ken Boa & Robert M. Bowman Jr.

God, I Don't Understand: Answers to Difficult Questions of the Faith

Ken Boa

Mere Christianity

C.S. Lewis

My Final Word: Holding Tight to Issues that Matter Most

Charles Colson

True Spirituality

Francis A. Schaeffer

Everything You Always Wanted to Know About God (But Were Afraid to Ask): The Jesus Edition

Eric Metaxas

Facing the Blitz: Three Strategies for Turning Trials Into Triumphs

Jeff Kemp

Hero

Derwin Gray

Gospel of Freedom: Martin Luther King, Jr.'s Letter from Birmingham Jail and the Struggle That Changed a Nation
Jonathan Rieder

Coaching and Playing:

The Mentor Leader: Secrets to Building People and Teams that Win Consistently
Tony Dungy

Sum It Up: A Thousand and Ninety-Eight Victories, a Couple of Irrelevant Losses, and a Life in Perspective
Pat Summitt and Sally Jenkins

Catch a Star: Shining through Adversity to Become a Champion
Tamika Catchings

One Yard Short: Turning Your Defeats into Victories
Les Steckel

Heart of a Coach
Fellowship of Christian Athletes

Online Resources

The following websites offer an abundance of material on personal growth, coaching resources and opportunities to "Winning Choices and make winning choices." Also, check out www.getinthegame.org or www. winningchoices.net for ongoing updates of relevant resources.

www.kenboa.org (or reflelctionsministires.org)
Huge variety of resources on worldviews, Christian living and Biblical commentary.

www.breakpoint.org
Daily discussions of today's culture from a Christian perspective.

www.davidjeremiah.org
Articles, radio and TV, devotionals, plus an online Bible.

www.focusonthefamily.com
Wide variety of media relating to today's culture

www.northpointministries.org
Resources related to the ministry of Andy Stanley.

www.summit.org
Youth-oriented educational resources from a Christian perspective.

www.yfc.net (Youth for Christ)

Wide variety of youth-oriented resources.

www.fca.org (Fellowship of Christian Athletes)

Wide variety of youth-oriented resources.

www.getinthegame.org

Complementary site to Winning Choices book.

www.worldviewweekend.com

Wide variety of multimedia discussions on worldviews.

www.josh.org (Josh McDowell)

Part of the worldwide Campus Crusade for Christ, or Cru, ministry.

www.seanmcdowell.org

Bringing truth to a new generation.

www.cru.org (Campus Crusade for Christ)

Dedicated to multiplying disciples who launch spiritual movements.

Younglife.org

Dedicated to presenting Christ to every adolescent.

www.netusa.org

Catholic Youth Organization events, retreats and blog.

www.kairosprisonministry.org

Addresses the spiritual needs of incarcerated individuals.

www.prisonfellowship.org

Addresses the spiritual needs of incarcerated individuals.

www.navigators.org

Discipleship and outreach with a multitude of resources.

www.RZIM.org

Ravi Zacharias ministries focused on apologetics in today's culture.

Winning Choices Endorsements

"At FCA, we understand the value of a strong coach-to-athlete relationship in producing winning results. Winning Choices leverages this relationship to create a sound, practical decision-making tool for the young generation. The football metaphor opens the door to the "kid on the street" who may otherwise shun the advice of more-experienced adults. The Biblical principles serve as a foundation and a filter to guide both coaches and quarterbacks in making morally tough choices. Undoubtedly, those who employ the ideas of Winning Choices will develop a winning edge in the game of life. "

Rick Isaiah – VP Field Ministry, Fellowship of Christian Athletes

Great Lakes Region

"Wow, it's tough to find a tool that combines the power of God' Word withthe simplicity of a football metaphor. Football is such a great game, what an unbelievable way to help young people face the challenges of today's culture. Winning Choices will help jumpstart the process of making great life choices consistently. Winning will be fun!"

Dave McDowell

Vice President, Athletes in Action

"During my career as a football player I learned the importance of making the right choices to achieve the goal of becoming a Champion on the field: working hard, developing discipline, building strong character, maintaining resolve, supporting teammates, receiving wisdom from others who had achieved excellence. A as a former minister to the incarcerated, I see the tremendous need for Prisoners to make a similar choice, to embrace these fundamentals of transformation, in order to achieve genuine success in life. Winning Choices is a tremendous tool for those in prison;

utilizing simple, accessible football metaphors, built on the strength of a Biblical worldview, to help them and those who work with them develop a plan to become true Life Champions!"

William Anderson – Former Executive Director, Prison Fellowship Ministries;

Co-founder of Angel Tree Football Clinic

"As an educator in a major university, I have witnessed thousands of young people struggle with making pivotal career and life decisions. Winning Choices provides a powerful game plan to help these young people develop the talent needed to make effective, ethical, and successful decisions. Developing these decision-making talents can have a profound impact on their future. It is a practical tool kit for individuals and groups who need guidance in creating a worldview that makes sense, and adopting the methods that can make that happen. As a former college football player and co-author of the Two-Minute Drill, I can attest to the power of the football metaphor being used in Winning Choices. As a Christian, I have experienced and witnessed the impact of adopting Biblical principles into my life and the lives of countless others. The combination of both of these elements in Winning Choices will offer the reader an opportunity to get their game plan together, move down the field, score and WIN in the biggest game of all... The Super Bowl of Life! Winning Choices will be a must-read for those who want to step off the sidelines and make a difference with their lives. "

Clinton O. Longenecker, Ph. D.

Distinguished University Professor

Director- UT Center for Leadership Excellence

Ernst & Young Entrepreneur of the Year & Jefferson Award Winner

"As author, Greg Papp, points out, we live in a "do what you view" world. That is, our worldview drives what we do. Over my career at Prison Fellowship and the Colson Center, I have witnessed the positive impact on people who learn to adopt and live out a solid, Biblical worldview. In Winning Choices, Greg takes the simple road, using the metaphor of something we all understand, pizza, to teach how our worldviews affect six critical elements of decision-making. He contrasts the scriptural view with contemporary alternatives including human secularism, political correctness and environmentalism to illustrate the need to build our worldview on the God of the Bible. Anyone hoping to understand and teach the basics of worldviews would benefit from reading Winning Choices."

Steve Bradford

Principal, Three Cords Strong LLC

Former VP Operations for the Chuck Colson Center for Christian Worldview

"Throughout my educational career, I had some great teachers but it was my coaches who made the biggest impact on my life. The coaches who really challenged and cared for me taught me incredible truths about how to live. Greg Papp's Winning Choices provides a wealth of practical tools to equip any coach to make a real positive difference in the lives of the athletes they lead. The materials and the website all fit together neatly with simple plans, great illustrations and powerful stories. Learning that the choices we make every day is a truth that is life changing. Knowing how to make great decisions is life transforming. It's time to Winning Choices!"

William E Brown, PhD

Senior Fellow of Worldview and Culture

The Colson Center for Christian Worldview

"On any given day, Youth for Christ Juvenile Justice Staff and Volunteers engage thousands of young people in one of the 1280 juvenile detentions centers across the United States. They build relationships inside the facility through a variety of programs in hopes of continuing those relationships when the teen enters back into their community. Finding relevant material that teens can relate to and understand is a constant struggle for our team. In Winning Choices, Greg Papp has provided a whole host of stories and tools that help teach how to make better choices. The metaphors of pizza and football enable workers to engage the upcoming generation in a language they can both understand and adopt in their own personal lives."

Eric Kelly

National Juvenile Justice Ministry Director

Youth for Christ Ministries

"I have always believed that if it's not worth doing something right, then it's not worth doing it at all. As a professional dedicated to helping drive improvement, I have witnessed countless examples of the impact of both good and bad decisions made by individuals and organizations. In Winning Choices, author, Greg Papp, lays out a straightforward approach to facing the challenges of making sound choices. He has done it right. Using the easy-to-understand metaphors of football and pizza, he provides tools for both teaching and implementing the skills of successful decision-making."

Tim Stansfield P.E., Ph.D.

President

IET Inc.

456

"As a regional director within the Prison Fellowship Ministries organization, I see the need on a daily basis to provide ideas and tools that can help improve the outcomes of choices made by prisoners. In Winning Choices, Greg Papp has created just such a package, using the metaphors of pizza and football to provide an easy to understand, practical approach for coaching those in need. Individuals who work with youth, prisoners or anyone else attempting to make better choices need to read this book. Stories from football, current day life and scripture highlight ideas that we can all incorporate in our efforts to mentor and coach others."

Joe Avila, Regional Director- Prison Fellowship Ministries

Western Region;

Co-founder of Angel Tree Football Clinic

"Whether you are on the football field or playing in the game of life, to win, you must get the entire team involved in the game. In a team effort, each and every role is critical in its additive value to a successful outcome. As an NFL player, I truly appreciated the various skills that teammates and coaches brought to the game. In my current role, I see that same need for total, selfless and even sacrificial individual investment in order to create a network of trust. That trust network then becomes the foundation for team achievement. In a complex world, no one wins on their own. In Winning Choices, author Greg Papp lays out ideas and tools for working together to make and implement winning decisions. If you are helping others learn to take their life to a new level, you will find this book ripe with real-life examples."

John Choma, President

The Leadership Huddle

Super Bowl XVI Champion

"Life is full of decisions that often are simply overwhelming. Greg Papp illustrates so poignantly in Winning Choices" a variety of simple steps, analogies and scripture that guide us through the most complex to simple life challenges, questions and decisions we face. From the high school athlete to the business professional, to the event planner like myself, Winning Choices provides simple steps for us all to use."

Janna Bowman, Head Duck

J. Duck Production

"Winning Choices offers a nice development of football terms. I like the way Greg used them to explain the Gospel it would be great for sports team chaplains or men's Bible study leaders to have and use!!"

Scott Smith

Area Assistant

Evangelism Explosion International